WITHDRAWN
UTSA Libraries

FIGHTING UNEMPLOYMENT
IN
TWENTIETH-CENTURY CHILE

PITT LATIN AMERICAN SERIES
CATHERINE M. CONAGHAN, EDITOR

ÁNGELA VERGARA

UNIVERSITY OF PITTSBURGH PRESS

Published by the University of Pittsburgh Press, Pittsburgh, Pa., 15260
Copyright © 2021, University of Pittsburgh Press
All rights reserved
Manufactured in the United States of America
Printed on acid-free paper
10 9 8 7 6 5 4 3 2 1

Cataloging-in-Publication data is available from the Library of Congress

ISBN 13: 978-0-8229-4679-3
ISBN 10: 0-8229-4679-3

Cover art: Copyright © "Colección Museo Histórico Nacional." Marcos Chamudes Reitich, Lota, 1951.
Cover design: Melissa Dias-Mandoly

To my family, los de aquí y los de allá

CONTENTS

Acknowledgments ix

Introduction 5

PART ONE

DISCOVERING UNEMPLOYMENT (1900s–1920s)

1. The Global Debate on Unemployment 23

2. Unemployment in Early Twentieth-Century Chile 37

PART TWO

EXPERIENCING MASSIVE UNEMPLOYMENT (1930–1938)

3. Fighting Unemployment 53

4. Social Assistance and the Rationalization of Aid 75

5. Protecting Consumers 96

PART THREE

THE ROAD TO FULL EMPLOYMENT

6. Incomplete Reforms   117

7. Full Employment and Labor Rights during the Long 1960s   137

Epilogue. Unemployment, Dictatorship, and Neoliberalism   153

Notes   163

Bibliography   215

Index   237

ACKNOWLEDGMENTS

Writing this book has taken longer than expected. It started as a conference paper for a seminar organized by Paulo Drinot and Alan Knight at the Institute of the Americas, University of London, in 2011. The workshop, the interesting conversations, and the research and writing of a book chapter that became part of the edited volume *The Great Depression in Latin America* raised so many questions that I dropped every other project to study the 1930s. The following year, I was at the Seminário Internacional Mundos do Trabalho in Rio, Brazil, when John French casually mentioned that if I wanted to study unemployment, I should start with its definition. Many years later, that remark became the central question for this book. Today, when the pandemic has shut down all academic activities, I am especially grateful to those conversations, formal and informal, at conferences, workshops, and seminars.

Throughout the years, I have received support from many institutions, colleagues, friends, and family members. During 2017–2018, I was awarded a one-year fellowship from the National Endowment for the Humanities. The fellowship allowed me to read, research, and write an entire draft. I also received support from the Mining History Association, as well as research and travel funding from California State University, Los Angeles. In Chile, the Instituto de Historia of the Universidad Católica (Santiago), Facultad de Filosfía y Humanidades of the Universidad Alberto Hurtado, and Instituto de Historia of the Universidad Católica de Valparaíso invited me to share my research.

I have crossed paths with many fantastic and generous scholars. Whether we shared a conference panel or only exchanged emails, their comments, readings, and overall support have made me a better historian, reader, and writer. Special thanks to Ted Beatty, Paulo Drinot, Leon Fink, Claudio Llanos, Brian Loveman, Gillian McGillivray, Diego Ortúzar, Jorge Rojas Flores, Pablo Rubio, Silvia Simonassi, Fernando Teixeira da Silva, Heidi Tinsman, and Peter Winn. I'm also fortunate to have a wonderful group of colleagues at Cal State LA. I am especially grateful for the friendship and support from Emily Acevedo, Kittiya Lee, Enrique Ochoa, and Ericka Verba. Lisa Munro edited the first draft of the book, and her comments and careful editing considerably improved the manuscript.

We cannot research without the work of so many librarians, archivists, student workers, and administrative staff. Thank you to the people at Cal State LA University Library, the International Labour Organisation in Geneva, Switzerland, the Biblioteca del Congreso Nacional, and the Archivo and Biblioteca Nacional in Chile. Special thanks to Melody Singleton, our department coordinator, who helped me navigate travel forms, research leaves, lost keys, and the campus bureaucracy.

At the University of Pittsburgh Press, it has been a privilege to work with Josh Shanholtzer. He offered clear guidelines and support, encouraging me to move forward when I was ready to give up. Two very supportive reviewers helped me strengthen the book. At the very last minute, José Ignacio González generously shared his map of Chile.

My family in the United States and Chile have supported me in incredible ways. This book is for all of you. To Mike, the most supportive partner I could have ever asked for. To Camilo, as you grow up (way too fast!), I love traveling, talking about history, and drinking good coffee with you. And to Manu, *mi niña hermosa*, your kindness and creativeness inspire me every day. This book is also for my parents in Chile, to my family in the south of the world, who I miss more than ever during this pandemic. To my mom, for her strength, optimism, and encouragement, and to my dad, for his calm advice and wise comments. I feel fortunate to have so many places I can call home. As Mike told me many years ago, I am a nomad, but a nomad with many homes—from our home in Santa Monica to the views of the Andes at my mom's home in Pirque; from my dad's and Ana María's beautiful house in Viña to Las Nevadas with Bernie and Rosa. Thank you all for your love and support.

Amid a global pandemic and a significant economic recession, I cannot stop thinking about the lessons of the Great Depression. If there is something to learn from the long history of unemployment and social welfare, it is the need to build a genuinely democratic social, political, and economic system. Today more than ever, if we want to transform social assistance, relief, and welfare, we cannot do it from the top but the bottom up. Experts should start listening to people.

FIGHTING UNEMPLOYMENT
IN
TWENTIETH-CENTURY CHILE

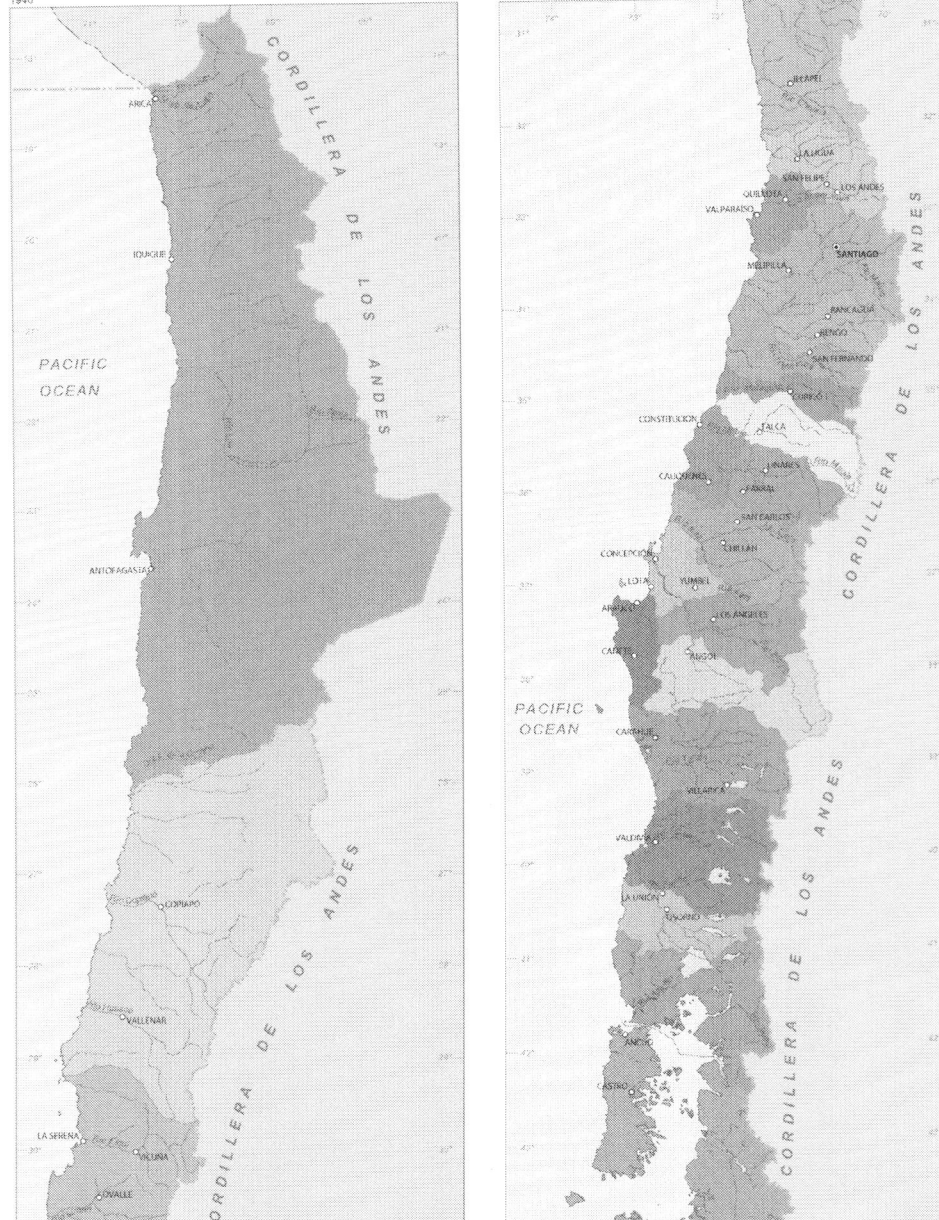

Chile in 1940

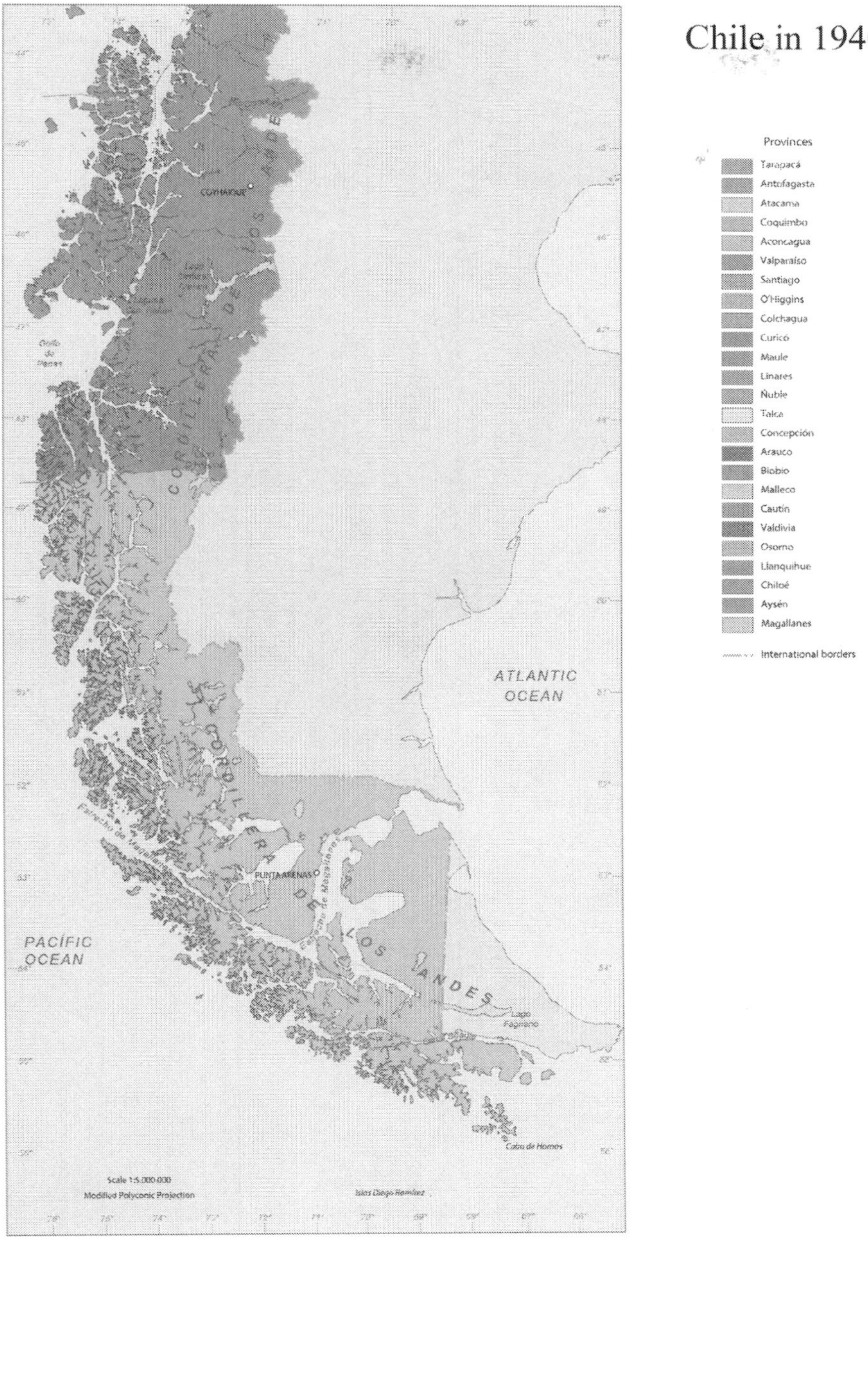

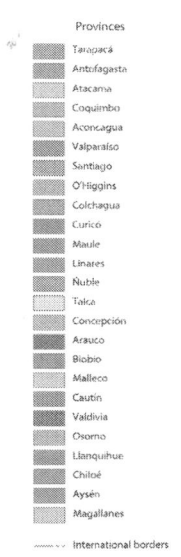

INTRODUCTION

Throughout the first half of the twentieth century, labor rights expanded dramatically in Chile, transforming the workplace and workers' place in society. New laws recognized trade unions, improved safety and working conditions, and banned child labor. To achieve social peace and respond to workers' growing activism, the state mediated labor conflicts and disputes. The Labor Department sent hundreds of appointed civil servants across the country to inspect working conditions and enforce labor laws. For workers, wage labor and formal employment opened access to other rights, such as health care and social security, symbols of progress and citizenship. In the union hall, workers created new forms of political, social, and cultural participation, which intertwined with a labor tradition dating back to the nineteenth century and the nitrate fields.[1] The institutionalization of labor relations, policy makers and social reformers argued, represented one of the greatest accomplishments of the country. As Moisés Poblete Troncoso, Chile's most influential and internationally renowned labor lawyer, explained in 1960, "the Chilean labor code is one of the most complete in Latin America."[2]

Despite its achievements, Chile's system of modern labor relations suffered from many problems. Legislation discriminated against agricultural workers, nearly 35 percent of the workforce in the 1950s; prohibited public employees from unionizing or bargaining collectively; and barely protected domestic workers, most of whom were women. Considered a milestone in Latin America, the social security fund gave health care benefits to workers and immediate family members but offered few retirement pensions until the 1960s. Because of economic instability and employers' opposition to labor laws, improving working conditions, negotiating salaries, and enforcing rights remained the most important and challenging union activity. High rates of inflation undermined workers' economic gains, while political oppression and abusive employers weakened workers' rights. Unionization also lagged and, until the late 1950s, was found largely in big industrial and mining plants, leaving other sectors relatively untouched.³ Workers' everyday reality was far away from the text of the law. Union leader Luis Solís noted in 1936 that although "labour laws have always been said to be advanced" and the country ratified international conventions, "it is a well-known fact that there is close collaboration between the employers and public authorities to suppress any too active trade [union]."⁴

Unemployment and job instability illustrate the limits of labor protections and economic modernization. Most workers could not count on labor rights or social welfare to ameliorate recurring economic cycles and dismissal. None of the labor laws enacted through the 1920s–1940s addressed unemployment. Approved in 1924, the contract law (Law 4053) offered little protection and did not guarantee job security. Social security, also established in 1924, did not cover the risk of unemployment until 1953. The Great Depression caused havoc in the country. Although over 120,000 people were out of work in 1932, the government responded by setting up emergency programs and protections for consumers instead of establishing long-term labor reforms. Social aid expanded in the 1940s but remained limited and in the hands of charity and religious institutions.⁵ The exception were white-collar employees in the private sector. To protect their middle-class status, Law 6020 of 1937 established unemployment subsidies and minimum wage for white-collar workers. However, they made up only a bit more than 10 percent of the insured workforce and contributed to personal saving accounts, not traditional social funds. In 1950, most working-class Chileans remained unprotected against unemployment.⁶

This book examines unemployment and job insecurity to explain labor tensions in Chile between the 1910s and the 1960s. This is not an economic analysis but a labor history of how workers, the state, and employers experienced, perceived, and defined unemployment and how the views of each of these groups shaped welfare policy. I argue that while the state adopted international standards to fight unemployment, local economic, political, and social forces transformed and limited these reforms.

International actors influenced national public policy, statecraft, and institutional practices in multiple ways. European political economists provided Chilean intellectuals with a technical lexicon to understand the labor market, including new concepts such as classifying the population as either economically active or inactive. The state also followed the recommendations of the International Labor Organization (ILO) to collect labor statistics and establish free placement offices. In the post–World War II era, foreign advisors, such as the Klein-Saks Mission (1955) and ILO experts, guided social security reforms and reorganized public administration.

International exchanges are only one part of the story. Interactions between workers, civil servants, and employers reveal a more complex reality.

As labor scholars have demonstrated, countless obstacles, including employers' vicious opposition to workers' rights and lack of public funding and commitment to enforcement, undermined labor laws and policies in Chile.[7] In his classic study of textile workers in the Yarur mill plant, Peter Winn demonstrates the enormous difficulties faced by labor to enforce basic rights, form an independent union, and bargain collectively. Similarly, Brian Loveman has shown that rural employers used all kinds of tactics to prevent labor inspectors from entering their properties. These works reaffirm the importance of looking beyond the law and examine the relationship between employers, civil servants, and workers. Civil servants such as social workers and labor inspectors were critical actors who understood and worked to resolve problems of the working class: unemployment, inflation, and employer resistance to unionization. Addressing concrete cases, these professionals interpreted people's needs and negotiated with employers, workers, and local political actors.[8] Their political loyalties and views about race, class, gender, and family infused public programs and institutions with new meanings.

By contrasting the local and the global, the text and the practice of labor laws, and different definitions of unemployment, this book illustrates the fractures deeply embedded in Chile's system of industrial relations. Scholars have long pointed out the limits of Chilean democracy. Elizabeth Lira and Brian Loveman have demonstrated how regimes of exceptions, the political and partisan role of the judicial power, and other authoritarian political practices limited democracy between 1925 and 1973.[9] From a labor perspective, the history of unemployment helps us understand the everyday limits to citizenship, social rights, and democracy in twentieth-century Chile.

A HISTORY OF UNEMPLOYMENT

Unemployment, Raymond Williams explains, is a complicated and controversial keyword. Its use and application reflect how societies perceive work and wage labor. The most important aspect of its meaning, Williams explains, "depends upon its separation from the associations of idle; it describes a social situation rather than a personal condition."[10] In Europe and the United States, the process of separating unemployment from idleness took place between the 1870s and 1910s. To better understand this process, historians have examined how states, political economists, and labor organizations understood unemployment.[11] They have focused on three major changes: definition (semantic/language), measurement (statistics), and legislation (labor laws and social security).[12] Labor scholars have shown how people responded to unemployment at the personal, community, and political levels, including through social mobilization and migration. Working people, they argue, contested narrow definitions of unemployment and eligibility criteria for direct relief based on race, gender, and political citizenship.[13] While these historical narratives focus only on Europe and the North Atlantic world, they suggest the need to examine how social categories emerged and influenced state policies. Moreover, development in the North Atlantic had a global impact as European social thought and, after 1919, the International Labor Organization (ILO) heavily influenced Latin American labor laws and unemployment policies across the globe.

Changing definitions of unemployment provide the starting point to understand how and why societies began to recognize unemployment as a unique social and economic phenomenon. Traditionally, societies had viewed unemployed as a personal and moral failing and criminalized vagrancy and poverty.[14] Alexander Keyssar, for example, explains that the term *unemployed* was ambiguous in the United States until the 1870s. It referred both to people "out of work and seeking it" and to those "who were simply 'not employed,' who were idle or not working."[15] Parallel processes took place in other parts of the world. In the late nineteenth century, the words *chômage* (French) and *Arbeitslosigkeit* (German) evolved in similar ways to their English counterpart.[16] The transition in Spanish took longer. In the early twentieth century, Spanish-speaking authors could not find a word in their language to define unemployment, preferring *chômage*. By the 1920s, Spanish words such as *paro* and *desocupación* became common.[17] However, arguing that these terms could refer to both the unemployed and people unfit or unwilling to work, experts in Spain and Spanish Latin America added the adjective *forzoso* (unavoidable or forced).[18]

By placing these semantic discussions in a historical context, scholars have reconstructed the birth of modern unemployment within the context of industrial capitalism, wage labor, and the rise of a regulatory state. Beginning in the late nineteenth century, both state agents and political economists looked to describe a new social and economic experience; wage labor had made unemployment visible. In *Capital* (1867), Karl Marx argued that capitalism not only caused unemployment but required a "disposable industrial reserve army" to increase production and maintain wages low.[19] Across the globe, economic recessions hit hard in industrial cities and affected thousands of factory workers. Unemployed workers began to protest regularly, demanding food and jobs. In 1886–1887, "unemployed demonstrations . . . caused near panic in London."[20] When helping the poor, states and charity organizations separated unemployed people from paupers and vagrants, but the differences were not yet clear. To explain the differences, European political economists turned to studying the labor market, demography, and the economic and social causes of unemployment. In 1909, the Italian scholar Manlio Andrea D'Ambrosio published *Passività econom-*

ica. He identified three reasons why people might not work: voluntary, biological, and social. Only the latter, D'Ambrosio claimed, meant unemployment.[21] By identifying and specifying these differences, experts set the stage for two streams of public aid: unemployment insurance for the workforce and social welfare for children, the elderly, and disabled people.

The extent to which people were themselves responsible for losing their jobs sparked continuous political and academic debates, shaping social insurance and aid. In the 1910s, William Beveridge, the author of the UK social security system, studied the impact of industrial production and economic cycles on urban workers. He argued that the "maladjustment between the supply of and the demand for labour" caused unemployment rather than workers' own failings. So, Beveridge argued, experts should pay attention to unemployment and not the unemployed.[22] This view represented a pivotal change both in social analysis and in state practices. If economic problems caused unemployment, personal or moral failures became less relevant. Because unemployment transcended the individual, it required public attention and a state response. Britain's shift from poor laws to public insurance illustrates these changes. Beginning in the sixteenth century, poor laws gave direct aid to the indigent but also forced people in need to labor in workhouses to redeem themselves. Receiving aid from workhouses and other similar institutions carried a negative moral stigma. Instead, the National Security Act (1911) created compulsory insurance and made unemployment subsidies a social right.[23]

Early twentieth-century experts also looked for reliable data.[24] The history of unemployment as a measurable category intersects with the rise of the field of modern statistics. In the second half of the nineteenth century, experts developed a scientific method to count and systematize economic, social, and demographic data. A symbol of modernity and statecraft, statistics were used by states to understand problems, design solutions, and rule people and territories. In nineteenth-century Italy, statistics "created a particular image of the national space, they gave a body to an abstract entity."[25] Yet despite the scientific claims of the science of statistics, race, gender, and class, as well as politics, influenced their use and shaped who, where, and how census takers counted people.[26] This was the case in early twentieth-century Chile, where census takers omitted women workers. By not recording informal and sporadic occupations such as laundresses, they made women workers invisible.[27]

Labor statistics made significant strides in the early twentieth century. Influenced by international debates, many Latin American countries opened statistical offices that focused exclusively on labor issues. In Chile, the Labor Department (Oficina del Trabajo), founded in 1907, included a small statistical desk and collected data on salaries, work accidents, and the number of workers per industry.[28] Although labor statistics became common worldwide, experts faced several challenges in measuring unemployment. No dependable sources of information existed. Data from trade unions, employers, local governments, and relief services offered incomplete information. Many countries recorded unemployed workers in the census. Conducted every ten years, the census only gave a snapshot of the problem.[29] While new public institutions, such as social security and unemployment insurance offices, started offering more exact data than previous sources, they only focused on the insured population. In addition, earlier statistical efforts had only counted the absolute number of people unemployed; the new statistics measured the workforce and unemployment rate (the percentage of unemployed people in the total workforce). Similarly, international experts attempted to standardize definitions across countries, using common measurable benchmarks such as age and time unemployed.

Between 1880 and the 1910s, industrial countries and political economists worked to define and measured unemployment. In the following decades, the rise of labor laws and social security consolidated a modern notion of unemployment and the role of the state.[30] As the state increasingly intervened in the workplace and labor-capital relations, it would also regulate the labor market. During the interwar period, new labor laws, social protections, and social security systems in countries such as Britain (1911), Austria (1920), and Germany (1927) regulated unemployment and increasingly protected workers. Nevertheless, despite ongoing pressures from the labor movement and progressive political sectors, unemployment insurance remained the exception, not the norm. Moreover, the early unemployment funds limited coverage to specific groups of workers (usually highly skilled workers), leaving many unprotected. Most insurance systems made workers present proof of unemployment and accept jobs offers from placement offices prior to receiving subsidies.[31] In some places, elites feared working-class idleness and vagrancy, views that were reinforced by ideas of race and gender, and opposed state intervention in the labor market. How to finance this new benefit also divided experts and politicians. The Great Depression and World War II accelerated the movement to implement universal insurance. In the Americas, the United States approved the Social Security Act in 1935, and Canada's Employment and Social Security Act faced many legal and political battles until it came into effect in 1941.

In contrast, we know very little about unemployment in Latin America during the first half of the twentieth century. Economic modernization, the rise of export-oriented sectors, industrialization, and rapid urbanization transformed people's lives and work habits. Wage and industrial labor became symbols of progress. State agencies, such as social security offices, provided benefits to working families and, along with industrial managers, attempted to transform workers into modern citizens. Historians of social welfare have analyzed medical and family benefits, mothers and children programs, and food policies. They have underscored the inner workings of welfare institutions; the influence of race, gender, and class on state formation; the role played by women as both targets of social policy as well as their work as welfare professionals; and the continuities and ruptures between early forms of philanthropy and modern welfare practices.[32] By looking at unemployment and the limits of unemployment policies, this book expands our understanding of social welfare in the region. While welfare systems provided rights and benefits to working families based on their status as formal workers, they failed to protect people from the risk of unemployment. Unemployment, underemployment, job instability, and, in later decades, informality limited the impact of social welfare in Latin America.

A TRANSNATIONAL HISTORY OF UNEMPLOYMENT

In 1923, Carlos Contreras Labarca, the future secretary general of Chile's Communist Party, published his law thesis, titled *La defensa del proletariado contra el riesgo profesional de la desocupación* (The defense of the proletarian against the professional risk of unemployment).[33] Writing in the aftermath of the 1921 economic crisis, he considered involuntary unemployment the "cruelest and most dreadful social risk threatening the stability" of working-class families. Like many of his contemporaries, he turned to European political economists to define, understand, and explain Chile's social and economic problems. He cited French authors such as Charles Gide, Leon Bourgeois, and Philippe de Las Cases. His work built on the conventions and the publications of the ILO; he was familiar with different European models of unemployment insurance. Although he belonged to the Communist Party, argued that wage labor and capitalism caused unemployment, and adopted a leftist lexicon as his thesis title, he did not cite any radical intellectuals and made only scattered references to Chile's labor movement. Like many other leftist writers at the time, in the short run, he endorsed reformist and regulatory approaches to labor problems.

Unemployment, the young communist lawyer concluded, was a modern, complex, and chronic problem, requiring the immediate and systematic attention of the state. He believed modern statistics and state intervention in the labor market could prevent unemployment. He also argued that public work projects, rather than in-kind aid, could better help the unemployed. Immigration, trade, and finances had tied workers' livelihood to the world economy, he concluded, making Chilean unemployment a reflection of a global phenomenon. His writing shows how growing international awareness about unemployment and the rise of state regulatory and technical approaches prompted interventions into the labor market, and it reminds us of the importance of placing labor history into a transnational framework.³⁴

Influenced by the transnational turn in labor history, scholars have studied how different countries came to share a similar regulatory approach to labor problems. Argentine historian Juan Manuel Palacio called this a "global process of development of social rights."³⁵ From Europe to the Western Hemisphere, experts and state agents confronted similar labor and economic problems: industrialization, urbanization, and the rise of labor conflicts. Despite significant national and regional differences, they enacted labor laws and created institutions and state bureaucracies, including labor departments, labor courts, and social security and professional welfare offices.³⁶ At conferences and international exhibits, they exchanged ideas and created "networks of experts."³⁷ These meetings became a "transnational sphere" or "space where encounters across national borders took place."³⁸

One of these spaces was the ILO. Founded in 1919, the ILO sponsored conferences, publications, and technical missions, as well as facilitated the exchange of ideas about work and labor legislation. Despite divergent views on how to achieve social justice, ILO conventions incorporated the essential demands of the labor movement and helped create universal labor standards.³⁹ The ILO was not the only transnational space for evolving approaches to government and modern industrial relations. Underneath this global exchange lay the circulation of alternative ideas such as anarchism, anarcho-syndicalism, and communism, which deeply influenced radical writers and many sectors of the labor movement. The Communist International and communist labor movements around the world challenged the ILO's exclusive emphasis on legislation and, instead, advocated to dismantle the entire capitalist system. Concerned about the growing influence of communism on the Latin American labor movement, Albert Thomas, director of the ILO, traveled to South America in 1925 to promote a regulatory approach to labor relations.⁴⁰

Debates about unemployment also circulated in the transnational sphere. During the 1910s–1920s, several conferences, publications, and experts' exchanges focused on unemployment. In 1910, the First International Conference on Unemployment in Paris brought together academics and public servants from all over the world, including small delegations from Argentina, Chile, and Mexico. In October 1919, the ILO convened in Washington, DC, and approved its constitution and six conventions. After endorsing the eight-hour workday for industrial workers, the most emblematic workers' demand, ILO representatives turned to the second item on the agenda: "preventing or providing against unemployment."⁴¹ Parallel to the ILO meetings and conventions, the Comintern, the Third International Organization of Communist Parties, addressed unemployment in its meetings and reports, encouraging communist parties around the world to fight against capitalism. Relatively untouched by the capitalist crises of the 1920s and 1930s, the Soviet Union offered a different road to fight unemployment. At the local level, the ideas of the Comintern intersected with more concrete demands, such as protections for the unemployed, better jobs, and social insurance.

While Latin American states and experts intently followed these debates, they also balanced the conflicting influences of the foreign and the local. Recent scholarship on transnational history has demonstrated that national and local actors not only received and implemented foreign recommendations, but they also contested, adapted, shaped, and transformed them. In other instances, some ideas and legislative responses emerged simultaneously in Europe and the Americas.[42] Although local actors often had only a marginal influence on global debates, they took part in the transnational sphere as selective and critical readers, translators, and intermediaries. As Paulo Drinot argues for the case of labor laws in Peru, "the legislative response to the labor question Peru was subject to a local translation."[43] Labor laws, then, expressed both international influences as well as "local assumptions about the character of Peruvian population." Not a literal translation, but an adaptation to local reality.[44]

The debate about unemployment shows the complex interaction between the global and the local. Latin Americans writing about unemployment at the time, such as Carlos Contreras Labarca in Chile and the Argentine Manuel Gálvez, used a Western European analytical framework but pointed out the specific political, economic, and social conditions of their countries.[45] They redefined unemployment within the context of economies dependent on commodity production and exports, the reality of rural labor, and what they saw as the unique social, cultural, and racial characteristics of Latin American workers. In doing so, they challenged a Eurocentric view of labor issues that had focused only on industrial workers.[46] By looking at these exchanges and negotiations, this book provides a more complex view of transnational exchanges and dialogues.

UNEMPLOYMENT IN CHILE

From the 1910s to the 1960s, Chileans debated how to help, protect, and control the unemployed. Influenced by both global and local actors, the state recognized unemployment as a social and economic problem, created institutions to help people find work, and collected statistics. International agencies, such as the ILO, informed debates in Chile, but local economic, political, and social conditions also shaped unemployment policies. Most of these policies, including placement services, did little to resolve workers' immediate problems. Chilean working families continued experiencing job instability and had few means to survive cycles of unemployment. By the mid-twentieth century, the ILO described Chile's unemployment policy as rudimentary and outdated. To explain the shortcomings of unemployment policy, I turn to the history of the national and global debates about labor and social laws, state responses to economic crises, the lived experience of social workers and labor inspectors, and workers' demands for job security. Throughout this period, four key elements influenced how state, expert networks, employers, and workers conceptualized unemployment.

First, massive unemployment, or *chômage*, attracted widespread attention, sparked a wave of social protests and labor activism, and frightened local elites, persuading the state to legislate basic work protections and welfare rights. The country witnessed three massive unemployment crises (1914, 1921–1922, and 1930–1933), and the state implemented measures that had become common in the global fight against unemployment. In 1914, the Labor Department estimated that 30,000 people lost their jobs in the nitrate fields. In response, the government opened placement services in railroad stations to register and place workers in construction and agricultural jobs. In 1921, 70,000 people were out of work. Many of them moved from the nitrate fields to the south of the country, and the government housed and fed unemployed miners and their families in public shelters. Displaced nitrate families occupied public spaces, frightening state authorities and local elites who associated unemployment and poverty with social and political turmoil. During the worst years of the Great Depression, between 1931 and 1932, at least 120,000 people were unemployed.[47] Unlike earlier crises, not only did nitrate and mine workers lose their jobs but also blue-collar workers and white-collar employees lined up at soup kitchens and scrambled to find temporary work in emergency programs. The government rationalized social aid, sponsored an ambitious program of public works, and set price ceilings for food and essential consumer products.

Second, in contrast to public policies adopted to meet short-term economic downturns, workers' own views about unemployment were broader than these visible crises, bringing together demands for job security and unemployment insurance. Urban workers underwent long periods of frictional unemployment (the time a worker is unemployed between jobs), and employment for agricultural and construction workers was seasonal and unstable. Sectorial crises, shortage of raw materials, or production restructuring affected many industrial laborers. Legislation and policy ignored these kinds of problems caused by seasonal and frictional unemployment, job insecurity, and informality. In response, the labor movement pressed the state to regulate and enforce work contracts. At the local level, unions included severance payments in collective agreements and protected their members. Reforms came slowly. Employers feverishly attacked the expansion of labor laws, arguing that employers' contributions to social security and contract stability crippled business and economic freedom. Moreover, they never recognized unemployment as a problem. Instead, they talked about labor shortages and workers' lack of work habits. Following the extensive reform of the country's social security system in 1953, blue-collar workers earned the right to unemployment benefits. Only in 1966 did the labor movement achieve its most crucial work victory: contract stability and stricter limits to arbitrary firing.

Third, while the Chilean state established a modern bureaucratic framework to counter unemployment, low public budgets and poor labor infrastructure limited the impact of these policies. Civil servants lamented the lack of funding and resources to enforce labor laws and improve working conditions. The inspectors of the Labor Department faced enormous obstacles to reach people employed outside the main urban areas, including lack of transportation, no funding to pay for gas (or for horses and saddles in the rural sector before the 1950s), and employers' antilabor practices. Lack of personnel also hindered the collection of statistics and the operation of placement offices. Furthermore, state agents' social, cultural, and political views determined how the state applied and carried out these reforms. Traditional fears of working men's vagrancy; ideas and expectations about class, gender, and family; and landowners' opposition to improving working conditions and labor relations in the countryside dissuaded government leaders from establishing long-term protections such as unemployment insurance. Journalists and politicians frequently argued that unemployment benefits would dissuade workers from finding employment.

Finally, Chileans believed that the state should create industrial jobs. In Europe, the modern concept of unemployment emerged, French historian Yves Zoberman argued, "linked to industrial society."[48] In contrast, Latin Americans understood unemployment in conjunction with the contradictions and vulnerabilities of export economies, peripheral industrialization, the poor development of labor markets, and their demographic and cultural problems. The face of unemployment in Latin America was not industrial workers displaced by technology and automation but rather workers in the export sector who lost their jobs because of changes in the international market. Because the instability of the export market, local experts argued, caused unemployment, only a national industry could offer stable jobs.

In the 1930s, diverse groups including leftist political parties and labor organizations demanded that the state develop new industries, support production, and open new land for "colonization." By the 1940s, the fight against unemployment became intertwined with the broader political agenda of industrialization and import substitution. When President Gabriel González Videla inaugurated the steel plant of Huachipato (1950), the symbol of the country's industrialization effort, he promised Chilean citizens more wealth, higher salaries, jobs, and a "more dignified and decent life."[49] By the 1960s, economists questioned whether national industry would in fact offer decent jobs to all Chilean working people. Rapid demographic growth, massive rural-urban migration, mechanization, and automation made unemployment a persistent condition.

Fighting Unemployment in Twentieth-Century Chile relies on a wide range of archival and periodical sources. Most of these sources, such as the reports of labor inspectors and social workers, echoed the perspective of the state and professional experts. However, these reports also include many details and observations, shedding light on the daily lives, views, and demands of the unemployed and their families. From this perspective, the Department of Labor holds invaluable documents to study labor issues from both a top-down and bottom-up perspective in twentieth-century Chile. Founded in 1907, the Department of Labor enforced labor laws and oversaw labor unions, including supervising board elections and collective bargaining.[50] The department appointed labor inspectors to work and travel throughout the entire country, leaving behind a paper trail of reports, letters, and telegrams about local working conditions. In addition, the archival collection of the Ministry of Development (Ministerio de Fomento) includes information on public work projects and gold mining sites in the early 1930s. The records of regional governments (called *intendencias*) address urban issues such as public shelters and consumer rights. In memoirs, theses, and periodicals, lawyers, social workers, and medical doctors thought about unemployment and reflected on how public policies both accomplished and fell short of their goals. To place Chilean history in a transnational framework, I turn to the digitized collection of the ILO and its physical archives in Geneva, Switzerland.

Despite the efforts of statisticians to record unemployment, numbers are unreliable and scattered. The census of 1920, 1930, 1940, and 1952 measured the size of the workforce and broke down information by economic activity. However, categories and terms changed regularly on the census, making it difficult to compare unemployment across time. A more reliable source of statistical information is *Estadística chilena*, a monthly publication of the Dirección General de Estadística de Chile. The journal included data from the Bolsa de Trabajo (the work placement service maintained by the Labor Department) and estimated the unemployment rate. Beginning in 1958, the University of Chile has regularly published unemployment surveys, the most accurate source of unemployment data to the present. Rationalizing these diverse statistical sources requires a methodology beyond the scope of this book. I relied on the outstanding work of economic historians who reconstructed salary and price series, inflation, and, especially for the 1960s–1980s, the unemployment rate.[51]

This book presents a chronological account of Chilean labor history to underscore the changes, breaks, and continuities in the history of unemployment. The first two chapters focus on how local and international actors discussed and responded to unemployment in the 1910s and 1920s. Chapter 1 examines the global and Latin American debates about unemployment in those years. The First International Conference on Unemployment held in Paris in 1910 and the conventions of the International Labor Organization (ILO) created a global framework to understand and cope with unemployment. International conferences and publications influenced Chile and Argentina, the first countries in Latin America to set up free placement services and statistical offices. By looking at these influences, this chapter demonstrates the connections and disconnections between global forces and local practices. Chapter 2 turns to Chile and the first policies to confront unemployment. Looking at the nitrate crises of 1914 and 1921, it shows how the instability of the export sector shaped public perceptions of unemployment and led to the first policies to protect workers. It contrasts workers' and social reformers' views about unemployment. While the labor movement focused on job security and contract protections, social reformers turned to the social consequences of large economic crises or chômage.

The second part of the book, chapters 3 through 5, focuses on the era of the Great Depression (1930–1938). The Great Depression unleashed political, economic, and social changes. General Carlos Ibáñez del Campo, known for his authoritarian political style and support for labor laws, governed Chile between 1927 and 1931. During the first year of his government, he had carried an ambitious agenda of economic and social modernization including public infrastructure. However, the international crisis quickly destabilized the government. The fall of exports reduced state revenues, and by 1931 the country defaulted on its foreign debt. Social discontent forced Ibáñez to resign. After his departure, President Juan Esteban Montero, a member of the Radical Party, governed as interim president and as elected president until June 1932. The crisis worsened and unemployment soared. Between June and October 1932, a chain of military and civilian leaders governed the country and proposed various solutions, including the brief but emblematic Socialist Republic. In October 1932, Arturo Alessandri, who had governed the country between 1920 and 1924 and briefly in 1925, won the presidential election and governed until 1938. He restored political order and stability, sought to implement the 1931 Labor Code, and encouraged legal unions, but also imposed unpopular economic stabilization policies.

Chapters 3 to 5 focus on this intense political and economic period. They analyze how despite political instability, the state implemented many different work and direct relief programs, such as public shelters and soup kitchens, as well as consumer protections. In these spaces, these chapters argue, unemployed families, welfare professionals, labor inspectors, and law enforcement agents negotiated on-the-ground definitions of unemployment, poverty, and need. Chapter 3 analyzes work programs during the Depression. It focuses on how the Labor Department worked to regulate internal migration, organize work relief programs, and enforce labor rights. These measures focused exclusively on working-class men, reinforcing views that unemployed men threatened the nation's political and social stability. Chapter 4 turns to social provisions and unemployed families. It discusses the professionalization of aid, showing the intersections between moralistic and modern notions of welfare and private charity and public social services. Chapter 5 analyzes protections for consumers and renters such as price and rent controls and minimum wages. These were some of the most emblematic reforms enacted during the Depression, suggesting the critical importance of consumer rights in the construction of a system of social welfare.

The last section of the book examines unemployment policies in the 1940s and 1960s. In 1938, the victory of the Popular Front opened a new political era in Chile. The social and economic role of the state expanded. President Pedro Aguirre Cerda committed to advance social justice and incorporated labor into the political system, but after his death in 1942, the Popular Front quickly disintegrated and became a center-right coalition. From WWII into the late 1950s, the country industrialized and modernized, while the politics of the Cold War and monetary instability undermined labor rights. Chapter 6 studies how the state-led industrialization efforts and a growing international consensus about social security impacted unemployment and social welfare policies in Chile. Despite some reforms, jobs remained unstable. Chapter 7 focuses on the long 1960s and the intersections between development, labor reforms, and employment policies. In 1966, the labor movement achieved its longest and most crucial work victory: contract stability and stricter limits on arbitrary firing, and in 1971, for the first time in the history of Chile, the country achieved full employment. However, the Pinochet dictatorship that came to power in 1973 dismantled workplace protections, returning workers to a state of persistent job insecurity. The epilogue notes that under the dictatorship, right-wing political leaders emulated conservative attacks on welfare around the western world, and a new generation of economists, the "Chicago Boys," eagerly implemented a neoliberal agenda that deepened economic inequality and job insecurity.

In the early 1980s, Chilean sociologist and playwriter David Benavente interviewed unemployed men and women in Santiago. The unemployment rate was over 20 percent, and nearly 260,000 people worked in emergency programs. In shantytowns, community organizations and the Catholic Church organized soup kitchens. This collection of oral stories vividly illustrates the drama of unemployment, the dismantlement of social welfare, and the rise of informality in the 1980s. A shoemaker, for example, reflects on his life and employment history. Originally from Valdivia, he learned his trade from his father and other older workers. He moved to Santiago in the early 1960s and, in 1963, started working in the J.C. factory. He became a union leader. One of his fondest memories was approval of the 1966 contract stability law, our "most important union victory." Working conditions deteriorated after the military coup, and he was arrested during a wildcat strike. After being released, the company alleged that his job position was obsolete and fired him. He unsuccessfully filed a grievance at the Labor Department. Searching for work became a frustrating experience. Although he received an unemployment subsidy, he explained, it "was miserable comparing to the salary I received in the plant." He had some savings and opened a family business. Working along his wife, children, and mother in law was challenging, and he missed his days as a factory worker: "this family job is the worst, the most unpleasant [job] . . . when one works in a factory, one has real coworkers . . . one can talk, one can argue."[52] His and other similar stories in this book reveal how Chileans navigated the transnational crisis of capitalism and political liberalism during the interwar years, the limits and contradictions of development and industrialization projects during the Cold War era, and the devastating impact of deindustrialization and neoliberal reforms in the 1980s.

PART I

DISCOVERING UNEMPLOYMENT (1900s–1920s)

CHAPTER 1

THE GLOBAL DEBATE ON UNEMPLOYMENT

In 1910, Luis Malaquías Concha Stuardo, a Chilean lawyer and son of the leader of the Democratic Party, went to study political economy at the University of Paris, La Sorbonne. Paris fascinated Latin American social reformers at the time. Home to the first *musée social* and a diverse intellectual community, the city of lights had hosted the 1900 International Exposition and sponsored a large pavilion dedicated to social and economic reform. The young lawyer attended one of Charles Gide's seminars. Gide, a prominent French economist, had authored numerous treaties that were widely read in Latin America at the time.[1] In September, Concha Stuardo was one of the few Latin Americans who attended the First International Conference on Unemployment. At the conference, he listened to Léon Bourgeois, a colleague of Gide known for his work on solidarity and mutualism. Bourgeois declared unemployment a global threat and "probably, the most serious of social ills."[2] Concha Stuardo also learned about unemployment in industrializing countries, the efforts of William Beveridge to build a comprehensive system of social insurance in Great Britain, and the US preference for "private" and "individual" solutions. Upon his return to Chile, he served in the Parliament (Chamber of Deputies, 1915–1918) and participated in the social legislation committee.[3]

Concha Stuardo's international experience reveals how models and ideas of social reform circulated at the time. Like him, many Latin American lawyers, medical doctors, and criminologists traveled to Europe, read treatises about political and social economy, and followed news from around the world. They built networks and exchanged ideas, influencing public policy, statecraft, and institutional practices.[4] They participated in international and regional meetings and joined organizations such as the International Conference on Unemployment. Like the US Progressive Era generation, Latin American social reformers negotiated between global and regional forces. Immersed in their social and economic reality, they implemented, adapted, and, sometimes, ignored international norms.[5] In Latin

America, as Daniel Rodgers argues for the case of Progressive Era politics, "nothing, to be sure, came through the transnational networks of debate and connections unaltered."[6]

During the first decades of the twentieth century, ideas about unemployment circulated across national borders and states. They were part of the larger debate about social legislation, the efforts to regulate the workplace, and the rise of scientific and technical approaches to solve social problems. Social reformers, political economists, and labor organizations agreed that the state should establish mechanisms to protect unemployed workers and improve the labor market. The First International Conference on Unemployment (1910) and, after 1919, the meetings of the International Labor Organization (ILO) established a global framework for understanding and confronting unemployment that included the development of labor exchanges or placement services, statistical departments, and, in some cases, unemployment insurance funds.

This chapter analyzes the global debate about unemployment between 1910 and the late 1920s. To trace the circulation of ideas, it focuses on the influence of the International Conference on Unemployment, the ILO, and foreign scholars on Latin America's unemployment policy. Although experts from the North Atlantic usually disregarded the reality of Latin America, their proposals provided regional experts a starting point to discuss the labor market and, in some cases, build new institutions such as statistical departments and placement services. The case of Argentina and its National Department of Labor, analyzed at the end of this chapter, illustrates the connections, dialogue, and disagreements between regional and international experts.

THE INTERNATIONAL ASSOCIATION ON UNEMPLOYMENT

Since the late nineteenth century, experts and international bureaucrats had discussed social reform through international conferences, exhibits, associations, and publications. These venues not only built long-term networks that circulated ideas around the world but also influenced local policies and statecraft.[7] In the case of unemployment, the Società Umanitaria de Milan hosted a small conference on unemployment in 1906 that coincided with the World Expo. The meeting "brought together scientists and activists, scholars and interested parties, to shed light on various facets of [the problem of unemployment], in order to draw attention of the public authorities."[8] Along with discussing the causes of unemployment, experts examined different instruments to solve the problem including labor exchanges and insurance. More importantly, presenters turned away from "the old moralist interpretation of unemployment" that blamed the unemployed and recognized its economic causes and "involuntary character."[9] Following the Milan meeting, a group of European professors and public servants started planning a larger conference to discuss and compare measures to confront unemployment. In 1910, they met again in Paris and founded the International Association against Unemployment.

The First International Conference on the Problem of Unemployment reflected a growing consensus on the need to regulate the labor market and protect unemployed families. The conference took place in Paris in September 1910 and brought together delegates from twenty-six countries. A wide range of specialists, professors, and bureaucrats attended the conference and agreed that unemployment posed one of the most serious and complex problems to modern society. They identified many political and economic obstacles to implementing an effective program to help the unemployed, but the delegates recognized the need to meet, compare policies, and collaborate across borders. The conference encouraged states to develop labor statistics, job placement agencies, and some form of unemployment insurance. These three elements became the basis of a modern and global policy on unemployment and a foundation for the ILO's view on unemployment.[10]

Drawing on growing acceptance of scientific and technical solutions to social problems, the delegates at the conference believed that they could solve unemployment through data collection and labor statistics. Since the mid-nineteenth century, statistics had become a widely accepted scientific tool to understand society and provide governments with information on economic, demographic, and social problems. An efficient statistical office symbolized a modern state.[11] Harold Westergaard, a Danish professor and expert in statistics and demography, summarized the conference's view on statistics. Labor statistics, he explained, revealed not only the number of jobless people, but also the causes and characteristics of unemployment. By collecting information on the unemployed (e.g., age, place of birth, language, educational level) and the duration of unemployment, local and national governments could better assist people out of work.[12]

Statistics was the first pillar in the fight against unemployment, but counting the unemployed proved difficult. Westergaard argued that "Unemployment is, undoubtedly, one of the most important problems and at the same time the most complicated problem of modern statistics."[13] Collecting unemployment statistics was a complex process that revealed how states, employers, and society understood work and defined the workforce.[14] Should labor statistics be limited to one industry or have a national scope? How could labor statistics count seasonal and agricultural workers? How could statistics differentiate between people "out of work" and those who "resisted work"? How did statistics consider the place of women, many of them who worked at home? How often should states collect unemployment statistics? Some scholars differentiated between the economically active and the economically inactive population, but the distinction still puzzled and divided sociologists, statisticians, and demographers.[15] In the end, the conference presenters considered statistics a vital part of a successful unemployment program and encouraged national governments to set up statistical offices.

The second pillar of the fight against unemployment, the conference presenters argued, was the placement office or labor exchanges. Throughout the nineteenth century, a wide range of systems, including public, private, and nonprofit agencies, helped people find work. By the turn of the century, public labor exchanges, either run by municipalities or by national authorities, had become common in Europe. Civil servants also used these services to distinguish between employable and unemployable individuals.[16] At the conference, presenters argued that placement agencies could coordinate employment policies and guarantee the operation of unemployment insurance systems. By advertising jobs, connecting job seekers with employers, and recording information and statistical data, placement agencies could contribute to fight unemployment. Alessandro Schiavi (from the Società Umanitaria de Milan) believed that a modern placement service should have a technical orientation, maintain a well-organized archive, and serve all workers.[17] Experts also explored the role of placement services in internal and international migration, arguing the importance of collaboration across borders. Because placement services had a long history in Europe, presenters were optimistic about their future. A municipal officer from Strasbourg believed that "of the three questions that the conference deals with (statistics, placement, insurance), the question of placement seems to me the most practical one."[18]

The most contentious issue at the conference was whether social insurance should cover the risk of unemployment. Many industrial nations had established some form of unemployment insurance, such as voluntary insurance and support for mutual aid societies and labor unions. While some European countries subsidized and supplemented benefits already provided by trade unions, known as the Ghent system, others, such as Great Britain and Germany, were considering state and compulsory insurance. The British National Insurance Act of 1911 represented the first and most ambitious effort to implement a broad social security coverage that included the risk of unemployment. Influenced by William Beveridge, author of *Unemployment. A Problem of Industry* and one of the conference presenters in 1910, the Act provided compulsory insurance to workers in certain trades mostly affected by unemployment at the time. Contributions from employers, employees, and the state funded the insurance, a tripartite system that became the norm in social insurance programs around the world.[19]

Experts could not agree on how and why to insure the unemployed. Raoul Jay, the French expert in social legislation, argued that the final goal was "general and compulsory insurance against unemployment."[20] Others were less confident. Some warned that implementing massive unemployment insurance programs could bankrupt social security offices, while others feared that a public agency would be unable to control the fair distribution of benefits. Supporters of public insurance questioned how a union and community-based system, basically a local arrangement, could respond to a national problem such as unemployment. At the heart of the debate about unemployment insurance was the control of the unemployed. Experts were concerned that insured workers would resist employment or quit their jobs in favor of public benefits. The Director of the Labor Statistics Office in Amsterdam, Ph. Falkenburg, argued that "the question is whether the unemployed had voluntarily left work or not, and the cases when the unemployed had rejected a job offered to him outside the city."[21] Falkenburg concluded that it was imperative to know the cause and reasons for the continuity of unemployment and, only based on that, allocate benefits. By selecting, supervising, and managing insured workers, insurance offices could guarantee the distribution of payments.

The conference had many shortcomings. Few representatives of the labor movement attended, and most participants favored social reform and a middle ground between communism and laissez-faire. It was also almost entirely a European event, with the exception of the United States; the rest of the delegations—from Australia, Canada, New Zealand, South Africa, Japan, Argentina, Chile, and Mexico—played no role in the discussion. The Argentine government sent two lawyers from the National Department of Labor, Juan G. Beltrán and Manuel Gálvez, and one diplomat, Belisario Montero. With three members, the Argentine delegation was the largest Latin American delegation and the only of the three attending to give a formal, although brief, presentation. Argentina also became the only Latin American country included as a permanent member of the International Association on Unemployment.

Most presentations ignored women workers and women's unique experience with unemployment. Only two speakers, the French socialist Lydia Pissarjevsky and A. J. de Marguerie (who did not list an affiliation), briefly addressed the problem of unemployment and insurance for women. Pissarjevsky, who represented the Comité international fémenin, stressed the difficulties of counting unemployed women: "The female worker deprived of her regular job commonly resorts to cheap labor, home work or, finally, prostitution."[22] Because of the informal nature of women's work, Pissarjevsky argued, unemployment insurance would not help women. Instead, she advocated promoting union rights, fighting against prostitution, establishing a minimum salary for workers in traditional female trades, such as seamstresses, and expanding women's political rights. In contrast, A. J. de

Maguerie argued that no differences existed between men and women, as both were industrial workers and resorted to home work in times of layoffs. Advocating the equality of women's experience also allowed Maguerie to demand equal treatment in economic life.[23] Both interventions were short and provide only a glimpse into the "women issue."

After four days of intense debates, presenters agreed to form the International Association on Unemployment, which maintained national sections and published a journal quarterly. Based in the Belgian city of Ghent, the association operated in Europe, but influenced debates and policies in other parts of the world. The association invited governments to create their own national sections and exchanged publications. In 1911, Luis Varlez, the secretary of the association, wrote to the director of Chile's Labor Department, Eugenio Frías Collao, and encouraged him to form a national section.[24] Chile did not create a national section, but the association's ideas (discussed in the next chapter) informed the country's unemployment policies. The annual meetings were interrupted by the First World War, and its journal stopped appearing in 1914. Throughout the 1920s, the association and its members' careers became intertwined with the work of the ILO, which became the leading voice in the global debate about unemployment.

THE INTERNATIONAL LABOR ORGANIZATION (ILO) AND UNEMPLOYMENT

The international debate on unemployment, job security, and social policy intensified after World War I. The war had awakened the old ghosts of social revolt. The Bolshevik revolution of 1917 shook the foundation of the existing capitalist and imperialist world order. In Western Europe, the end of the war created a broad political consensus to legislate and establish social protections for all citizens.[25] In Germany, the Weimar Republic (1919–1933) expanded the role of the state in social policy and built the foundations of the welfare state, including the approval of a comprehensive and compulsory unemployment insurance (1927).[26] In Latin America, countries such as Argentina and Chile had experienced high rates of unemployment during WWI and implemented the first measures to count and assist the unemployed.

In this international context, social and labor reform became part of the peace negotiations and the Treaty of Versailles (1919). In Part XIII, the Treaty called for the creation of the ILO to advance labor rights and social justice throughout the world and, hence, contribute to peace. Following the Treaty of Versailles, representatives from thirty-nine countries met in Washington, DC, Albert Thomas, the first director of the ILO, remembered: "A mission was given to us by the Peace Treaty to found universal peace in social justice."[27] In Washington, the delegates drafted a constitution and approved six conventions. The agreements covered fundamental labor rights: hours of work (industry); unemployment; maternity protection; night work (women); minimum age (work); and the night work of young persons (industry). These conventions represented a global consensus about labor rights, and while the ILO lacked the power to enforce the agreements, it nonetheless influenced both international and national debates about labor justice.

The ILO convention on unemployment was influenced by the European debate and a sense of postwar urgency. Before the conference, Arthur L. Fontaine (former director of France's Labor Department) and Harold B. Butler (a civil servant from the British Ministry of Labor) consulted with several governments and prepared a report on the problem of unemployment. The report mostly focused on Europe and the United States. Only four Latin American countries (Argentina, Bolivia, Chile, and Peru) replied to the survey sent by the organizing committee. The war, Fontaine and Butler concluded, had transformed the global economy, and cyclical economic recessions and technological innovation had made unemployment inevitable. The authors identified four kinds of unemployment: cyclical unemployment, seasonal unemployment, casual labor, and unemployment caused by changes in the industry (e.g., reorganization, new machinery). Their report described the standard measures to fight unemployment, such as employment placement offices, relief work, statistical data, control of immigration, and insurance. But the report had a grim tone. They concluded that "the study of the problem of unemployment is still undeveloped in most countries; and its range does not appear to be adequate even where it exists."[28] The committee, thus, urged the International Labor Office to coordinate the collection of global information and statistics and to recommend states to implement measures to protect workers and jobs.

Building on Fontaine-Butler's report, the ILO convention No. 2 (1919) required all signing members to collect and provide statistical information on unemployment; establish a free and public system of employment agencies; and extend these protections to immigrant workers and colonial territories. The convention brought together the two elements discussed at the First International Conference on the Problem of Unemployment: (1) reliable statistics and (2) placement and exchange offices to regulate the labor market. However, it left out universal unemployment insurance, only compelling countries that had already established insurance to cover immigrant workers. Instead of advocating universal insurance, the ILO agreed to extend special protection to groups of workers more vulnerable to unemployment. In 1920, the ILO approved the "Unemployment Indemnity in Case of Loss or Foundering of the Ship" that protected mariners and ships' crew in the event of a shipwreck.[29] In 1921, the ILO recommended that governments implement measures to prevent unemployment among agricultural workers, such as forming cooperatives and developing supplemental forms of income for seasonal workers.[30] Only in 1934, during the Great Depression, the members of the ILO approved a convention recommending the distribution of relief to the unemployed and the establishment of unemployment insurance (compulsory or voluntary).[31]

Throughout the 1920s, the ILO argued that unemployment threatened social and political stability and caused labor unrest. While the problem was global, the work of the ILO focused exclusively on industrial countries, and references to Latin America were marginal. In 1921, Albert Thomas appointed Max Lazard, the general secretary of the International Association on Unemployment, to lead a technical commission to study the problem.[32] The commission surveyed measures and remedies implemented around the world, such as employment and placement agencies, relief work, and assistance and insurance.[33] A different commission focused on statistics and definitions of unemployment. Confronted with diverse national realities, local definitions, and systems, the commission argued that "internationally comparable statistics" required a "formal definition of involuntary unemployment."[34]

Emphasizing a comparative approach among nations, the ILO proposed a universal definition of unemployment: "Unemployment is the condition of a worker who is both able and willing to work, but is unable to find employment suitable to his qualifications and reasonable expectations." The last part sparked long debates. Countries debated who a worker was and what willing and able to work meant. South Africa raised the question of "men disabled in the war, willing to work, but incapable of doing so *in their ordinary occupations.*" Chile, one of the two Latin American countries surveyed, pointed out "the difficulty of deciding in practice whether the expectations of the worker are reasonable or not." In the end, the commission revised the original definition. For purpose of collecting statistics, it argued, governments should use the following definition: "Unemployment is the condition of a worker (meaning thereby any person whose actual or prospective normal means of livelihood is employment under contract of service) who is both able and willing to work under contract of service, but who is without work and finds impossible owing to the stare of the labour market to obtain such work."[35] Despite its global discourse, the ILO analyzed unemployment as a European problem.

LATIN AMERICAN UNEMPLOYMENT AND PAN-AMERICAN SCHOLARS

In the 1920s, many Latin American governments embraced the legal and technical solutions proposed by the ILO. Latin Americans had a long relationship with the ILO dating back to the 1919 convention. In the early 1920s, Albert Thomas, ILO's first director between 1919 and 1932, traveled to South America to promote the ideals of the ILO. Latin American labor experts, such as Moisés Poblete Troncoso, regularly participated in the ILO meetings and maintained a close relationship with Thomas.[36] Despite these connections, Latin American nations did not endorse all recommendations. In the late 1920s, few countries had public placement offices or had ratified the ILO unemployment convention before the Great Depression. Unemployment insurance was unknown in the region, labor statistics were rudimentary, and public placement offices had limited impact and existed alongside for-profit agencies.[37]

Racial, gender, class, and cultural stereotypes shaped how employers and social reformers interpreted work and nonwork in Latin America. During the expansion of the export sector (1860s–1920s), employers in the region complained about labor shortages and the lack of skills and working habits among the poor. The *escasez de brazos* (labor shortage) became a rallying cry for employers, who advocated restrictions on workers' mobility, supported antivagrancy laws and debt peonage, established abusive recruitment systems, and sponsored foreign immigration.[38] By repressing and controlling workers, investors and public authorities looked to develop a modern labor market, consolidate wage relations, and create a proletarian workforce.[39] Reformers, state authorities, and law enforcement viewed healthy men who did not work as vagrants, and vagrancy, they argued, threatened social stability and economic growth.[40] This view left no room for the unemployed. Racialized views on indigenous and agricultural workers also influenced labor policies and definitions of work and nonwork. As Paulo Drinot demonstrates in the case of Peru, legislators, welfare professionals, and elites defined workers as factory and urban laborers, excluding indigenous workers.[41] Definitions of work also ignored women employed in the informal urban economy such as laundresses, peddlers, and occasional seamstresses. If vagrants, indigenous people, and working-class women were not workers, they could not be unemployed.

In the early twentieth century, local and foreign political economists became interested in understanding the consequences of economic instability in Latin America. They paid attention to the impact of the global market on their countries, arguing the need to build stronger institutions to support and protect local production. For many experts at the time, international events such as World War I foretold the difficulties of economies depending on the export of primary products.[42] Although there were only scattered mentions to the labor market and unemployment, these references unveiled the existence of new forms of unemployment, especially in urban areas and export regions with a well-developed labor market.

The work of Leo Rowe illustrates the growing visibility of unemployment in the region. In the 1910s, the Carnegie Endowment for International Peace published a series of studies on the economic impact of World War I. While most of the studies focused on Europe and the United States, two of the volumes addressed conditions in Latin America (Peru and Chile). Leo S. Rowe authored the two Latin American volumes. A political scientist and "an authority on Pan American relations and policy," he was a well-known figure in South America and had received honorary degrees from several Latin American universities, including the Catholic University in Santiago, Chile, and San Marcos in Lima, Peru. Rowe was part of a large group of US scholars who traveled, studied, and wrote about Latin America during the first half of the twentieth century. This group, historian Ricardo Salvatore argues, contributed to build new knowledge expertise about the continent, extend academic networks, and strengthen Latin America-United States diplomatic and economic relations.[43]

Rowe was one of the first to write about unemployment in Latin America. While his studies on Peru and Chile focused on the overall economic problems of these countries, he also discussed the labor market, employers' attitudes and policies, and the relationship between unemployment and wages. In Chile, Rowe explained, the war affected national finances and banking, aggravating the traditional instability of Chile's currency. He dedicated a special section to labor conditions, arguing that "the difficulties and hardships encountered by Chilean merchants and manufacturers as a result of the European War sink into insignificance when compared with the widespread suffering and misery which the paralization of commerce and industry entailed upon the working classes."[44] In the nitrate districts, workers fled the region and migrated south, forcing the state to "maintain at public expense a large army of workers and their families." Unemployment also affected industrial workers in urban areas. In some cases, factories had made efforts to keep the workforce by reducing wages. The economic crisis did not affect agricultural production, Rowe argues, but unemployment in the North had caused "a superabundance of farm labor" and reduced wages.

He visited Peru in 1915. Like in his analysis of Chile, he described the characteristics of the country's economic structure and financial and fiscal system, paying special attention to the export sector. Drawing on data about customs and internal revenues, he concluded that Peru was in "the most unfavorable economic, financial and governmental situation." The war, then, aggravated the ongoing economic crisis, forcing the state to adopt a series of emergency measures and reduce public expenditure. He dedicated a special chapter to labor conditions. He recognized unemployment as a problem. Unskilled laborers in Lima and Callao, Rowe argued, quickly felt the impact of the economic crisis. In other places, conditions varied. In the mining industry, companies maintained the workforce by reducing wages and benefits. Not all economic sectors suffered the impact of the war. Sugar and cotton production increased, but these employers did little to improve workers' lives and salaries.[45] In sum, Rowe identified the impact of the economic crisis on the labor market, the increase in unemployment in urban areas, and the efforts of mining and agricultural entrepreneurs to adjust to economic instability.

Rowe used a modern framework to explain economic and labor problems in South America. He provided clear and direct information on how the labor market worked, different employers' policies, and the fluctuation of wages across the countries. In the case of Peru, he emphasized the systems of labor recruitment and the inflexibility of the labor market. However, he did not completely displace cultural, gender, and racial arguments. For example, he pointed out that Chile's dependency on foreign capital and the export market caused massive unemployment in the nitrate fields, he also argued that the lack of the "habit of saving" contributed to people's poverty.[46] In the following years, the influence of US scholars, technical missions, and businesses increased in the continent. They analyzed social and labor issues and recommended states to reform institutions and policies.

ARGENTINA AND THE FIRST UNEMPLOYMENT POLICIES ON THE CONTINENT

Argentina was the first Latin American country to develop a modern definition of unemployment. Not only rapid economic change and foreign migration had transformed the labor market and consolidated wage relations, but Argentine scholars had long been part of the intellectual networks that crossed the Atlantic.[47] In 1910, at the First International Conference on the Problem of Unemployment in Paris, Juan G. Beltrán explained to his European colleagues that "involuntary unemployment does not exist in Argentina, where, in contrast, the labor force is insufficient."[48] He may not have considered unemployment a problem, but still, the Argentine government had sent an official delegation to Paris. Three years later, Manuel Gálvez, who had accompanied Beltrán in Paris, argued: "In the Argentine Republic not only the special problem of unemployment but the vast problem of insecurity of the working life remains in its integrity."[49] What happened between 1910 and 1913? How and why did Gálvez acknowledge unemployment not only as a socioeconomic problem but as one of the most serious?

In Argentina, the characteristics of export agriculture, urban growth, and the pattern of European immigration made unemployment a national problem.[50] In 1913, Gálvez published his comprehensive study on unemployment in Europe and Argentina in the *Boletín del Departamento Nacional del Trabajo*. That same year, the National Department of Labor (DNT) began measuring unemployment, and the federal government established a national network of placement offices. In 1916, DNT reported that workers were enduring "low wages, more difficulties finding a job, more days unemployed, and the increase in the price of consumer products."[51] Unemployment reached 19.4 percent in 1917.[52] The economic recession made massive unemployment more visible, but the transnational debate on unemployment offered the DNT and people like Gálvez a framework to understand the problem.[53]

In his study, Manuel Gálvez explored the social and economic aspects of unemployment both in Europe and in Argentina, negotiating between global ideas about unemployment and the local reality. Influenced by the 1910 Paris Conference, Gálvez highlighted the role of statistics, placement agencies, and social insurance in the global fight against unemployment. He mostly focused on European countries and addressed Argentina only in the last section. Similar to the claim of European unemployment experts and most social reformers, he placed himself outside political debates and maintained that "social or political doctrines" had no place in his study.[54] This position of "non-political expert" was emblematic of the social reform movement. His study was widely read and influenced not only Argentina's labor policies but also Chile's first efforts to confront unemployment. When the Chilean government organized the first public placement office in 1914, they turned to Gálvez's study, the only Latin American treaty on unemployment policies.[55]

Gálvez argued that job instability affected both rural and urban areas in Argentina. While massive unemployment only occurred during an economic crisis, Argentine workers faced seasonal unemployment and enormous difficulty finding work after being laid off. Without social protection, the life of the Argentine worker was insecure. Because unemployment was the "most important and complex social question," it was the responsibility of the state to protect workers and regulate the labor market. Building on the conclusions of the Unemployment Conference of 1910, Gálvez urged the Argentine state to develop a minimum program that included: regular collection of statistical data, the establishment of a national system of placement, and regulation of immigration. Nevertheless, although he recognized the benefits of public insurance for the unemployed, he considered it "premature" for Argentina.

While Gálvez conceptualized the problem of unemployment, Alejandro Bunge, director of the statistical office of the DNT, developed methods for analyzing and understanding the labor market.[56] Beginning in 1913, Bunge began collecting data on employment and unemployment in the city of Buenos Aires. National newspapers, Bunge explained, set off public alarm when they announced that 100,000 people remained out of work. But "how many were the unemployed?" Bunge asked himself. To find the answer, the statistical office conducted surveys across the city, interviewed factory owners, and studied the demographic data on occupations included in the last national census. Despite the alarming news, the data did not show a dramatic increase in the number of people out of work. To draw larger conclusions, Bunge needed to collect information periodically and compare numbers across a longer period of the time.[57] In 1914, the DNT started conducting periodic surveys, called *censos de desocupados*. The surveys remained limited to urban workers in Buenos Aires and those who "spontaneously" registered themselves as unemployed, which meant that the numbers were incomplete. Despite these limits, the surveys made the problem visible. In 1916, the DNT counted 10,073 individuals without a job in Buenos Aires, but it estimated the real figure probably closer to 15,000.[58]

The Argentine government also looked to curtail the abuses committed by private employment agencies and organized a national and public system of placement.[59] In 1912, the National Department had opened a national registry of placement and ordered the inspection of private agencies. Complaints had arrived at the office daily, revealing the abuses committed by private labor recruiters.[60] In September 1913, Law 91,148 created a system of no-cost and public placement agencies, the first such effort in Latin America. The law called for two offices in Buenos Aires, one in each provincial capital, as well as one in Rosario and Bahía Blanca.[61] In tandem, provincial governments started organizing placement agencies. Despite the enthusiasm of the DNT, national placement offices had a limited impact and could not eliminate the abuses committed by private recruiters, especially in rural areas, such as the sugar plantations in Tucumán.

Other Latin American countries implemented similar measures, although the impact of the reforms varied. In revolutionary Mexico, Article 123 of the Constitution of 1917 declared that "the service of job placement will be free for all workers." The Constitution did not specify how to enforce labor rights across the nation, and the violence and political instability of the following years delayed the enforcement of rights. In 1931, the Mexican Federal Labor Law (Ley Federal del Trabajo de México) established the mechanisms to enforce labor laws. The law declared that the Department of Labor would organize a system of free placement offices and allowed only some private agencies to operate.[62] In addition to Argentina and Mexico, a system of national employment agencies was first established in Chile (1914), Colombia (1928), Dominican Republic (1929), El Salvador (1931), Peru (1933), and Uruguay (1934).[63]

Between 1910 and 1930, economic downturns, growing social pressures from below, and the rise of progressive political leaders coupled with the influence of European social theorists and experts led to the discovery of unemployment in Latin America. Countries such as Argentina and Chile (discussed in the next chapter) devised mechanisms to regulate the labor market, recognized the need to curtail the abuses of private job recruiters, and believed that a scientific statistical method could inform the state.[64] Nevertheless, they dismissed other reforms. For example, Gálvez considered unemployment insurance premature. Others highlighted the differences between agricultural Latin America and industrial Europe. In 1936, speaking at the Labor Conference to the American States, Chile's minister of labor, Alejandro Serani Burgos, reflected on the differences between Latin America and European countries and the United States. He explained that "There is a whole series of factors which result in conditions, social and economic, being different in our country . . . such as the distribution of population which is small as compared with the United States or with Europe, the cultural level of our own working masses and other geographical and racial factors."[65] In the following years, these views influenced how Latin American states adapted and shaped global recommendations regarding unemployment, including unemployment insurance.

CHAPTER 2

UNEMPLOYMENT IN EARLY TWENTIETH-CENTURY CHILE

Throughout the 1910s and 1920s, Chilean lawyers, political economists, and social reformers identified unemployment as a new social and economic problem. In the pages of the magazine of the Labor Department, *Revista del Trabajo*, public servants wrote about the employment crisis in the North and the consequences of "workers' unemployment" [*desocupación obrera*]. In 1914, the government opened the first public placement service to assist unemployed nitrate workers. Carlos Contreras Labarca, the future leader of the Communist Party, published his law thesis, *La defensa del proletariado contra el riesgo profesional de la desocupación* [The defense of the proletarian against the professional risk of unemployment] in 1923. The following year, Jorge Baraona, a lawyer and member of the Conservative Party, published *El paro forzoso* [Forced unemployment]. In the 1920s, labor laws began regulating the work contract, but employment protections for blue-collar workers were minimal and difficult to enforce, especially in smaller and isolated plants.

The crisis of the nitrate industry, the national debate about social laws, and European political economists shaped Chile's first unemployment studies and policies. Witnessing the massive layoff and displacement of nitrate workers in 1914 and 1920–1921, local experts identified the export sector as the birthplace of mass unemployment in Chile. Influenced by global debates, social reformers believed that a modern public placement system and a statistical office could help improve the job market. But, as many Latin American reformers, they distrusted the unemployed and feared that uncontrolled migration, radicalism, and workers' social habits could threat the country's social order. The first unemployment policies, thus, were both about helping people to find jobs and about exerting control over workers, migrants, and their families.

The experience of unemployment, E.P. Thompson argues, precedes its understanding or discovery by social reformers. In early Victorian England, policymakers did not consider unemployment a social problem, although radical groups and trade unions addressed the issue as early as the 1820s.[1] Similarly, job instability was not new to Chilean workers. Since the late nineteenth century, labor organizations had established mutual aid funds, attempted to control the hiring and firing of workers, and fought for employment protections. Without social insurance, working families migrated and resorted to pawning their few belongings to cover the costs of medical emergency and survival during times of unemployment. During the nitrate crisis, workers strove to control both their jobs and their independence, while radical labor organizations demanded broader economic and political reforms. In the process, workers demonstrated a sophisticated understanding of the capitalist system. If reformers expected people to work for low wages under abusive conditions in the countryside for the sake of the moral importance of work, people made rational economic decisions, rejected low-paid and abusive work, and navigated the placement system established by reformers in 1914.

THE NITRATE ECONOMY AND CHILE'S CHÔMAGE

In Chile, the cycles of boom and bust of the nitrate industry brought about massive unemployment or *chômage*. Between the 1880s and the 1920s, the mining and export of nitrate sodium were the engine of the Chilean economy. Although British investors controlled the production and commercialization of nitrate, taxes on exports generated revenues for the government. The profits made possible public investment in infrastructure and the modernization of the country. The growth of the nitrate industry and its large workforce stimulated economic growth across the nation, opening a market for cheap consumer goods such as textiles and agricultural products.[2] Like other export commodities in Latin America, the market was unstable; despite government' efforts to control stocks and production, oversupply was common.

The nitrate economy gave birth to a unique labor culture. The Atacama Desert was a distant region, isolated and underpopulated, the driest desert on earth. Conquered by the Chilean army during the War of the Pacific (1879–1884), it became home to a migrant working-class community and a network of dispersed production complexes (called *oficinas*). The average *oficina* employed around three hundred people, although the largest one, Agua Santa in Tarapacá, employed more than six hundred workers.[3] Thousands of people arrived from the south of Chile and neighboring countries, such as Peru, Bolivia, and Argentina. Peons followed the promises of labor recruiters, called *enganchadores*, and traveled for days in cramped train wagons and steamships, with little food or water. The reality of nitrate fields was far from migrants' expectations and recruiters' promises. Workers faced harsh and unsafe working conditions, employment insecurity, and precarious living arrangements. The company script (used instead of national currency) and the abusive company store became the symbols of labor exploitation and created many conflicts. Over time, workers adjusted to wage labor and industrial discipline and built a proletarian labor culture and identity. In 1890, they organized, for the first time, a general strike that involved workers from fields to ports. By the turn of the century, local and general strikes were frequent, bringing the labor question to the forefront of national politics.[4]

While economic cycles caused periodic unemployment in the nitrate industry, the characteristics of the workforce, including its radical history and pattern of migration, made unemployment a national problem. During economic downturns, nitrate companies reduced and suspended production and dismissed workers. In response to the economic recession of 1885–1889, for example, employers fired nearly 50 percent of the nitrate workforce.[5] In the absence of labor laws regulating the work contract, workers faced layoffs without notice or economic compensation. Many of them waited in the ports of Antofagasta and Iquique for conditions to improve.

In the first months of 1914, the international price of nitrate started declining, and by July, the First World War interrupted international trade. Nitrate piled up in ports, and, as in the past, *oficinas* closed and laid off their workforce. In 1913, more than 54,000 workers were employed in the nitrate industry. By late 1914, the Department of Labor calculated that near 55 percent of the nitrate workforce was unemployed, estimated at approximately 33,000 people.[6] In the northern cities of Antofagasta and Iquique, commercial and port activity declined; scores of laid-off workers desperately roamed the streets in search of food and shelter. In Antofagasta, official soup kitchens distributed between 4,500 and 5,000 daily food rations, mostly to women and children.[7] Not only did unemployed workers find survival difficult in the North, but public authorities became concerned with control of these large groups of unemployed workers.

Nitrate workers had historically resorted to migration and geographical mobility to cope with the cycles of the export market. After 1914, assisting the return of unemployed nitrate workers to central and southern Chile also became a matter of public policy. Regional authorities, in collaboration with the Labor Department (founded in 1907) and foreign consulates, provided economic assistance and transportation to laid-off workers to return to their places of origin. In 1914, the Peruvian government sent a steamship to repatriate nearly 9,000 workers, most of whom had come to Tarapacá from communities in the Central Andes.[8] The Chilean government allocated funds to cover transportation and food for workers moving south; about 30,000 people were on the move.[9] In August of 1914, the National Congress authorized the Ministry of Interior to spend up to one million pesos to transport and feed unemployed workers and their families. Three months later, the government required an extra 700,000 pesos for those purposes.[10]

Most laid-off workers never returned to their birthplace, which they had left because of poverty. Instead, they stayed in larger urban areas, such as Santiago and the port of Valparaíso. The rest of the country could see the crisis on the faces of displaced strangers and laid-off workers, but a sharp decline in industrial production also worsened economic conditions in larger cities.[11] In 1914, the Labor Department estimated that industrial unemployment affected 3,785 workers in Valparaíso (nearly 44 percent of the industrial workforce), 1,059 workers in Santiago, and 616 in Valdivia.[12]

Along with arranging for the evacuation of workers from the North, the Chilean government started counting the unemployed and organized the first public placement service. In October 1914, the Ministry of Industry and Public Works created an office to oversee the job market and coordinate the distribution of blue-collar workers across the country.[13] The first system of placement was organized along the railroad stations across the country, where supervisors collected information from job seekers and employers and reported to the Labor Department in Santiago. Original plans called for placing unemployed nitrate workers in public and agricultural jobs, but the telegrams from regional authorities attested to the difficulties of placing the unemployed in new positions. In addition, the national railroad company alleged lack of funding and personnel and did not always cooperate with the new agency.[14]

The impact of official placement was limited. Based on the statistics of the Labor Department, historian Peter DeShazo estimated that placement only reached about "a quarter of the total number of the unemployed" during 1914–1915 and a fifth in 1921–1922.[15] Additionally, not all workers stayed in their new jobs. In December 1914, the Labor Department recognized that it had no information about 20 percent of the total number of workers placed, nor could it determine whether they had ever arrived to the job.[16] Turnover was high in agricultural jobs, as a combination of low salaries and poor and oppressive working conditions drove nitrate workers away. On the outskirts of Santiago, for example, the Labor Department placed 114 unemployed workers on the property of a Mr. Monreal, but after two months, only 20 remained. The rest either left or were fired. In San Vicente Tagua Tagua, landowners complained that nitrate workers were not suited for agricultural work and were heavy drinkers.[17]

Beginning in 1914, the nitrate economy entered a negative cycle and crises became more recurrent and deeper.[18] Markets conditions improved in 1916–1918, but by 1919 the accumulation of nitrate stocks and the development of synthetic nitrate threatened the industry. The end of the nitrate boom was approaching. Massive layoffs started again in 1920; 20,000 nitrate workers lost their jobs that year. The recovery of the labor market was slow, and only began improving after 1923 to collapse again in 1930.[19]

The nitrate crises evidenced Chile's fragile social infrastructure. Without institutions to manage the unemployed, the state resorted to emergency measures and funding. Between 1919 and 1922, the Congress increased funding for unemployed workers: 300,000 pesos in July 1919; 5 million for transportation and 550,000 pesos for other expenses in November 1921; and 5.8 million for shelters in October 1922.[20] While the placement office attempted to find jobs for laid-off workers, authorities opened public shelters and provided basic assistance to displaced nitrate miners and their families. In mid-1921, at the peak of the crisis, government shelters housed 48,000 people. Of the people living in the shelters, 16,000 were in the north; 12,000 in Valparaíso; and 20,000 in Santiago. At the time, Santiago had a population of just over 500,000 people, while Valparaíso had about 180,000.[21] In April 1922, there were fifteen government shelters in Santiago and one in Limache, near the port of Valparaíso, and a total population of 14,000 people, including children and women.[22]

The instability of the nitrate international market affected the Chilean economy, including the labor market and salaries. During the golden years of the nitrate boom, between 1880 and 1913, historian Mario Matus argues, there "was an increasing demand for workers," which improved salaries in many economic sectors. Nevertheless, inflation, especially after 1905, constantly threatened working-class incomes. Beginning in 1914 and until the Great Depression, the nitrate market became more volatile and crises more frequent and profound.[23] These cycles produced waves of migration from and to the northern nitrate mines. In times of economic crisis, large masses of unemployed workers concentrated in ports and larger cities, and salaries and working conditions deteriorated.[24] During the 1921–1922 recession, President Arturo Alessandri warned, unemployment in the nitrate regions affected 55,000 people; more than 47,000 men, women, and children moved south. The nitrate recession also affected other economic sectors, and Alessandri pointed to 9,422 unemployed people in the copper mines, 486 in glass factories, 3,000 construction workers, 1,200 coal miners, and 10,000 people in the shipping industry.[25]

With few legal resources and protections, workers turned to social and labor mobilization.[26] In shelters in Valparaíso and Santiago, unemployed nitrate workers formed committees, organized rallies, and exchanged ideas. In 1921–1922, workers protested in and around the public shelters, spreading fears about masses of radicalized workers wandering throughout the cities. About 300 people from nearby shelters marched to the Plaza Yungay, in downtown Santiago, on the evening of April 16, 1922. The demonstration lasted until midnight. For three hours, the crowd listened to labor activists and communist leaders. The incident was not unique: "'Shelter' residents (*albergados*) repeat these demonstrations so often," the police chief lamented, "that the police has to distribute its forces in a way that produces serious irregularities in the service." A few days later, the chief of police called in mounted troops to dissolve a demonstration of about one hundred people gathering in front of the police station in Quinta Normal, not far from Santiago's Central Railway Station.[27]

JOB SECURITY AND THE LABOR MOVEMENT

The nitrate crises showed the lack of contract protections and the need to regulate layoffs. In the nitrate fields, workers faced chronic unemployment and economic instability, as nitrate companies constantly laid off workers as the international market changed. To prevent social turmoil, employers fired and evicted workers overnight without any prior notice. Strike demands and settlements included employment protections as early as 1890. Following the General Strike of 1890, nitrate employers agreed to pay workers in cash, instead of tokens, as well as provide a fifteen-day notice in case of dismissal. However, after reestablishing public order and production, employers reverted to their previous practices and abrogated or ignored the agreements. In the early twentieth century, the government mediated labor conflicts and proposed employment protections to regulate firing and layoffs.[28]

By 1921, most nitrate companies had adopted the fifteen-day severance pay. However, the minister of the interior recognized that no laws existed to regulate the layoff of workers, which complicated government's negotiations with both workers and employers. If employers dismissed their workers without payment, the state provided for the unemployed, including paying for transportation and shelter. In his annual report, the minister recalled that the government, "obtained from the majority of nitrate and mining companies in the north, the payment of transportation costs and a severance pay to laid-off workers. This made workers' situation less distressing, and it relieved the state coffers."[29] Despite the minister's optimism on the agreement, not all nitrate employers accepted the terms. While no laws guaranteed its payment, workers considered severance pay a legitimate right and their only safeguard to confront unemployment.[30]

A disagreement over the terms of layoffs sparked the San Gregorio strike of 1921, the most violent nitrate strike at the time. Laid-off workers in San Gregorio demanded a small service indemnity from the company.[31] In January 1921, the Gibbs House, one of the largest British nitrate investors, ordered a stop in production at its San Gregorio nitrate plant, located in the province of Antofagasta. It fired its entire labor force of three hundred workers. When the company refused to give workers the traditional fifteen-day severance pay, workers occupied the town. The workers found support from the Chilean Workers' Federation (FOCH) and national labor leader, Luis Emilio Recabarren.[32] Workers refused to leave town, Recabarren wrote in *La comuna*, "without compensation (*desahucio*) and without assurance of finding work."[33] In February, hundreds of FOCH's supporters joined the San Gregorio workers in a massive demonstration. The troops stationed in town fired on the crowd, leaving around seventy people dead and more than one hundred wounded.[34] The incident, which became a symbol of the political and labor repression of the 1920s, demonstrated workers' efforts to control the terms of layoffs, employers' opposition to compensating workers, and the state's limited ability to enforce labor agreements.

In addition to severance pay, some groups of skilled workers attempted to control the labor market and the process of hiring and firing. After a series of strikes and conflicts with contractors, in 1916, maritime unions established a system of rotation (*redondilla*) in Iquique and, in 1919, in Antofagasta.[35] The system of *redondilla*, the maritime union newspaper explained, equally distributed job assignments among "the comrades registered to work" to prevent abuses committed by contractors.[36] The system only lasted a few years. In 1921, employers declared a lockout, and the government abolished the system of rotation, providing port companies broad discretion in the selection of personnel. Adducing the need to "increase workers' efficiency and discipline," the government dismantled the protections that had, for six years, distributed work and given the union a voice in that distribution.[37] Anarchist writer José Santos González Vera accused the government of creating "unemployment" among port workers to benefit commercial and port companies, and, above all, allowing management to "reject workers not because of their professional incompetence but because of their rebellious ideas."[38] Following the lead of maritime workers, bakers, printers, and foundry men also established registries of workers, but closed shops and seniority were unknown in Chile.[39]

From a larger political perspective, organized labor criticized economic policies and the lack of democracy. Throughout the 1920s, the FOCH argued that ineffective economic policies and the government's unwillingness to confront British imperialism had caused the nitrate crises. For the Left and the labor movement, the crisis revealed the intricate relationship between capitalism, economic imperialism, and unemployment. In a volatile international market and facing the threat of synthetic nitrate, nitrate producers and buyers (distribution houses) attempted to control price and supply. In 1919, the Association of Nitrate Producers had brought together most producers in an effort to improve marketing, modernize production, and, most importantly, establish export quotas. In 1921, under the leadership of the Gibbs House, buyers created what came to be known as the "nitrate pool" to unify stocks and distribute them in common. These practices focused on maximizing profits or, in times of uncertainty, minimizing losses, but had little consideration for workers' well-being and employment security. The government attempted to negotiate both with the association and with the pool to prevent a deeper economic recession.[40]

In 1921, the FOCH accused the "nitrate pool" of speculating, accumulating stocks, and manipulating the price and supply of nitrate. The pool was "responsible for the unprecedented economic catastrophe that the country is currently suffering. There are more than 40,000 hungry unemployed, who despite having energy, they must live of shameful charity."[41] That same year, José Santos González Vera, novelist and anarchist journalist, denounced the schemes of foreign companies and the lack of effective government action: "The owners of the nitrate complexes in consortium with Mr. Gibbs & Cía. have created in our land the problem of unemployment." The "inept" ruling class, continued González Vera, did not oppose their tactics, preferring to leave people in public shelters.[42]

Nitrate employers, labor and leftist leaders argued, had caused unemployment and manipulated the market to benefit and protect themselves. Their diagnosis of the export market, either controlled by foreign companies or foreign commercial houses, became a recurrent argument in the political thought of the Latin American Left. In the aftermath of the Mexican Revolution, political movements and intellectuals across the continent, such as APRA in Peru, called for the nationalization of natural resources. In Chile, historian Rolando Álvarez demonstrates, the Communist Party proposed the nationalization of the nitrate economy. Communist representatives argued in the National Congress that the nitrate economy should benefit the nation, provide stable work, and guarantee the well-being of its workers.[43] In the following decades, economic nationalism became the cornerstone of the Left and its demand for nationalization and industrialization. Industrialization and control of natural resources could also help overcome the cycle of unemployment. In tandem with these larger economic and political projects, labor unions would use collective bargaining, the court system, and direct action to protect their jobs and improve employment conditions

SOCIAL LEGISLATION AND UNEMPLOYMENT

Beginning in the early twentieth century, social reformers across the Americas called attention to the need to regulate living and working conditions. They proposed new types of legislation and asked the state to intervene in the workplace to protect working people against exploitation, unhealthy working environments, and exorbitant rents for inadequate housing.[44] In 1907, the same year that police troops massacred protesting nitrate workers in Iquique, the Chilean government established a Labor Department and approved the law of Sunday rest. The Labor Department began studying the labor question and collecting labor statistics. But the approval of labor laws was a slow process, spanning almost two decades from 1907 to 1924. Meanwhile the Parliamentary Republic continued to deploy troops to repress strikes and social protests across the country.[45]

Although two large unemployment crises had shaken the country, protections for the unemployed only appeared on the margins of social reform projects. In 1919, a group of senators from the Conservative Party presented the first labor reform project. Inspired by the Papal encyclical *Rerum Novarum*, these "aristocratic catholic" legislators, as James Morris called them, recognized the role of the state in the workplace. They asked for the regulation of labor contracts, as well as the establishment of work protections and a minimum salary. They admitted the importance of legalizing and regulating labor conflicts and industrial relations. Otherwise, they warned, trade unions would not be "agents of progress and order" and would cause "a wave of disorder and anarchy."[46] The project addressed the question of social insurance, proposing that labor unions create mutual funds to protect their members in case of accidents, disease, death, and unemployment.[47] However, the proposal did not specify how the insurance system would work. Unemployment was merely listed as another social risk.

The movement for social legislation gained strength with the presidential election of Arturo Alessandri in 1920. "In 1920, a new era started in Chile," wrote the emblematic labor lawyer Francisco Walker Linares. Walker meant that Alessandri's election signaled the end of the absolute power of "the privileged caste in the country."[48] During his campaign, Alessandri had mobilized the working class and used populist rhetoric, promising to end social injustice. Entrenched congressional opposition, the economic recession of 1920–1922, labor conflicts, and military pressures quickly destabilized his government. In 1920, Alessandri asked Moisés Poblete Troncoso, the director of the Labor Department, to draft a labor code as an alternative to the proposal of the Conservative Party. Poblete produced a comprehensive plan that included 600 articles and incorporated most of the ILO recommendations, some workers' demands, and the legal discussions on social laws of the last decade.[49] Poblete's project, Walker reflects, was "comprehensive but . . . unrealizable" and sank in Congress.[50]

Poblete's proposal on unemployment insurance was ambitious and stemmed more from the ILO conventions than the Chilean reality.[51] He suggested a system of compulsory unemployment insurance to cover workers formally employed, who were at least fifteen years old and earned less than 3,600 pesos per year. The insurance system excluded seasonal, agricultural, and domestic workers, as well as public employees. To receive unemployment benefits, workers would register at the Placement Agency of the Labor Department, demonstrate their physical ability to work, and accept the first job available. Financed by mandatory contributions of workers and employers, as well as an annual contribution of the state, the insurance fund would offer registered unemployed workers two pesos a day for no more than three months.[52] His insurance proposal found little support in the Congress and was quickly forgotten.

The efforts to enact social laws faced ferocious political opposition. Only after a group a group of young military officers led by Carlos Ibáñez del Campo arrived in the National Congress in September 1924, legislators approved a package of seven labor laws.[53] These laws became the backbone of Chilean labor code and established compulsory social insurance (sickness and disability), work accident compensation, mandatory labor contracts, and unionization rights. A system of arbitration and conciliation would mediate collective labor conflicts and individual disputes between workers and employers. A few months later, in April 1925, the National Congress approved a law to protect working mothers and guaranteed provision of childcare in the workplace.

Chile's first broad labor legislation (1924) did not include protections for the unemployed. The employment contract law (Law 4053) established rules of employment in workplaces with at least ten workers, with the exception of agriculture and retail industries and domestic work. It guaranteed some standard rights: an eight-hour day, the prohibition of child labor, basic safety conditions, and special protections for women workers. The law also regulated the length of the contract and the grounds for termination. Employers could legally and immediately fire workers in case of dishonesty, absenteeism of more than two days, intentional damage to property, and failure to complete work. Employers could also dismiss workers without cause by providing a six-day notice or the payment of the equivalent of six days of work. If workers had moved for their jobs, employers had to cover the costs of transportation for the worker and their family.[54]

In 1931, the Labor Code incorporated the employment contract law (Law 4053), extending its benefits to all manual workers without exception. The six-day warning remained intact for blue-collar workers, and the law only further obligated employers to give workers an hour a day to search for work during the six-day warning period time. Domestic workers, now covered by labor laws, had the right to a fifteen-day warning, but could be fired without warning or compensation if employers believed they had been "disrespectful." In the countryside, the Code, although rarely enforced, provided seasonal workers with six days' warning and *inquilinos* (the resident laborers) with a two-month notice. Employment conditions were better for white-collar employees in the private sector. If employers had no reason to fire an employee, the law required that they provide a one-month notice or the equivalent to one month's wages, as well as severance pay equivalent to one month's wages per year of service.[55]

The new employment protections fell short of the demands of the labor movement. For three decades, nitrate workers had struggled for rights in cases of contract termination. The six-day warning in case of contract termination did not guarantee payment, as employers could give a notice instead of paying the extra days. The vague grounds for termination without warning or compensation still gave employers considerable room to fire workers at will. For example, at the National Hat Factory in Santiago, workers could only take a ten-minute break per shift (each shift was about four hours), could not talk with their coworkers while operating the machinery, had to show respect for their supervisors, and were responsible for keeping the machinery in good shape. Penalties for violating the factory rules ranged from a small fine and deductions from pay to immediate firing.[56] At the José Robinovitch foundry, strict rules prohibited employees from leaving the workplace without authorization or fixing breakfast or tea. Workers were immediately fired after missing work for two consecutive days without a legitimate excuse and fined for late arrivals and other misconduct.[57]

Employers constantly fired workers for breaking internal regulations. In the Anaconda copper mines, employees' behavior in the camp or even inside their home could be considered grounds for contract termination. Sixto Mondaca Julio was found drunk inside his home and in possession of two bottles of *pisco* (brandy). While he alleged that the bottles belonged to a guest, drunkenness, even in the privacy of his home and during nonworking hours, was enough to get him fired without notice or compensation. Under the regulations (*reglamento interno*) imposed by the company and ratified by the Labor Department, firing Mondaca Julio and evicting him from the camp without compensation was entirely within the company's rights, showing the enormous power of employers.[58] In other words, despite the enactment of labor laws, as the Gath & Chaves department store labor newspaper stated in 1926, workers remained vulnerable to dismissal. "In the workshops and factories, one can hear when a brother is fired from his job because of economic reasons or an insignificant mistake, after years of service, without any consideration for his efforts. . . . Not a small tip, not even a word of thanks for his daily sacrifices, the worker only takes with him the dry notice of the six days of warning . . . the law does not establish more, then, one has to resign himself to suffer with patience the innumerable vicissitudes that come with forced unemployment."[59]

Enforcement of labor contracts faced many obstacles; wrongful termination and unpaid salaries were among the most common cases in labor courts.⁶⁰ Employers evaded their legal responsibilities, exposing workers to unsafe working conditions and insecurity, while employees had few resources to prove unfair firing to receive monetary compensation. Between 1924 and the enactment of the Labor Code in 1931, the regulatory system excluded some workers entirely, such as domestic and agricultural workers, creating a series of conflicts and ambiguities in certain industries. In southern sawmills, employers argued that as an agricultural complex, the rules of employment did not apply to them. The Molvén sawmill, in Mulchén, employed more than four hundred workers without a contract in the late 1920s, showing the limits of employment protections.⁶¹

The enactment of labor laws paralleled employers' efforts to increase control over the work process as well as maintain discipline on the shop floor. Across larger industries and modern mine complexes, such as the US-owned copper mines, management established welfare departments and strict internal regulations that extended company's influence beyond the workplace and into workers' homes and everyday lives.⁶² In the South, coal companies hired professional social workers to enter workers' homes and promote modern ideas of family.⁶³ While some companies committed to improving working and living conditions, the regimentation of the work process increased pressure on the labor force and undermined workers' independence. New company rules allowed employers to fire workers for disrupting internal discipline, talking, smoking, or missing work. The employment contract law gave workers basic employment protection in case of firing but also reaffirmed employers' control over the workforce. In the following decades, unions would defend workers from employers' arbitrary abuses and organize wildcat strikes and walkouts

The demand for unemployment insurance never found widespread support among legislators, reformers, and politicians in Chile. Most of them saw it as a foreign measure unsuitable for countries such as Chile. Jorge Baraona argued that unemployment insurance was unnecessary in Chile because the country still had undeveloped natural resources that could stimulate the economy and provide jobs.⁶⁴ Like Baraona, Carlos Cañas O'Ryan, a medical doctor at the retirement fund of railroad workers, also saw unemployment insurance as too complicated, especially in terms of defining risk, calculating the compensation, and funding it.⁶⁵ Wilson Hernández also opposed unemployment insurance, citing economic reasons and cultural idiosyncrasies of Chile versus Europe. He distrusted Chilean workers and believed that they would use "subterfuges to improperly obtain a subsidy."⁶⁶ Additionally, he stressed Chile's economic vulnerability, which would make unemployment insurance so large as to be impractical. On the other hand, labor leaders and leftist politicians did not articulate a larger demand for unemployment insurance as a priority. Instead, they strove for regulating the work contract, the process of hiring, and the payment of service indemnities on termination of employment.

Throughout the 1920s, Chilean lawyers, political economists, and social reformers identified unemployment as a new problem of the national economy. They reacted to the massive layoff and displacement of nitrate workers, making the export sector the birthplace of mass unemployment. They supported state intervention in the labor market and the establishment of basic protections such as placement services and labor laws. If they identified the economic causes of unemployment, they also highlighted the "moral" and "racial" decline of unemployed men and the need to differentiate between vagrants and unemployed. When the Great Depression hit the country, experts were still struggling to count and define unemployment.

PART II

EXPERIENCING MASSIVE UNEMPLOYMENT (1930–1938)

CHAPTER 3

FIGHTING UNEMPLOYMENT

PUBLIC PLACEMENT AND WORK RELIEF PROGRAMS

> When the future of the country demands sacrifices,
> You have no right to avoid them
> And you must resign yourself to work and earn less.
> —GENERAL CARLOS IBÁÑEZ DEL CAMPO, 1931

In 1930, Guillermo del Fierro oversaw the Labor Department's provincial office in the city of Copiapó. It was a small office, with only five people to serve the entire province of Atacama. He taught workers about labor laws, supervised union elections, handled inquiries and complaints from workers, and visited mining camps; but long distances, limited transportation, and little funding obstructed his work. When unemployment soared in the first months of 1930, del Fierro opened a job placement service in the railroad station of Pueblo Hundido, near the Anaconda copper mine of Potrerillos and six hours from Copiapó. He placed people in agricultural work and the construction of the Lautaro reservoir, the most important construction project in the province. Like other labor inspectors and experts on unemployment, he believed that helping people find work and assisting employers secure a workforce would improve the labor market.[1] However, by July 1930, few local employment opportunities and increasing numbers of people out of work made the traditional job placement system obsolete.[2]

People like Guillermo del Fierro were the first public officials to respond to the economic crisis in 1930. Working in the northern provinces of Tarapacá, Antofagasta, and Atacama, they witnessed the downfall of the nitrate and metal mining industries and recorded the rise of unemployment. Inspectors were the human face of the Labor Department. Despite limited resources, they visited plants and labor camps, attempted to enforce labor laws, and responded to the pressing needs of the people who lost their jobs. Their work was a sign of the growing influence of the state in the workplace and in workers' lives. During the first three decades of the twentieth century, Chile had built a modern system of labor relations that included the regulation of work contracts and working conditions, the legal recognition of labor unions and collective bargaining, and the mediation of the state in labor disputes. This system required the state to create agencies such as the Labor Department (1907) and hire a growing number of public servants.[3] Although the Labor Department's size, budget, and functions had expanded, its resources were not enough to meet the growing demands of labor.[4]

This chapter examines how the Labor Department handled unemployment between 1930 and 1933. The rapid deterioration of economic conditions, political instability, and widespread fears about social turmoil influenced unemployment policies. In 1930, the Labor Department transported and relocated nitrate and mine workers, recommended the reduction of the workweek in industrial plants, and attempted to enforce labor laws. Labor inspectors also turned to the traditional placement system, expecting to regulate the labor market. None of these efforts were simple tasks. Inspectors negotiated with unemployed workers who challenged norms that limited workers' autonomy and with employers and other state agencies that considered labor laws an obstacle to economic recovery. Following the fall of the Ibáñez dictatorship in July 1931, the Labor Department and the Department of Public Works established work relief projects and employed about 60,000 people. Relief faced many hurdles. The stigmatized view of the unemployed as idled and radicalized individuals, as well as problems financing and managing public works sites, made work relief highly controversial and discouraged the establishment of long-term reforms such as unemployment insurance.

UNEMPLOYMENT AND NITRATE WORKERS (1930–1931)

In January 1930, Ernesto Ortíz Wormald, the retired military general in charge of the Labor Department's placement service, reported that about 6,000 nitrate workers had lost their jobs in the provinces of Tarapacá and Antofagasta and the Association of Nitrate Producers had shut down 56 of its 128 plants.[5] Although the nitrate industry employed 58,493 people in 1929, Ortíz Wormald was not particularly concern about the layoffs.[6] During the first months of 1930, nitrate production and exports declined; as in the past, the Labor Department and provincial authorities expected nitrate to rebound quickly. They saw the crisis and unemployment as a problem of the export sector and the nitrate industry and were unaware of its impact on the rest of the country. In February, Ortíz Wormald argued that there was "no unemployment in the country," and the recent layoffs in the nitrate districts were "momentary."[7] Despite his initial optimism, working and employment conditions deteriorated. By February 1931, 28,661 nitrate workers had lost their jobs, and 47,893 people (including men, women, and children) had moved south.⁸ In September, the total number of unemployed nitrate workers reached 32,619, and 58,394 people had moved out of the nitrate provinces of Tarapacá and Antofagasta.⁹ Between 1929 and 1932, nitrate exports dropped about 85 percent, and the industry never recovered its pre-Depression levels.¹⁰

The Labor Department used labor laws and services such as the placement office to control layoffs and regulate the transportation and relocation of nitrate workers and their families. It relied on two legal instruments. First, the employment contract law (1924), discussed in chapter two, defined work contracts and required employers to provide a six-day notice to workers dismissed for reasons beyond workers' responsibility. The law also required employers to pay workers and their families for transportation costs in case they had to move.¹¹ This last issue was especially important in the nitrate industry, where most workers had migrated from other parts of the country. Second, the Labor Department had the authority to supervise and prevent "unexpected and large layoffs." In 1929, when hundreds of laid-off workers from the copper mine of Chuquicamata had unexpectedly arrived in Santiago, the Ministry of Social Welfare reaffirmed employers' responsibility to alert the Labor Department if planning to fire more than fifty workers. In a memorandum sent to all regional authorities, the Director of the Labor Department required employers to give local authorities a twenty-day notice for all massive layoffs and to submit a list with the number, occupation, and destination of all dismissed workers and their family members.¹²

By enforcing the contract law and managing large layoffs, the Labor Department expected to prevent the concentration of large numbers of unemployed people in northern cities and ports. At the local level, inspectors struggled to guarantee workers' rights in a volatile economic environment. Instead of sending workers home and paying transportation costs, some employers had relocated workers within the nitrate industry. Bad working conditions and low salaries created an intolerable situation. Overcrowded labor camps, the *intendente* of Tarapacá warned, endangered "the hygiene and health of its residents," and many workers asked the office for help.¹³ Northern ports and towns quickly felt the impact of the nitrate crisis, forcing the Labor Department to cover travel and living expenses. A diverse group of people including single mothers, dock and railroad workers, and urban laborers could not find work and required assistance to pay basic living expenses. Emilio Valdivia Rojas, for example, was married, had five young children, and had worked in the port of Iquique between 1920 and 1929. In 1931, he had no work, no savings, and was about to be evicted from his house. His only hope was moving in with his wife's relatives in Tocopilla, 143 miles south, but he had no money for the trip.¹⁴

Following layoffs, unemployed nitrate workers faced a long and uncertain journey. From their workplace in the Atacama Desert, they rode the railroad to one of the two main nitrate ports, Iquique or Antofagasta. There, employers provided a third-class steamship ticket to Valparaíso and railroad tickets from Valparaíso to Santiago and then from the capital city to their final destinations in the Central Valley and the south of the country. Not all nitrate workers followed the same route. Because of family ties or the expectation of employment opportunities, some nitrate workers traveled to the port of Coquimbo and wandered through the small towns and agricultural valleys of the Norte Chico.[15]

Despite the route they took, travel conditions were miserable. Workers rarely received third-class tickets. Instead, they traveled on boat decks and ate little. Drinking, gambling, and fights became common aboard.[16] Steamships and railroads often lost and mishandled workers' luggage. After many workers complained about missing luggage, a labor inspector lamented that the Association of Nitrate Producers and the steamship companies refused to protect the "interests of the unemployed workers."[17]

Many times, nitrate families spent the night in Santiago, boarding in one of the cheap guesthouses located near Central Station. The daily reports pictured a chaotic and grim atmosphere. On March 7, 1931, at about 10 p.m., the train from Valparaíso arrived in Central Station with 141 men, women, and children from the nitrate fields. An employee of the Association of Nitrate Producers met them at the station and distributed the group in two hostels, El Viajante and Europa.[18] But as the number of displaced people soared in the following months, travel arrangements deteriorated, abuses increased, and the large number of people traveling and looking for assistance created a permanent state of emergency around Santiago's railroad station.[19] The movement of nitrate workers across the country and the everyday display of poverty sparked a sense of national crisis and, as the next chapter analyzed, forced the Labor Department to provide additional services such as shelters, soup kitchens, and medical care.

Along with managing the relocation of nitrate workers, the Labor Department used its placement services to distribute nitrate workers in available jobs. The office had not changed much since the last nitrate crises of 1914 and 1920: unemployed workers registered at the Labor Department or other regional offices, employers submitted their labor needs, and the Department arranged the transportation of workers. But the Placement Office lacked personnel, resources, and information to handle the increasing number of unemployed people.[20] More importantly, the placement strategy failed when the crisis extended to other economic areas, and jobs in mining, manufacturing, transportation, and construction became scarcer. The Department of Labor only placed between one-half to two-thirds of registered

TABLE 3.1 NUMBER OF REGISTERED AND PLACED BLUE-COLLAR WORKERS, 1932–1933

MONTH	REGISTERED	PLACED
December 1931	55,733	17,496
January 1932	56,180	7,114
February 1932	63,930	1,967
March 1932	74,960	3,179
April 1932	75,349	4,421
May 1932	79,263	2,366
June 1932	90,570	4,282
July 1932	96,780	4,926
August 1932	101615	5,973
September 1932	101,202	5,611
October 1932	n/a	n/a
November 1932	102,105	4,344
December 1932	97,990	5,345
January 1933	79,574	9,216
February 1933	69,578	8,840
March 1933	52,559	7,515
April 1933	53,384	6,146
May 1933	47,621	2,759
June 1933	47,598	2,992
July 1933	41,928	2,464
August 1933	41,880	2,079
September 1933	46,650	2,946
October 1933	49,057	4,464
November 1933	48,637	5,234
December 1933	45,014	5,352

Source: *Estadística chilena*, 1933.

workers, and the number of unplaced workers consistently increased from 1930 to 1932 (table 3.1). Santiago Wilson Hernández, minister of social welfare in early 1932, argued that "faced with the magnitude of unemployment, placement services played a very modest role." The problem, Wilson Hernández continued, was that "there were no jobs for the unemployed."[21] This was not a just a nitrate crisis but the largest economic depression in the history of capitalism, making traditional placement services ineffective.

The massive migration of nitrate workers and the failure of the placement system created tensions between the Labor Department and provincial authorities, reviving traditional fears about social and labor upheavals. Whether the Association of Nitrate Producers or the Labor Department had paid for transportation costs, inspectors expected nitrate workers to settle with family members or in places where they could find jobs. The Department had little power to limit people's mobility or verify the information workers provided. Did Emilio Valdivia Rojas, the port worker described above, ever settle with his in-laws in Tocopilla? Or did he, as many other unemployed men, leave his family behind and start searching for work somewhere else? Indeed, throughout the entire period, provincial authorities and local elites protested the arrival of unemployed people, especially nitrate workers. In the South, the governor of Traiguén protested the "wandering" of unemployed nitrate workers in his province, whom he described as "a floating population of vagrants."[22] Similar accounts came from all over the country. In the face of massive unemployment throughout the country, provincial authorities pleaded with the Labor Department to restrict the migration of nitrate workers. Throughout 1931, unemployment became a national problem.

UNEMPLOYMENT BECOMES A NATIONAL PROBLEM

In February 1931, the Labor Department recognized that the "problem of unemployment is worse every day" and called for new studies and effective solutions, such as reducing wages and working hours.[23] Indeed, the nitrate industry showed no signs of recovery, and the entire Chilean economy felt the effects of the world depression. The price of copper, the country's second export commodity, plunged from 17.47 cents per pound in 1929 to 7.03 cents in 1931. Agriculture, manufacturing, and construction also plunged throughout 1931, and the country experienced a devastating economic crisis.[24] The Department recommended industries with more than 200 people to shorten the workday from eight to five hours or the workweek from six to five days.[25] Throughout the country, labor inspectors supervised layoffs and enforced labor laws, assuming the cost and responsibility of guaranteeing workers' survival (e.g., food, shelter, transportation). Because of the crisis, they also legitimated wage cuts, payments in kind or scrip instead of cash, and other business strategies to reduce labor costs.

Like in other parts of the world, the crisis showed the contradictions of companies' welfare discourse and capital's inability (or unwillingness) to protect workers in times of economic insecurity.[26] Large mining and manufacturing companies avoided shutdowns by reducing production. They fired single and unskilled workers to protect workers with large families and maintained some of their paternalistic practices such as company housing and in-kind benefits (e.g., fuel, food).[27] These were informal practices; neither seniority nor family status legally protected Chilean workers from layoffs. If large companies continued their corporate social welfare practices, they also harassed and co-opted labor inspectors, refused to comply with labor laws, and used layoffs to purge the workforce of radical elements.

The cases of large-scale copper and coal mines illustrate the tensions between corporate social welfare and companies' financial decisions. In the copper mines of Chuquicamata, Potrerillos, and El Teniente, US-owned copper companies suspended all construction work, froze investment, and decreased production.[28] The average annual production of these companies fell from 248,000 tons in the period 1925–1929 to 178,000 tons between 1930 and 1934.[29] Moreover, the *Anuario Estadístico* estimated that employment in the large-scale copper industry fell from 12,376 to 7,966 between 1931 and 1933.[30] The collapse of the copper industry impacted the overall Chilean economy, as well as local employment, salaries, and working conditions. Companies cut salaries and working hours, but assisted unemployed workers, especially those with families.[31] In El Teniente, the Kennecott Copper Corporation fired about 1,400 workers between March and June 1931, many of them single, unskilled, and transient laborers.[32] In Potrerillos and Chuquicamata, management imposed a 10 percent wage cut in December 1931 yet allowed some jobless families to stay in company houses.[33] While labor inspectors welcomed companies' efforts, many working families found the terms unacceptable. In the case of Potrerillos, for example, more than 500 workers resigned and left town following the wage cuts.[34]

In coal towns, such as Lota and Coronel, companies had also reduced work, fired unskilled and single workers, and operated the mines only three to four days a week by the end of 1931. Companies allowed unemployed families to stay for free in company houses and access charcoal for cooking and heating, while labor unions provided a small subsidy to members who lost their jobs.[35] In September 1932, the Ministry of Labor paid an official visit to coal mining towns; officials reported that coal miners worked three days a week and earned an average wage of seven pesos per day, but also noted 2,500 registered unemployed miners. Despite the coal companies' efforts to assist workers and their benevolent discourse, the report pointed out, many obstacles prevented enforcement of labor laws. Particularly in the case in Lota, the report concluded, the company "has a semi-feudal power in this region" and owned or influenced all local commercial activities. The report also mentioned that the company manipulated local authorities by giving them free housing, coal, and other goods. As a result, the report concluded, the local labor inspector did not enforce labor laws, a practice that the working community resented.[36]

Small and medium-size copper mines were more unstable than large-scale mining; reducing production was financially and technically impossible. In the province of Coquimbo, a region of small mines, copper production fell from 2,783 tons in 1930 to 110 in 1932.[37] In many cases, labor inspectors reported that small mines had not paid salaries for months, illegally reduced benefits, charged exorbitant prices in company stores, fired people without previous notice, or abandoned their properties to evade all legal responsibilities. The dramatic stories from small mining camps struck by the crisis involved men, women, and children living in dire geographical conditions without access to food, legal assistance, or transportation. In these conditions, labor inspectors not only had to deal with the reluctance of employers to follow the law, but also overcome the physical difficulties to reach isolated communities. The obstacles to enforce labor laws were enormous; nevertheless, inspectors filed reports and sued employers in labor courts, prevented starvation, and relocated people at the expense of the state.

Elisa de Bordos was a small copper mine located twenty-eight miles from Copiapó near the Yeso railroad station. On the eve of the Depression, the company employed forty-three people, many of them married and with large families that lived in a small camp near the mine. The mine had a history of labor abuses, which a previous labor inspector had pointed out in a report in February 1930. In May, the manager announced the shutdown of production for an indefinite period. When a labor inspector arrived, he found a desperate situation: unpaid salaries, almost no food left at the company store, and many women and young children starving in the camp. The hands of the inspector were tied, while companies should not shut down without paying the workforce, Elvira de Bordos had no means to fulfill its obligations at the time. The inspector adapted the terms of layoffs because of the dire economic circumstances and accepted the company's promise to pay workers' salaries in the next thirty days. In the meanwhile, the Labor Department relocated the workers and their families, many of whom moved in with relatives in the area. In the Elvira de Bordos mine, as in many other small mines and companies, the government paid to relocate and feed workers, while employers vanished to avoid legal obligations.[38]

In the first months of 1931, the Labor Department confronted the deterioration of working conditions in construction sites. Because it relied on export revenues, the Chilean state's finances suffered the consequences of the world recession; state revenues declined about 60 percent between 1930 and 1932.[39] In February 1931, General Ibáñez ordered Teodoro Schmidt, Director of the Department of Public Works, to suspend payments to private contractors. Although Schmidt reassured private firms that the suspension was temporary, working conditions quickly deteriorated.[40] Between February and July 1931, many contract companies stopped work, while others alleged they were unable to pay workers in cash.[41] In May 1931, the Ministry of Social Welfare authorized contractors both to pay workers every other month and to advance part of their salaries in tokens valid at company stores.⁴² This emergency and temporary solution allowed contractors to overlook some fundamental labor rights such as workers' right to be paid regularly and in cash. In the case of railroad construction projects, the Railroad Department negotiated with contractors to ensure that cash payments would not be less than 10 percent of workers' wages, arguing that it was "better for the working class to have a job that could guarantee their subsistence than complete unemployment."⁴³

Uncertainty, as well as employers' abuses, increased on construction sites during the first months of 1931. Working conditions at Barriga, Wachholtz, Alessandri & Cia firm in Valdivia typified the instability and deprivation construction workers endured in 1931. Like other private contractors, Barriga, Wachholtz, Alessandri & Cia had not received regular payments from the government. In April 1931, the company and its subcontractors had employed about five hundred workers to construct the railroad in Maullín but laid off about two hundred people and planned to fire another two hundred men in the following weeks, cutting its workforce to one hundred. Local authorities encouraged the company to lower salaries to keep as many workers as possible.⁴⁴ The construction company, then, fired all its workers and rehired them under new contracts, offering to pay 10 percent of salaries in cash every two months and the remaining salary in scrip. While the agreement may have prevented further layoffs, workers complained they did "not receive a cent in cash for their work" and prices at the company stores were about 40 percent higher than in the free market.⁴⁵ At the National Congress, Abraham Quevedo, the communist deputy, supported workers' demands and accused company stores in Maullín and other railroad camps of charging "exorbitant prices."⁴⁶ In a later visit to the camps, the labor inspector dismissed workers' complaints, arguing that the company store system offered some advantage to workers, although he did not detail what these advantages were.⁴⁷ At the end, the Labor Department had prevented a massive layoff in Maullín, but failed to enforce existing labor laws.

During the first six months of 1931, labor inspectors reported massive layoffs in coal mines, construction sites, and manufacturing plants. In May 1931, the Labor Department recognized its inability to solve the problem of unemployment with traditional methods and institutions, asking labor inspectors to help people as they could. In many cities, authorities instructed law enforcement to tolerate street vendors. In Santiago, local authorities organized the men and women living in one of the many shelters to "sell dry fruit" on the street, wearing white aprons and bonnets, providing people with prunes and raisins packed in standardized cardboard boxes.⁴⁸ In large industrial plants and construction projects, the Labor Department encouraged employers and workers to create special funds to help those who had lost their jobs. In Puerto Montt, workers at the Dickerhoff &

Widem construction firm contributed part of their meager weekly salary to a collective emergency fund, though the company had promised the Labor Department it would match workers' contributions.[49] These strategies only helped at the local level and were quickly exhausted, many of them unpractical or without much impact on people's well-being or the national unemployment rate.

Economic conditions deteriorated during the winter months of June–July 1931. Workers participated in a wave of protests and strikes across the country to demand that General Ibáñez resign. His inability to confront the economic crisis had made his authoritarian style intolerable. On July 26, 1931, Ibáñez fled the country. Juan Esteban Montero assumed as provisional president.[50] Economic and social conditions across the country were desperate, and local authorities demanded a national response. The *intendente* (the head of the province) of Concepción warned the minister of the interior that "the problem of unemployment in the province of Concepción is now beyond the control of local authorities." Private organizations were unable to help, the *intendente* argued, and the government should find a "solution" to unemployment.[51] Congress representatives also brought attention to the dire needs of their districts. Carlos Elgueta, a member of the Radical Party, asked for emergency funds to help unemployed families in the coal towns of Coronel and Lota.[52]

Jobs were the solution to unemployment. While the remedy was obvious, explained social worker Leo de Bray, the question of who should provide work for the unemployed was less clear.[53] As of the 1910s, previous chapters demonstrated, Chilean social reformers believed that an imperfect labor market and lack of information caused both labor shortages and unemployment, while massive unemployment (called by the French word *chômage*) was cyclical and a problem of the nitrate industry. By collecting statistics, negotiating with employers, understanding employers' needs, and regulating internal migration, the Labor Department expected to find temporary work for nitrate workers in agriculture and construction sites. For the next fifteen months, political and economic instability, as well as military interventions, shook the foundations of Chile's republican tradition.[54] Despite this instability, state intervention in society and the economy increased, and the Labor Department devised new ways to help the unemployed. In August 1931, the provisional government led by Juan Esteban Montero moved from placing workers in the private sector to organizing and financing work relief programs.

WORK RELIEF, 1931–1932

During the Great Depression, governments around the world turned to public works to provide jobs for the unemployed, increase people's consumption and purchasing power, and reactivate national economies.[55] As a mechanism to replace "direct assistance" with "productive assistance," the ILO explained, massive public works projects put millions of workers on construction sites in countries such as Germany and the United States.[56] Work relief was an attractive idea, David Crew argued in the case of Germany, because "it promised to preserve welfare clients' commitment to industrial labor discipline and their intellectual and physical abilities to resume wage labor when the opportunity arose."[57] But these programs reproduced gender, racial, and class divisions. In the United States, the Works Progress Administration (WPA) created programs for different types of workers: young and old, intellectuals and artists, people of different races, and men and women.[58] In Germany, work relief programs maintained traditional gender roles by giving women jobs that reinforced homemaking skills.[59]

Though Chilean social reformers and government officers looked to these international experiences to legitimate the establishment of similar programs, they developed their own national version of public work. In Chile, the government only offered jobs to working-class men, while women, children, and white-collar employees, as the following chapter analyzes, received food and shelter. Unskilled workers and peons were the largest unemployed group, but also the most visible one. Elites and public authorities viewed unemployed men as suspicious, fearing they would lose work habits and physical strength, commit immoral or unlawful acts, and radicalize fellow workers and neighbors. Teodoro Schmidt, Director of the Department of Public Works, argued that charity and direct aid "leads, inevitably, to a person's moral and physical ruin," while work disciplined men and limited the influence of radical ideas.[60] Physical work, he argued, provided unemployed men with an income to support their families and, more importantly, prevented their degradation.

The first efforts to provide work for the unemployed were municipal initiatives. From 1930 on, local governments faced the arrival of unemployed nitrate workers and the closure of local industries. Unable to place the unemployed in the private sector, authorities used municipal funds to start small projects, such as road and building repairs, employing as many people as possible. Little support from the central government, ongoing migration, and growing numbers of unemployed people quickly exhausted local funding. In Valparaíso, local tax revenues and commercial activity declined and, in June 1931, the major explained that the city had no more money to finance public works projects.[61] Powerless, provincial authorities asked the central government to control the movement of unemployed nitrate workers and provide emergency funds for public works projects. The crisis required a national response.

The depth and length of the crisis undermined local resources, and both direct assistance and work relief became the responsibility of the national government. The transition from a local to a national response to unemployment took place under the Montero administration (August 1931–June 1932). Work relief programs expanded during the months of the Socialist Republic (June–September 1932) and ended during the government of Arturo Alessandri (1932–1938). Between May and July 1931, the Ibáñez administration had shut down most public works projects, creating widespread discontent and insecurity among construction workers. In July, the *New York Times* reported that acting president Montero was considering "hiring 10,000 workers for public projects, such as extending a park along the Mapocho River in Santiago, beginning railroad improvements and starting other projects where manual work could be used."[62] In August, Montero ordered the Department of Public Works to restart public works projects, hire as many people as possible, eliminate piece work, and establish a fixed wage. In the past, contractors had selected the workforce; now, the Labor Department recruited workers. Construction work had become relief work and a "welfare system," Schmidt lamented. The department hired people regardless of lack of skills or experience and prioritized the number of workers employed over efficiency or productivity.[63] The more technical orientation of the Department of Public Works clashed against the social orientation of the Labor Department. Conflicts between the engineers and the labor inspectors over working conditions and salaries became frequent.[64]

Public works expanded rapidly in the last months of 1931. The number of paid workers increased from 2,585 in August 1931 to more than 30,000 in January 1932.[65] The Department of Public Works hired unemployed workers in all its divisions, including road construction, irrigation, architecture, railroad, and hydraulic projects. Road construction remained the most important division, employing about a third of the total workforce by the end of December of 1931 (see tables 3.2 and 3.3). Throughout the country, unemployed men repaired potholes, removed debris from shoulders, and laid gravel. Although working conditions varied across divisions, location, and skills, they were generally unappealing and sparked many protests.[66] With the exception of urban projects, workers lived in temporary camps, far away from their families, and paid for food and lodging. The characteristics of the workforce revealed the extension of unemployment. In Isla de Maipo, a rural community in the Province of Santiago, 220 unemployed men worked on road construction projects by 1932. The men came from all over the country, and while most of them were single and listed as "day laborer" as their last occupation, many were miners, as well as bricklayers, carpenters, and painters.[67]

TABLE 3.2. UNEMPLOYED WORKERS HIRED BY THE DEPARTMENT OF PUBLIC WORKS BETWEEN AUGUST 3, 1931, AND JANUARY 2, 1932

WEEK	ROADS	IRRIGATION	ARCHITECTURE	RAILROAD	HYDRAULIC	TOTAL
Aug. 3–8	1,510	1,075	0	0	0	2,585
Aug. 8–15	2,130	1,075	0	0	0	3,205
Aug. 15–22	3,454	1,075	159	0	0	4,688
Aug. 22–29	6,320	1,075	375	0	0	7,770
Aug. 29–Sept. 5	8,064	1,300	568	0	0	9,932
Sept. 5–12	10,837	1,300	869			13,006
Sept. 12–19	12,807	1,200	980			14,987
Sept. 19–25	14,274	1,674	1,589			17,537
Sept. 25–Oct. 3	13,934	1,877	2,049			17,860
Oct. 3–10	18,153	1,922	2,406	390		22,871
Oct. 10–17	19,160	2,046	2,503	590		24,299
Oct. 17–24	19,305	2,079	3,117	918		25,419
Oct. 24–31	21,381	2,124	3,440	850		27,795
Oct. 31–Nov. 7	22,150	2,049	3,608	1,137		28,944
Nov. 7–14	22,613	2,268	3,820	1,385		30,086
Nov. 14–21	22,804	2,313	4,193	1,507	50	30,867
Nov. 21–28	21,266	2,439	4,607	1,933	60	30,305
Nov. 28–Dec. 5	21,841	2,434	5,449	1,933	102	31,759
Dec. 5–12	20,593	2,456	5,641	2,155	102	30,947
Dec. 12–19	20,209	2,461	5,669	2,201	124	30,664
Dec. 19–26	20,035	2,520	5,341	2,180	123	30,199
Dec. 26–Jan. 2	20,118	2,354	5,476	2,140	120	30,278

Source: ILO-BIT Archives (Geneva), Unemployment U 15/01/12.

Low wages symbolized the dreadful working conditions in public construction projects. Work relief projects established a minimum wage of three pesos per day, an income that did not provide enough money for basic subsistence. In road construction projects in the Province of Santiago, day laborers spent about one peso per day on food and lodging.[68] In Puerto Montt, workers employed in road construction also earned three pesos per day, but received half of their wage in food.[69] In August 1931, a group of six legislators of the Democratic Party including Juan Pradenas, Leonidas Leyton, and Santiago Wilson asked the government to increase the daily wage of workers in construction projects from three to five pesos, arguing that the current wage was "insufficient to meet the most urgent needs in life."[70] In September, the minister of development (*fomento*) informed the National Congress that it would increase wages from three to four pesos for married workers, but it would maintain the three pesos per day for single workers.[71]

TABLE 3.3. WORKERS EMPLOYED IN ROAD CONSTRUCTION BY PROVINCE IN 1931

PROVINCE	WORKERS	INVESTMENT (PESOS)
Tarapacá	393	17,3100
Antofagasta	461	199,165
Atacama/Coquimbo	1,260	488,120
Aconcagua	2,810	1,387,980
Santiago	7,420	3,593,011
Colchagua	1,439	483,330
Talca	816	240,676
Maule	498	183,176
Ñuble	1,100	438,354
Concepcion	991	257,390
Bio-Bio	971	389,462
Cautín	1,150	379,200
Valdivia	880	336,879
Chiloe	600	122,748
Aysén	164	112,501
Magallanes	516	164,925
Total	20,615	8,950,017

Source: ILO-BIT Archives (Geneva), Unemployment U 15/01/12.

The controversy over a minimum wage in public works projects continued throughout the entire period, intensified by the increase in the cost of living and widespread labor protests. In November 1931, a labor inspector in Temuco explained that former nitrate workers refused to labor in isolated construction sites for three pesos a day.[72] In December 1931–January 1932, the National Congress discussed authorizing emergency funds to expand public relief projects and addressed, once again, the minimum wage problem. In the Chamber of Deputies, Juan Pradenas lamented that the Senate had rejected establishing a minimum daily wage of five pesos in public construction projects across the entire country. He described a desperate situation in labor camps throughout the country, where thirty thousand people worked, many sleeping in "poorly built shacks." A "humane salary" of five pesos, pleaded the democratic deputy, would allow "workers to eat better, purchase some clothes and, if possible, look after their families."[73]

While economic conditions and the government's bankruptcy made increasing wages difficult, the substandard working and economic conditions of rural workers remained the Achilles' heel of discussions about a minimum wage for the unemployed.[74] The minister of development opposed increasing wages, arguing that "to pay 5 pesos to workers in road construction, when their fellow workers in the countryside earn a lower salary, will cause more difficulties." Similarly, Elías Errázuriz Larraín, a representative of the Conservative Party and member of one of the oldest elite families in Chile, warned that rural workers would flee the countryside for public works projects, disrupting production.[75] In reality, the landowner class was more preoccupied about maintaining a rigid control over their workforce and stopping the enforcement of social laws than increasing production. In the following months, conservative legislators and landowners often returned to this comparison and the hypothetical fear of an exodus of rural workers of biblical dimensions. Although some agricultural peons sought construction jobs and left low-paying jobs in nearby haciendas, authorities usually turned them down.[76]

Isolation, low wages, and poor working conditions made work relief projects unattractive. Inspectors visited shelters and compelled workers to accept jobs, but some of the unemployed rejected jobs in construction or quit after a few days, while others organized and demanded better conditions. In the port of San Antonio, the labor inspector failed to convince unemployed workers to accept a daily wage of three pesos, and many just walked off the job.[77] In the Culimo water reservoir in Illapel, workers struck in October 1931 and demanded written labor contracts, wage increases, medical assistance, and price controls in company stores.[78] That same month, workers building the Polpaico road also called a strike.[79] Most labor inspectors could not keep workers in camps for long periods of time. In November 1931, nitrate workers repairing a road in Curarrehue, near the border with Argentina, asked contractors for time off and free transportation to visit their families living in shelters in Temuco.[80]

Labor inspectors and other state authorities blamed activists and organizers for the rising discontent in urban areas and shelters. In November 1931, for example, a labor inspector in the town of Calera communicated to his superior the presence of "communist elements." Many of these "elements," he argued, came from other parts of the country and were encouraging workers in the local cement plant (El Melón) to walk out of their jobs.[81] Similar communications came from other labor inspectors, evidencing the political, social, and labor unrest at the time. Indeed, both the Communist Party and the Federación Obrera de Chile (FOCH) were reaching out to the unemployed and organizing unemployment councils throughout the country.[82] But it was not only the presence of formal organizers but the arrival of nitrate workers with a common history of labor struggle, migration, and radical politics.[83] These traditions, Thomas Klubock argues in the case of copper workers, became part of "a shared historical past."[84] A few years later, in 1934, unemployed men, many of them from the nitrate fields, working in gold panning sites and the construction of the railroad tunnel Las Raíces in Lonquimay participated in the Ranquil peasant uprising.[85]

Although most of these conflicts were local, direct actions over working conditions, salaries, and the enforcement of labor laws, they were not isolated events. They took place in a time, both at the national and at the international level, of intense political, social, and labor conflicts.[86] Since the last days of Ibáñez, protests and rallies had become a daily occurrence. In the nitrate port of Iquique, for example, demonstrators gathered on September 1, 1931, to protest "the horrible poverty" and reaffirmed their rights as "wage earners (*asalariados*)."[87] They demanded unemployment insurance, rent control, jobs, aid to families in need, and the end of Compañía de Salitres de Chile (COSACH).[88] Similar rallies, called *comicios públicos*, took place around the country, bringing together large crowds of unemployed and underemployed people.

Despite public support for work relief programs, unemployment increased during the Montero administration. In October 1931, the provisional government had presented an emergency bill to Congress that would support a comprehensive plan to fight unemployment. In his speech, Manuel Trucco (provisional vice president) encouraged legislators to provide work and assistance including food, lodging, and clothing to about eighty thousand people out of work. The bill included the creation of a new state agency to supervise and coordinate all unemployment policies, the establishment of an unemployment fund, and support for "productive" activities. Citing the recent French experience in public works, he argued that public works projects should support production and the economic reconstruction of the country, discouraging financing ornamental and beautification projects.[89] In the following months, legislators discussed the project, arguing the need to devise mechanisms to put people back to work. Many believed that the solution was to support new economic activities such as commercial fishing and agribusinesses that could increase production and offer employment. Other legislators argued the need to place the unemployed in rural settlements, where they would work the land and contribute to decongest cities. In the end, the unemployment bill languished for months in the National Congress, moving back and forth between the House of Deputies and the Senate, and usually postponed because of "lack of time" or other political priorities.[90]

In April 1932, Law 5105 allocated a budget of 152 million pesos to finance public works projects, pay previous commitments, and provide direct relief to the unemployed. Public works were the largest item in the budget (about two-thirds of the total budget) and included large infrastructure projects, such as the construction of military installations and barracks, new bridges, and the improvement of port facilities throughout the entire country.[91] The budget allocated funding to develop new economic industries, such as gold panning and fishing, but was not, according to Roberto

Yunge, Director of the Department of Labor, a comprehensive work relief project. Indeed, in March, Yunge had written a confidential letter to the Ministry of Social Welfare, lamenting that the Congress had "destroyed" the original plan, "modified, cut short, and at the end, its objective distorted."[92] That same month, more than 75,000 people had registered at placement services. By August, the number of registered unemployed had reached 101,000, but only represented, the national statistical office argued, about two-thirds of the total number of unemployed people.[93]

The Montero administration had failed to resolve the crisis. Protests and discontent soared. In April, the government declared stage of siege. From the tribunes of the National Congress, Juan Pradenas (Democratic Party) accused President Montero of returning to the old times of the Ibáñez dictatorship and suppressing civil and political rights. The government, Pradenas denounced, "has declared state of siege, arrested workers and students, censored independent media."[94] In the following months, the economic and political crisis worsened.

NEW INDUSTRIES AND JOB CREATION: UNEMPLOYMENT PROGRAMS AND SOCIALISM

On June 4, 1932, a military intervention overthrew the Montero administration and a *junta* integrated by Carlos Dávila, Marmaduke Grove, and Eugenio Matte declared Chile a Socialist Republic. For the next three months, Chileans witnessed a succession of socialist-inspired military juntas that, although brief, accomplished influential reforms, such as price controls (chapter 5) and university autonomy and gave birth to the Socialist Party.[95] The new political leadership promised Chileans it would resolve the economic crisis through economic nationalism, accusing previous governments of "giving the national wealth to foreign capitalists." In contrast to the previous "mistakes of economic liberalism," the leaders of the Socialist Republic argued they would "feed the people, dress the people, and shelter the people." To do so, the government promoted national production, regulated consumption, and assisted the unemployed.[96] Though they called themselves socialists, Paul Drake argues, the leaders rejected both "capitalism and communism," "stressed state planning more than class conflict," and were far from advocating a radical redistribution of the means of production.[97]

State planning and economic nationalism influenced the fight against unemployment during these months. On the eve of the June revolution, Carlos Dávila had criticized the government's approach to work relief because it only provided a short-term subsidy and not permanent work. In contrast, he called for the creation of state companies that could offer "permanent jobs" and resolve the "country's fundamental economic problems" such as its dependency on the export market and monetary instability.[98] In July, the government merged all state agencies serving the unemployed and formed the Dirección General de Cesantía. Under the authority of the Ministry of Development, this new state agency considered job creation and economic and industrial development the engine of economic recovery.[99] In August, the government decreed that "the main objective of the Socialist State is to safeguard that all the country's inhabitants have stable and paid work."[100] The government allocated 10 million pesos to provide work and direct relief to the unemployed and 160 million pesos to the development of mining, agriculture, and industrial production. These measures were not that different from previous discussions to fight unemployment, the idea that economic development could create jobs for all Chileans remained a central idea in the future fight against unemployment.

In a context of political and economic instability and with limited access to foreign exchange and loans, developing new economic activities was almost impossible. The exception was gold panning, a rudimentary mining practice that became a symbol of work relief and economic recovery in the early 1930s.[101] In 1931, the state had started promoting gold panning, offering credit, supplies, and technical assistance to small mining entrepreneurs. The Montero administration (1931–1932) provided additional funding to develop gold production, subsidizing contractors willing to invest. In exchange for these subsidies, producers had to sell the state their entire production. Requiring very rudimentary technology and with a secure market and a large pool of available workers, gold panning expanded between 1931 and 1932. In August 1932, the minister of development Víctor Navarrete announced the "The Gold Campaign" and offered additional subsidies to contractors who hired unemployed workers.[102] Benefits to private entrepreneurs (contractors) included a monetary daily subsidy of two pesos per unemployed worker and the recruitment and transportation of the workforce.[103] The government promoted and subsidized the exploitation of gold, Navarrete recalled a few years later, "with the dual purpose of giving the unemployed a job and obtaining foreign exchange."[104]

Thousands of unemployed men found work in the booming gold panning industry, but employment and working conditions were precarious. Throughout 1932, the number of people working in gold panning sites increased from 1,200 to 36,300, and the Gold Campaign promised to hire at least 40,000 workers.[105] In 1932, the Labor Department described conditions in gold panning sites as "*sui generis*" or peculiar. There were no work contracts, and the Labor Department only required contractors to provide minimal documentation of working arrangements, method of payment, and food and housing conditions. While contractors had to provide health care in case of work accidents and contribute to the workers' social security fund, they did not need to build permanent labor camps.[106] In the South, gold was found in ravines and creeks, and the rain, cold temperature, and humidity made work strenuous and dangerous. Workers lived in provisional camps and earned three pesos per day (the government paid two-thirds of workers' salary), and the supply of food was always a problem.

Gold panning was far from solving the economic crisis, only offering unstable and precarious jobs to unemployed workers. Low cost of production, rudimentary technology, and a growing demand for gold attracted small entrepreneurs, but it offered few opportunities for economic development and industrialization. As on public construction sites, labor inspectors constantly reported problems recruiting, keeping, and controlling the workforce.[107] By August 1932, increasing political and social instability as well as poor employment arrangements jeopardized work relief projects in both construction and gold panning. Teodoro Schmidt, for example, denounced a permanent state of "indiscipline and disorder" across construction sites and especially in urban areas.[108] In Santiago, construction workers had participated in political demonstrations, formed work councils, and obtained a wage increase and improved working conditions.[109]

THE PROMISES OF STABILITY AND ECONOMIC RECOVERY (1932–1933)

In September 1932, Ernesto Oelckers Schwarzenberg, *intendente* of the southern province of Chiloé and member of one of the most powerful German families in the region, reported to the minister of the interior that 1,935 people were still unemployed in the province. He asked for funding to develop an ambitious public works agenda.[110] Most of the province's unemployed were in Puerto Montt, the largest provincial city with a total population of about 16,000 people.[111] Oelckers was especially concerned about how lack of work, poverty, and food shortage were undermining the province's social peace. In November, he reported "a large number of people wandering through the streets, without work or food, and dedicated to illegal activities to support themselves."[112] A mob, he warned, had threatened the local mill and other stores in the city, and the FOCH had organized a few public meetings in town.

Like Oelckers, local authorities, elites, and law enforcement agents wrote extensively about unemployed people's idleness.[113] Since the beginning of the crisis, they had suspected displaced nitrate workers of political radicalism, warned the central government about the presence of outsiders, and associated the unemployed with social and political trouble. By the end of 1932, they argued that public relief programs had not only encouraged idleness, but also created a new class of "professional unemployed," who lived off state aid and did not deserve aid. Similarly, they criticized the Labor

Department for financing, with little control, the transportation of nitrate workers, transforming the unemployed into vagrants. In 1930, people had feared the unemployed, now they blamed populist policies for encouraging vagrancy and threatening the country's social fabric. Nevertheless, they continued asking the national government to finance public construction projects, considering work the most efficient tool to discipline the unemployed. Government efforts to create work responded both to the pressures of local elites and provincial authorities and to the need to help the poor.

Economic insecurity, inflation, high rates of unemployment, and political conspiracies became the new normal under Carlos Dávila, the last of the "socialists" to rule the country. The government had increased spending on public works and relief, but also boosted inflation. As Albert O. Hirschman argued, those policies "resulted in near financial panic and contributed powerfully to" its "downfall."[114] Dávila resigned in September 1932. Arturo Alessandri won the presidential election in October 1932. Alessandri, who had governed the country between 1920 and 1924, promised to "reconstruct the Republic" based on "respect for its fundamental institutions." In January 1933, he called for a "political, economic, social, and moral recovery of the country."[115] To reestablish political order, he reinforced presidential power, controlled the military, and repressed radical movements, while his minister of finance, Gustavo Ross, reduced the public debt and inflation and stimulated industrial and mining production.[116]

The new government's approach to unemployment maintained the traditional emphasis on statistics and placement, but Alessandri also took steps to control the unemployed, reduce the distribution of aid, and place workers in the private sector. First, the government restructured unemployment services and placed them under the Ministry of Labor.[117] In February 1933, it ordered all regional authorities to conduct a national census of unemployed workers and their families that included information such as age and former occupation.[118] To collect data, the government provided local authorities with a single definition of unemployment. In 1933, then, the unemployed was defined as "a manual worker," who did not work "because of factors outside his control," but had "the moral capacity to work according to the social laws in force."[119] This new effort to count and define the unemployed separated the employable from the unemployable, defining vagrants, but also abandoned women and children, as unemployable.

In March, national newspapers claimed that the unemployment office had committed a series of irregularities in the purchase of food and allocation of railroad tickets among other problems.[120] Although the government claimed that these problems came from previous administrations, Alessandri organized an *ad honorem* council to oversee the national allocation of benefits and the purchase of food and, above all, exert a strict control over the distribution of benefits.[121] In tandem with the reorganization of unemployment services, the stabilization and austerity policies of Gustavo Ross called for slashing public expenses to reduce inflation and the public debt. Ross ordered the Department of Public Works to cut expenses, increase efficiency, and reduce the workforce. By July 1933, Teodoro Schmidt argued, the Department had fired about fifteen thousand people from public construction and, by December 1933, only 11,227 workers remained employed.[122] Instead of a massive relief work program, the new administration gave the private sector stimulus, credits, and tax exemption to increase production and employment.

Behind the economic and fiscal ideas of the government and its political supporters was a general view of the unemployed as a social problem and, in many cases, joblessness as a "voluntary" state. In the decree that reorganized unemployment services, Alessandri argued that many unemployed workers "resisted" job offers because of "the idleness they have lived for some time as well as the unhealthy propaganda of political agitators."[123] Idleness and radical ideas, the president believed, had turned the unemployed into a mobile vagrant group. Labor inspectors and local authorities reinforced this view, criticizing unemployed men who turned down low-wage jobs. In 1933, for example, a group of unemployed workers who went to build a railroad line near Nueva Imperial returned after a few days of work, alleging that the work was "too heavy" for the amount of money (a daily wage of six pesos). In response, the labor inspector argued that "it would be convenient to take some measures because in general unemployed men do not want to work, because they are used to being unemployed, as a profession, and accustomed to living in public shelters."[124]

Throughout 1933, wide sectors of Chilean society distrusted the unemployed and believed they did not want to work. Amanda Labarca, a progressive educator and writer, argued in March 1933 that the peon "easily gets used to that terrible hybridity of begging and idleness."[125] On a lighter note, the magazine *En viaje* ironized the presence of unemployed men in the streets of Santiago. The journalist described Santiago in 1933 as a city of beautiful women, active commercial life, and attractive promenades. In this idyllic environment, unemployment, the writer argued, was a personal choice. "To be unemployed," the author argued, "is to have the right to many benefits and considerations that they never had when they had jobs in which it was necessary to work. They say that when one of these 'unemployed' is offered a job that they do not like, they usually answer 'in no way we can accept such a small proposal . . . I am not anybody! I am an unemployed, sir.'"[126]

By 1936, the Servicio de Cesantía reported that unemployment had almost disappeared in Chile. In December, the service had only distributed

15,701 food rations, most of them, to women and children. Men receiving free food, the service argued, were indigent and unable to work.[127] The government had reestablished political and constitutional order and favored economic recovery. A more favorable external market, special economic stimulus, available credits, and tax exemptions had reactivated mining, nitrate, agricultural, construction, and industrial production.[128] The experience of work relief projects was short lived. Widespread concerns about working men's idleness combined with poor working conditions had undermined most work relief projects. Providing work did not resolve unemployment, the Servicio de Cesantía stated, because unemployment was a "social" problem. By a social problem, the commission explained, it meant "the idiosyncrasy of our people, their adventurous and wandering spirit, their moral indifference to all commitments and obligations that could limit their freedom, and their unpredictability."[129] This view deeply influenced future unemployment and social policy, emphasizing work programs for the employable and, as the following two chapters will show, aid for mothers and children and protection for formal workers, working-class families, and white-collar employees.

CHAPTER 4

SOCIAL ASSISTANCE AND THE RATIONALIZATION OF AID

On the eve of the Great Depression, the term "unemployed" (*cesante*) was still ambiguous and referred both to a person who had lost a job (usually a man) and to dependent family members. Newspapers and official reports sometimes characterized "abandoned" women and children as unemployed and at other times called them indigent. Statistical records also used the term indistinctly, and while these records often broke down numbers into the categories of men, women, and children, they also applied the generic label of "unemployed" to anyone affected by job loss.[1] The census of 1930, the first national census to record unemployment in Chile, defined the unemployed as a person who "usually practices an occupation, a profession, or a trade, but who is unemployed or without occupation the day of the census."[2] The census did not specify a length of time someone had be out of work to be considered unemployed, but it broke down figures according to sex and age. The census also classified the unemployed as part of an "inactive population" and under occupation, listed them as head of household.

No official consensus existed on how to define unemployment in 1930. When public servants responded to massive unemployment and organized emergency programs in the early 1930s, they also started drawing lines between workers, family dependents, and indigents. They divided people between the employable and unemployable and deserving and undeserving poor. The employable, as chapter 3 indicated, were healthy working men. To prevent them from losing their work ethic and becoming vagrants or radicalized, the Labor Department placed them in public works projects across the nation. For them, direct relief was temporary and associated with their willingness to work. In contrast, the unemployable (women, children, and the elderly) required food, shelter, and medical attention. In addition, social workers drew a line between blue-collar and white-collar families and between those who deserved and did not deserve aid. These categories reflected changing notions about work, the influence of ideas of class and gender on unemployment policies, and the impact of the Great Depression on the rise of the welfare state.[3]

This chapter turns to social provisions and unemployed families during the 1930s, showing the daily efforts of social workers and labor inspectors to distribute emergency aid and how these experiences shaped unemployment policies. The distribution of aid required new welfare institutions and practices. In the 1920s, the Chilean state had regulated working conditions and established social security benefits (old age, disability, and death and health coverage) for formal workers. The Office of Social Security (Oficina de Seguro Obrero) had developed special health and social programs to serve the needs of mothers and young children. While additional public programs and philanthropic institutions assisted women and children in need, no formal provisions existed for people who were not workers, including the unemployed, informal workers, dependent people without formal relationship with a worker, and indigents. In the absence of an institutional framework to help unemployed families, welfare professionals advocated centralizing the distribution of aid, creating new public offices and services inspired on modern ideas of social assistance, and separating people in need according to class, gender, and capacity to work.

LOCAL GOVERNMENTS AND DIRECT RELIEF

Around the globe, community, labor, mutual aid, philanthropic, and religious institutions as well as local governments, first assisted the unemployed. In the case of Chicago, historian Lizabeth Cohen argues that private charity, ethnic community institutions, and informal networks assisted unemployed workers and families at the beginning of the Great Depression. These resources were limited, and over time, "could not handle the enormous demand for assistance."[4] In Canada, city governments provided unemployment relief until 1933, when the federal government assumed that responsibility. Canadian cities may have had fewer resources, but their programs responded to local realities and needs.[5] Chilean municipalities and provincial authorities established their own system of relief and work programs in the early months of the crisis. Without access to emergency funds and with only limited support from the national government, they relied on private donations and the collaboration of philanthropic and religious institutions.

The case of the northern province of Coquimbo shows an example of early forms of local relief. A mining and agricultural region, and a middle point between the nitrate fields and the central valley, the province had a high rate of unemployment, little economic activity, and many displaced nitrate workers.[6] Steamships from the North carrying unemployed nitrate families regularly stopped in the port of Coquimbo; many disembarked and settled in the area. In April 1931, Nicasio Green Gross, the *intendente*,

TABLE 4.1. DONATIONS AND FUNDRAISING EVENTS IN LA SERENA AND COQUIMBO, FEBRUARY–APRIL 1931

SOURCE	AMOUNT (PESOS)
Police officers	47.80
Business sector	410
Fundraising at "Chalet Serena"	244
Fundraising (soccer game)	311.80
Fundraising at the Royal Movie Theater	633
La Serena Soccer Club (direct donation)	104
Bishop of La Serena (direct donation)	100
Rotary Club (direct donation)	1,000
Elementary School teachers of La Serena (direct donation)	150
Sindicato Industrial El Tofo (direct donation)	500
Sociedad Artesanos (direct donation)	616.40
Municipalidad (direct donation)	100
Total funds collected	4,217

Source: Jorge Aguirre Fariñas to Intedente of Coquimbo, La Serena, April 20, 1931. ARNAD, DT, volume 242.

reported more than 7,000 unemployed men, women, and children in his province.[7] He marshalled local resources and organizations such as municipal councils, police officers, local businesses, and community members to manage the huge influx of unemployed people. Indeed, he explained, all aid to the unemployed came from "private donations, municipalities, public fundraising, and benefits offered from diverse institutions."[8] As in many provincial cities, police officers (*carabineros*) became the central figures in the organization of relief.

In La Serena, the largest city in the province of Coquimbo, police officers organized fundraising events and collected money and food from local individuals and institutions such as the Rotary Club, the Bishop, and labor unions (Table 4.1). When the mayor relocated unemployed families squatting in the outskirts to the shelter, he transported them in trucks provided by neighbors. Local growers and businesses donated milk, fresh produce, and coffee, which complemented a food ration otherwise limited to beans, sugar, and bread (Table 4.2). Charity groups also organized direct relief actions. The Sociedad de Señoras (a women's association) received five lambs and one pig from local landowners. With these donations, they prepared a special meal for about 260 unemployed people. Another day, schoolgirls distributed little baskets of food among unemployed families in La Serena.[9] The work of charity, though often symbolic, nonetheless had a long tradition of assisting the poor and, during the first months of 1931, became an important source of aid in local communities.[10]

TABLE 4.2. DIRECT DONATIONS IN LA SERENA, FEBRUARY–APRIL 1931.

DONOR	DONATION
Félix González	602 liters of milk
	2 sacks[1] of potatoes
Carlos Boos	7 sacks of Malta coffee
	2 sacks of wheat
	1 sack of lentils
	200 liters of beer
Eleuterio Fredes	50 squashes and some corn
Antonio La (ineligible)	2 sacks of carrots
	Some squashes
Line Naranjo	12 kg dried figs
Francisco González	10 kg bread
Alberto Carvajal	40 squashes
	2 sacks of potatoes
Rosario Cortés	13 squashes
Alberto Solar	25 squashes
	2 sacks of potatoes
Emilio Donoso	4 sacks of potatoes
Mariana Hernández	100 packs of cigarettes
	6 squashes
	50 kg potatoes
Román Mery	2 sacks of potatoes
Guillermo Marín	4 sacks of beef jerky
Federico Arces	1 sack *sémola*
	1 sack of flour
	Some produce

Source: Jorge Aguirre Fariñas to Intedente of Coquimbo, La Serena, April 20, 1931. ARNAD, DT, volume 242.

1. One *saco* (sack) weighs about 110 pounds.

Local resources drained quickly. In the case of Coquimbo, the city ran out of money and suspended the distribution of food rations by May 1931.[11] As in other parts of the country, the geographical extension and duration of the crisis required a national response and greater coordination among the different institutions assisting the unemployed. Social workers and other welfare professionals argued that the state should distribute aid according to modern notions of relief. The organization of a national response, the next section suggests, did not displace local and private institutions, but built on the traditional collaboration that characterized social assistance in twentieth-century Chile.

A NATIONAL RESPONSE

The fall of General Ibáñez in July 1931 represents a turning point in how the government responded to the economic crisis. In the last eighteen months, Ibáñez clung to orthodox economic ideas and the gold standard, but the country's dependency on the export market and foreign loans sank the Chilean economy.[12] Ibáñez had also relied on local governments, the Catholic Church, and private charity to feed and shelter the poor, but those resources were almost gone by July 1931. Unemployment and poverty, combined with the government's decision to cut expenditures, made the economic situation unbearable. Workers, university students, teachers, public employees, and the military protested and quickly destabilized the government. Presidential elections took place in October 1931, and elected president Juan Esteban Montero assumed power in November. In the following months, political leaders abandoned Ibáñez's orthodox economic policies and, by April 1932, completely dropped the gold standard. Nevertheless, rising state expenses put new pressures on the national economy and, as economist Gabriel Palma argues, monetary inflation quickly replaced deflation.[13] The circulation of paper money, which had dropped from 500 to 392.8 million pesos between 1929 and 1930, increased to 429.6 million in 1931 and 788.3 million in 1932.[14]

From a social policy point of view, the fall of Ibáñez marked the beginning of a national campaign of relief that reorganized social services and allocated emergency funds to feed and shelter the unemployed. In August 1931, the government formed an unemployment board (Comité Central de Ayuda a los Cesantes) and established new national guidelines to organize direct relief.[15] The board brought together the many public and private institutions serving the poor, such as hospitals, child welfare clinics, and soup kitchens. Led by the minister of social welfare, Dr. Sótero del Río Gundián, board members included Roberto Yunge (director of the Labor Department), Teodoro Schmidt (director of Public Works) and Horacio Campillo (archbishop of Santiago), as well as representatives from the volunteer association of firefighters, the Red Cross, the police corps (*carabineros*), the national railroad company, medical doctors, and the Rotary Club. Members of business associations, such as the Sociedad Nacional de Agricultura and the Cámara de Comercio, also participated. Absent from the committee were representatives of the labor movement or elected officials.

The mission of the unemployment board, Adriana Izquierdo, a social worker, argued, was "the management, organization, and administration of aid."[16] Many of the services overlapped with other public and private services, and government authorities looked to streamline duties and allocate funding. Provincial cities formed their own unemployment boards (Comités de Auxilio de Cesantes). Led by the highest jurisdictional authority, the labor inspector, and prominent regional citizens and business leaders, provincial committees organized and supervised the distribution of assistance, maintained statistical records of aid recipients, and communicated with the central office in Santiago. In Valdivia, for example, the president of the committee was the *intendente* (Víctor Navarrete Concha). Other members included the labor inspector (Guillermo del Fierro); the mayor of Valdivia (Alfredo Oettinger); the police lieutenant (Adolfo Fleck Deischler); and influential community members, such as Enrique Werkmeister (owner of a local furniture factory) and Clemente Holzapfel (a medical doctor).[17] In Valparaíso, Juan Carlos Gómez Leyton argues, the provincial committee's composition reflected "conspicuous representatives of the port [Valparaíso] dominant class."[18]

The Catholic Church supported the work of the committee and organized relief. In June 1931, the archbishop, Horacio Campillo, ordered all local parishes to open soup kitchens "to feed and clothe the needy."[19] In August, Campillo joined the unemployment board. The church was in a privileged position to respond to the crisis. It not only had physical infrastructure (parish buildings, dining halls) and presence throughout the country but the experience and the material and human resources to distribute aid.[20] The parish soup kitchens became the basis of social assistance, and the Catholic Church fed near 16,000 people in Santiago.[21] Among those working with the Church were the many laity groups working with the poor, such as the Society of Saint Vincent de Paul, a voluntary organization of Catholic youth dedicated to charity work. In 1931, the conferences of Saint Vincent de Paul sponsored some parish soup kitchens in Santiago, raised funds, and distributed aid.[22]

The story of direct relief for the unemployable, as Donna Guy has argued for the case of child welfare programs in Argentina, reveals how public social programs collaborated, conflicted, and intersected with a wide range of private, religious, and philanthropic institutions. Private and religious organizations influenced modern notions of assistance on philanthropic organizations, as well as shaped understandings of charity and moralistic ideas about state services. This collaboration, Guy has demonstrated for the case of Argentina, also implied that the state provided subsidies to private and religious organizations serving the needy.[23]

The Junta de Beneficencia provided a model on how to structure the collaboration between private and public agencies. Originally, the Junta was a philanthropic and medical organization and oversaw hospitals and hospices. Over time, its work expanded to include larger issues affecting the well-being of the urban poor, such as child welfare, mental hospitals, and public health campaigns. The Junta de Beneficencia also oversaw social assistance and, as the next section explains, promoted the professionalization of social work. In 1917, the Junta became a semipublic agency and, in 1927, one of the departments of the Ministry of Social Welfare.[24] Even though the Junta was part of the Ministry of Social Welfare, its national and provincial boards continued to include prominent members of the elite, emblematic professionals, and members of the hierarchy of the Church. Additionally, limited funding made the Junta dependent on private charity and donations, and many of its institutions and services remained in the hands of the philanthropic organizations or the Catholic Church, such as the nuns working as nurses in hospital wards.[25]

Throughout the 1930s, the state grew as a provider of social services, and aid transformed from private charity into a system of public welfare. However, the shift from private to public aid was incomplete, and the collaboration and intersection of both streams became the basis of Chile's modern welfare system.

SOCIAL WORKERS AND THE OFICINA DE SOCORRO IN SANTIAGO

Santiago offered a testing ground for direct relief in the early 1930s. A city of near 700,000 people, it not only received many unemployed nitrate workers, but also had a high rate of local unemployment. Factories had closed down, abandoned children roamed the streets, and working-class families struggled to buy food and pay rent. In 1932, a typhus epidemic threatened the lives of the city's most vulnerable population, including the unemployed. However, the city also had initiated large public works projects, such as the construction of the National History Museum, and offered better salaries and conditions than road construction in rural and isolated areas. Santiago's social and urban infrastructure was also better than in provincial cities, with more labor inspectors, social workers, medical doctors, and government officials, as well as private and philanthropic organizations. Indeed, most social workers lived and worked in the capital city. Of the 123 social workers employed in 1932, only ten worked outside Santiago and most worked in hospitals or social security regional offices.[26] As a large city, Santiago had its own problems but was also more prepared to provide for the poor.[27]

In Santiago, Roberto Yunge, director of the Labor Department, organized a relief office (*oficina de socorro*) to distribute aid and supervise public shelters.[28] Married to a social worker, Clara Williams, he brought on board a number of influential women with experience in organizing aid, relief, and assistance: Luisa Jörissen (Director of the Escuela de Servicio Social Elvira Matte Cruchaga), Leo de Bray (Director of the Escuela de Servicio Social de la Junta de Beneficencia), and Elena Hott (Jefe de la Oficina de

Asistencia Social). By bringing social workers to the forefront of the fight against unemployment, Yunge endorsed a scientific and modern model of relief and paved the way for the incorporation of welfare professionals and women into the Labor Department and the Social Security Office.

Together, these professional women represented the growing influence of social work in Chile and the prominent role of women in social and welfare institutions. In 1925, the Junta de Beneficencia had opened Chile's first social work school. Directed first by Jennie Bernier and later by Leo de Bray, both hired in Belgium, the school trained about thirty female students per year. The program lasted two years, and students—women between the ages of twenty and forty—took courses in psychology, social medicine, and nutrition and, during the summer months, pursued internships in a public or private office.[29] A few years later (1927–1929), the Catholic University opened its own social work school, named for Elvira Matte Cruchaga. Both schools, historian María Angélica Illanes argues, emphasized a scientific approach to social problems, incorporated transnational ideas about aid, and contributed to the professionalization of social assistance. In the following years, social workers played a "mediating" role in the implementation of social policy, connecting working families to the state.[30]

At the relief office, social workers did more than distribute benefits; they shaped social policy, determined when and how the state assisted the poor, and defined who deserved and did not deserve aid. The way welfare professionals categorized the poor, Alice O'Connors argues for the case of the United States, influenced not only on the distribution of aid but also how experts understood and explained poverty.[31] In Depression Era Chile, social workers applied the casework approach, a method of social investigation developed by Mary E. Richmond in the late 1890s in the United States, as the basis of social assistance. The casework method surveyed individual and family needs and relied on empirical observations to classify people according to their social and family status.[32] While many social workers, most of them from middle and upper-class families, looked at the poor from a paternalistic and moralistic perspective, their approach was not charity work but a scientific and rational organization of social assistance.[33]

Building on their professional training and influenced by transnational debates about aid and assistance, Chilean social workers organized a modern office of relief in Santiago. In order to distribute aid, they studied the poor and, then, "classified" and "categorized" people according to their needs."[34] First, they observed and assessed people's needs. People asked for help, and social workers evaluated whether they deserved assistance. Based on the casework method, social workers conducted surveys "to establish the economic condition and social condition, as well as the needs, of the applicant."[35] To cover the entire city, the schools of social work divided the

TABLE 4.3. RATIONING CENTERS IN SANTIAGO (ESCUELA ELVIRA MATTE CRUCHAGA), 1932

CENTER	NUMBER OF FOOD RATIONS	SOCIAL WORKER
Salto	5,400	Julia Gajardo
Hipódromo	1,470	
Recoleta	885	
Mirador	2840	Estela Rossi
O'Higgins	1715	
Yungay	3821	Sofía Campos
Buen Pastor	627	
Andacollo	1217	
Ecuador	1557	Olimpia Castillo
Erasmo Escala	1375	

Source: Adriana Izquierdo, "Como se organizó la ayuda a los cesantes y la participación que a ella le corresponde a la escuela de servicio social Elvira Matte de Cruchaga," thesis, Escuela de Servicio Social Elvira Matte de Cruchaga, July 1932, 16.

city in half: the Escuela Elvira Matte worked in the north part of the city and the Beneficencia school in the southern neighborhoods. Between 7:00 am and 6:00 pm, volunteer social workers, usually students, visited people's homes, conducted surveys, took notes, and recorded personal information. In the first months of 1932, they conducted an average of 300 daily visits and recorded information about more than 6,000 families.

Second, after the survey, social workers systematized the information and established instruments of control. At the relief office, they classified all the cases according to the kind of help people requested and provided families with a relief identification card (*carnet de socorro*) to record the amount of help they received.[36] Third, they appointed a social worker to supervise, coordinate, and follow up on the distribution of aid, which until then had been in the hands of parishes and private organizations.[37] In sum, they had observed a social problem, classified the poor according to social categories, diagnosed problems, designed a solution, and assigned aid. Finally, they followed up with delivery of assistance and services.

The rationing center became the workspace of the social worker. At the center, they could follow up their assigned cases and supervise the distribution of aid. By July 1932, thirty centers in Santiago served around 61,000 adult rations and 5,751 infant rations (sugar and oatmeal) per day.[38] The centers offered registered families two cooked meals per day. In addition to providing food, the centers coordinated other aspects of aid and assistance, such as the distribution of clothes (*ropero del pobre*), housing issues and evictions, recovery of pawned goods, medical services and hospitalization, and job applications. Each social worker supervised between two and three centers and was available for a few hours twice a week (Table 4.3). While at first the relief office had relied on volunteers and students, the rationing centers now formally hired social workers, who received a monthly salary of 300 pesos. At the center, the social worker "normally addresses all the requests made by unemployed people: relocations, registrations, difficulties, and problems."[39] When she was not at the center, the social worker conducted home visits, met at the central relief office, and negotiated with different public and private agencies to find solutions for people in need.

Many young professional women found their work at the rationing center overwhelming; but the experience reinforced their commitment to social work. Some of them, like Adriana Izquierdo, wrote their theses based on their social work or published well-written articles and memoirs about their work. Inés Oliveira was a still a student at the Beneficiencia when she accepted a job at the Centro de Racionamiento San Crecente in Ñuñoa, Santiago. She published a short article about her experience in the journal *Servicio Social*. She handled more than 500 cases and conducted about 230 home visits per month. She compared the work of the relief office to a "railroad network that crosses the city." Like a railroad, the relief office crossed the city, and the centers were like railroad stations "visited by thousands of disoriented travelers. Hungry, cold, dying, they look for bread, a roof, clothes; in other words, a haven for their social torments." Her work was simple: to find a solution for people to "remain alive."[40]

Outside the capital city, local governments and provincial unemployment boards fed the poor. They built on the previous local arrangements that had been in place and had no resources to implement a scientific approach to aid. In December 1931, the Ministry of Social Welfare distributed 400,000 pesos in emergency funding to provincial authorities to assist and feed the unemployed.[41] However, the money always ran out, and cities scrambled to feed people in need. In a heavily centralized country like Chile, less funding existed for smaller cities outside the capital, and local authorities had to make constant efforts to obtain—and justify—aid from Santiago. In Cañete, Province of Cautín, for example, the city provided food to 150 families, distributed by police officers, local businesses, and female charity organizations.[42] The southern port of Constitución provided one meal per week to 5,000 unemployed families, which consisted of beans or lentils, potatoes, salt, and rabbit meat. However, the city suspended the service in February 1932, once it ran out of funding.[43] In Valparaíso, Chile's second largest city, six soup kitchens fed more than 20,000 people per month in early 1932.⁴⁴ Letters from provincial authorities described their efforts to organize some form of relief system and how hard they found it to implement modern notions of assistance outside the capital city.

PUBLIC SHELTERS

Beginning in the early twentieth century, public shelters (*albergues*) served as temporary facilities to house and feed, mostly but not exclusively, unemployed nitrate workers and their families. In response to the fluctuations of the nitrate labor market and its cycles of migration, as chapter 2 showed, the state had opened emergency shelters in the main cities and ports during the economic crises of 1914 and 1920–1921. Overcrowded and poorly maintained, many people blamed shelters for chronic social problems, including epidemics, radicalization, and crime. Santiago Wilson Hernández, a lawyer and minister of social welfare (*bienestar social*) in 1931, called shelters "centers of promiscuity" and racial degeneration.⁴⁵ Adriana Izquierdo, a Catholic social worker, described shelters as places of "disorder, resistance, subversion, committees with communist ties, and political weapons against the government."⁴⁶ Similarly, María Benavides de la Cruz, also a social worker, believed that many people, especially men, quickly adapted to the life of shelters and eventually refused to go back to work. Unemployed men, Benavides argued, developed a "reluctance to work, dissatisfaction with low wages, rejection of situations [jobs] outside Santiago, diverse excuses to reject certain jobs, etc."⁴⁷

Because of these past experiences and criticism, the government hesitated to open shelters in the early 1930s. In March 1931, the Ministry of Propiedad Austral decreed the placement of unemployed men on public land a service that would not only offer work and means of survival, but also a way to avoid "every possibility to return to the shelter system" and its "unfortunate material and moral consequences."⁴⁸ As massive numbers of workers fled the nitrate districts, and state offices failed to place them in the private sector or on public land, the need for shelters became inevitable. In addition, government authorities feared that roving unemployed nitrate workers could cause a social, sanitary, and political crisis if they continued roaming the streets. In April 1931, the *intendente* of Aconcagua opened a shelter in Valparaíso to control and supervise migrant nitrate workers. In the previous month, many nitrate workers had settled in the port, formed an unemployment committee (*Comité de cesantes*), and established links with local labor organizations. Unemployed nitrate workers, a report from the *Intendencia* explained, had also refused agricultural jobs and demanded better working and salary conditions, which created anxiety among local businesses and landowners. A public shelter, local authorities argued, could help organize the placement system and limit the influence of local

TABLE 4.4. PUBLIC SHELTERS IN SANTIAGO, 1931

SHELTER	MEN	WOMEN	CHILDREN	TOTAL
Santa María	314	280	508	1,102
Bascuñán	251	140	232	623
El Salto	1,140	1,260	800	3,200
Esperanza	233	97	180	510
Total	1,938	1,777	1,720	5,435

labor organizations. Located on Chacabuco street, not far from the local government and the Navy buildings, the shelter only provided a place to sleep and breakfast, while police officers exerted strict control over the residents.[49]

Between 1931 and 1932, the number of public shelters increased throughout the nation, but the number of people housed in the shelters represented only a small percentage of the total unemployed population. By December 1931, public shelters existed in almost every large and medium-size city. A labor inspector who visited unemployment services in the northern provinces (Tarapacá, Antofagasta, Atacama, and Coquimbo) reported three shelters in Iquique (563 people) and one in Tocopilla (300 people), La Serena (1,075 people), and Vicuña (63 people). A shelter also operated in Copiapó, but the inspector did not list the size of the population.[50] The largest and best organized shelters were located in Santiago and included Bascuñan Guerrero (Parque Cousiño), El Salto (Recoleta), Esperanza (Portales/Estación), and Santa María (Recoleta).[51] Together, they offered the unemployed a place to sleep and regular meals to 5,435 people (table 4.4).[52] In addition to the shelters located within the city, the government opened a shelter in Buin, next to a military barrack, twenty-two miles south of Santiago.

In Santiago, each public shelter had an appointed social worker, a few volunteers (usually students from one of the two schools of social work), representatives of the Red Cross, and two or more police officers on duty to maintain public order.[53] Despite these efforts, life in the shelters was precarious, and shelters continued to symbolize failed social policy.

A description of the Santa María shelter illustrates how a typical shelter was organized and operated. Under the direction of Gabriela Prats, a social worker, the shelter was located at the intersections of Santa María and Walker Martínez, just a few blocks north of Plaza Italia in Recoleta. The shelter was essentially a warehouse [*galpón*], covered by a calamine roof with an open space for ventilation between the walls and the roof, making the building especially cold and humid during the winter. Inside the shelter, provisional rooms made of cardboard provided some privacy to the 220 families (more than 1,100 people) who housed there. The entrance con-

TABLE 4.5 WORK ACCOMPLISHED BY THE CENTRAL COMMITTEE OF THE RED CROSS IN SANTIAGO'S SHELTERS (BASCUÑÁN, EL SALTO, AND SANTA MARÍA) DURING 1931

TASKS AND ACTIVITIES	NUMBER OF PEOPLE, SERVINGS, OR UNITS
Wound dressing	6,919
Shots	506
Patients examined by doctors	472
Prescriptions filled	10,720
People admitted to hospitals	15
Haemotherapy	57
Pieces of clothing distributed	9,125
Preparation of baby bottles	197,826
Breakfast and afternoon snack for children	282,787
Servings of milk for sick people	41,129
Servings of milk for families	1,200
Units of bread	48,576

Source: *Memoria de la Presidenta de la Cruz Roja de las Mujeres de Chile Sra Carmela Prieto de Ramírez, 1931* (Santiago: Imprenta Lagunas y Quevedo, 1932), 10.

tained a reception desk, and inside the building was a dining hall, kitchen, and small office spaces for the police, the Red Cross, the social workers, and the *gota de leche* (child welfare clinics). Maintained by the Ministry of Public Welfare, the shelter also relied on donations of food and clothes from private organizations as well as neighbors.[54] For example, the Society of Saint Vincent de Paul donated clothes and blankets to both the Santa María and the Bascuñán shelters.[55]

Influenced by the social reform movement, shelter administrators implemented medical and family-oriented programs. During the first decades of the twentieth century, mothers and children had been at the center of Chile's social reform movement, as medical doctors and institutions had increasingly taken control and medicalized childbearing and child-rearing practices to reduce the infant and maternal mortality rate.[56] As Ann Blum has demonstrated for the case of welfare policies in revolutionary Mexico, medical ideas intertwined with eugenics and efforts to transform families, children, and family relations.[57] Despite their emergency character, then, Santiago's shelters offered social and health care workers opportunities to interact with the poor and implement reform policies. Social workers organized workshops and distributed reading materials for women that reinforced their roles as housewives and mothers. For example, they taught women "habits of hygiene, childcare, feminine tasks such as knitting, sewing, etc."[58] Volunteers of the Red Cross screened educational films, provided milk to infants, and distributed information about hygiene and infant care.[59] The preparation of baby bottles and children's meals became volunteers' most important daily activities (Table 4.5), a clear reflection on their concern about nutrition and children's health.

The shelters brought together state and private institutions to assist the poor and included both male and female professionals and volunteers. The lines between different agencies usually blurred, but conflicts were also frequent. In early December 1931, Luisa Pfau, a medical doctor and director of the educational department at the Dirección General de Sanidad, questioned the professionalism of Red Cross female volunteers.[60] A few days after Pfau's report, a local newspaper blamed volunteers for the high rates of infant mortality in the shelters. Medical doctors, the paper argued, looked at the problem "with professional criteria and estimated that [it] was better to prevent diseases than to cure them. Instead the Red Cross looked at the same problem with the criteria of a healer." The newspaper article also described what it saw as a lack of professional training of the volunteers, describing "the incapacity and lack of preparation of volunteer nurses of the Red Cross. They [the nurses] lack discipline, spirit of sacrifice, and technical preparation to perform their duties." While nurses studied for three years under the supervision of the Medical School at the Universidad de Chile, the volunteers from the Red Cross only completed a three-month course.[61] In the end, the minister of social welfare backed up the work of the Red Cross, and volunteers continued serving the shelter population. The state neither had the resources nor the personnel to replace private institutions, and the collaboration continued.

Provincial shelters had fewer resources and professional personnel than the ones in Santiago, and only offered the most basic services. In Valparaíso, a generalized decline in commercial, port, and industrial activity caused high rates of unemployment. The port also received many migrants from the northern nitrate province.[62] In early July 1931, the province maintained three public shelters (two in Valparaíso and one in Viña del Mar) with a total population of 822 people. Local authorities recognized that the shelters had turned away many people, and they expected to open new shelters in the towns of Quillota, Los Andes, and Putaendo. The local Red Cross provided most of the medical services, especially for children and pregnant women, and residents received three daily meals: coffee and bread for breakfast, bread and beans for lunch, and "*carbonada* or a stew with meat and bread" for dinner.[63] Services and conditions were precarious. In April 1932, a labor inspector denounced that the shelter in Limache did not provide the regular services of a midwife, but instead "a private midwife offers free services when she is not busy. But she does not have any medicines not utensils, not even a comfortable or hygienic department where to attend" people.[64]

A nitrate port, Iquique experienced the economic crisis from its outset. Although most of the unemployed only briefly stayed in the port before moving south, the city maintained at least four public shelters between 1931 and 1932. In August 1931, the Labor Department reported 456 people distributed in three public shelters in Iquique (206 men, 71 women, and 179 children).⁶⁵ In February 1932, the number of people in public shelters reached 613 (198 men, 119 women, and 296 children). Residents were not only nitrate workers, local authorities explained, but also local families, who were unable to pay rent and had been evicted from their homes. Lack of funding, weather conditions, and poor building infrastructure made living conditions in Iquique appalling. In the Lazareto shelter, people slept outdoors, only covering themselves with a *saco*, and children suffered from the intense "heat, sand, and flies." People suffered from malnourishment, and the labor inspector feared that many children were about to die in a few days. Residents had limited access to water, soap, or clean clothes, and he noticed a complete state of "uncleanliness." There was no reference to social workers or other professional personnel in Iquique, only the biweekly visits of the sanitary authority and the provincial labor inspector.⁶⁶

In other places, conditions were just as precarious. In Temuco, the shelter had only been open for a few months in 1931 when in August, the Department of Labor closed it down after its residents refused to "repair the streets in exchange of food."⁶⁷ In Talca, three shelters housed a total population of 648 people by September 1931, and conditions were described as "terrible."⁶⁸ Other cities refused to open shelters, providing only provisional lodging that offered workers a place to stay while they waited to be placed in agricultural or public works projects outside the city. In Valdivia, where about 1,170 people were unemployed, the provincial unemployed board offered regular meals but opposed opening a local shelter. Shelters, the authorities in Valdivia explained, were too expensive to operate and required special safety and health measures. More importantly, they believed that shelters encouraged "the habit of idleness."⁶⁹ In Linares, some homeless unemployed stayed in the police station, but there were no regular services.

Government authorities used shelters to house and feed the poor, but also to control and, in some cases, to "educate" the unemployed. In and around public shelters, police officers maintained public order, enforced the law, and repressed protests. In Concepción, police officers had a special unit to control shelters.⁷⁰ In most cases, they viewed unemployed men as suspicious and criminalized behaviors such as drinking and hanging out in public areas. In El Salto, the largest public shelter in Santiago, the police reported that unemployed men consumed alcohol and committed "excesses" in the neighborhood. They ordered residents to find work, stating that "under no circumstances would they accept that the [unemployed] are swarming around the city streets or around the mentioned shelter [El Salto]."⁷¹ Other accounts of El Salto highlighted conflicts between government authorities and residents. For example, a document from the Communist Party explained that when the minister of public welfare, Santiago Wilson, visited the shelter and tried to force single workers to work for three pesos in road construction, workers "kicked him out," and the police threatened to open fire.[72]

Despite documents that portrayed shelter residents as drunks and vagrants, residents in shelters organized committees and elected representatives to improve and negotiate the distribution of aid. In October 1931, the leaders of the Bascuñán shelter denounced delays in the daily delivery of milk, which usually arrived around lunch time, leaving children without breakfast.[73] While many of these incidents were very specific and local, they also built on nitrate workers' history of organized resistance within a national context of protest and political turmoil.[74] Some shelter residents belonged to the Communist Party, while others sympathized with anarchist organizations. They attended meetings and rallies organized by the Federación Obrera de Chile (FOCH) and the Anarchists' Casa del Pueblo. When government authorities expelled six workers from the Bacuñán shelter because of drunkenness (three men) and robbery (three men), the six men and the president of the shelter committee, went to a meeting of La Casa del Pueblo. Supported by anarchist leaders and three unidentified members of the National Congress, they denounced police brutality and contested the accusations.[75]

Although only a minority of unemployed workers stayed in public shelters, shelter residents symbolized the broad and devastating social consequences of the economic crisis. The desperate situation in shelters across the nation became a rallying cry of leftist political parties and labor organizations. In Temuco, the FOCH supported the organization of an unemployed local committee in December 1931. Among their demands, the committee wished to control the distribution of food in shelters, alleging that the administrators of the shelter were stealing it, and they requested that police officers leave the shelters. In case the provincial government rejected their demands, they threatened to open their own soup kitchens and start their own fundraising.[76] While the *intendente* rejected their demands and police officers continued to maintain order in the shelter, shelter residents without affiliation to the FOCH became part of a new committee to distribute food.[77]

WHITE-COLLAR EMPLOYEES

In July of 1930, a labor inspector in Valparaíso described the gloomy conditions faced by white-collar employees (*empleados*) and their families. Both public servants and white-collar employees in the private sector had lost their jobs, but they remained invisible. The inspector explained that "unlike blue-collar workers, they [white-collar employees] do not register at the Secretaría de Bienestar or display in public their unemployment condition, making it difficult to determine their number. This is a serious social problem because the unemployment of white-collar employees impacts many homes and families; and because of their roots and homes, they cannot easily move somewhere else."[78] During the worst months of the Depression, between June and December of 1932, about 16,000 white-collar employees registered at the placement office. Nevertheless, they were only a fraction of the total population of unemployed white-collar employees. First, the number of registrations at the placement office did not include public employees, many of whom had lost their jobs in the last months of the Ibáñez administration. At that time, most white-collar employees did not register, nor seek help from the Labor Department. In early 1933, more than 14,000 white-collar employees registered, but, according to a newspaper, "these figures are incomplete because of [workers'] negligence."[79]

White-collar employees were a highly diverse group of wage earners. In 1930, the census counted 172,600 employees, of which 80 percent were men.[80] According to the Labor Code of 1931, the difference between a white-collar and a blue-collar worker was the "predominance of intellectual over physical work."[81] The distinction between intellectual and physical work was not always clear, and in the following years many groups of skilled blue-collar workers obtained the status of white-collar employees. Labor laws also differentiated between public employees and employees in the private sector. In the private sector, employees could unionize and engage in collective bargaining, but public employees enjoyed a higher degree of job security and a better pension system. Nevertheless, they shared a similar social status, way of life, and viewed themselves as respectable families.[82]

During the Great Depression, although many white-collar employees lost their jobs and only source of income, no public works program existed to help them. Their savings disappeared, but their social status and sense of respectability prevented them from seeking aid in shelters or soup kitchens. In Vallenar, the governor argued that white-collar employees "are the ones who suffered the most because of the lack of work and the state of crisis that the country is going through. Their [class] status prevents them from reaching the soup kitchen of the unemployed in search of a ration and bread for themselves and their families."[83] Luis E. Miranda, a white-collar worker, described the suffering and needs of unemployed white-collar employees in the early 1930s. Having been unemployed for more than a year, Miranda could not feed his two small children, pay for medical assistance for his wife and, more importantly, maintain his middle-class status. Hopeless, he criticized the lack of adequate relief and assistance for people of his condition. "I, as a white-collar employee in the private sector," Miranda argued, "need more help than blue-collar workers. While they have the shelter and preferential help from everyone, we, who belong to the middle class, and our families and children are the ones who suffer the most."[84]

The situation of white-collar families illustrates not only how ideas of class, social status, and family shaped social assistance in the 1930s but also how people used those terms to articulate larger political demands. By highlighting their social status, educational level, and family situation, white-collar families tried to separate themselves from manual workers. Unlike manual workers, they dressed up for work, and their image as an employee of *cuello y corbata* (literally "collar and tie") symbolized those everyday differences. Manuel N., in his letter to the minister of public welfare, talked about problems that "only affect the middle class" and argued that this class "suffered the most."[85] White-collar employees faced the "unique" problem of maintaining a certain status and a public image of respectability, as well as the high social costs of seeking help. Middle-class families needed money to pay for rent and food, but they could neither beg nor accept a low-paying manual job.

Whether they were part of a larger organization or writing as independent citizens, white-collar employees demanded a different kind of social assistance. In September 1931, during a rally in Iquique, the FOCH declared that white-collar employees were in a "worse condition" than blue-collar workers and received no help from the government.[86] Organized by city, workplace, or profession, white-collar employees addressed their demands to the state. For example, in December 1931, a group called the Sociedad de Empleados Públicos Cesantes asked the government for immediate relief. The group presented a list of about forty members who required immediate help. Although the government had already formed the relief office and extended aid, members asked to distribute aid, including food and other in-kind benefits. They opposed the intervention of social workers, arguing that "the paperwork that imposes the visit of a social worker is extremely painful for the people of the culture and the social condition of former public servants."[87]

The Relief Office separated the distribution of aid between white-collar and blue-collar families and established a rationing center that exclusively assisted private white-collar employees. Instead of eating at a soup kitchen, they received food and produce to cook at home. Classification and proof of status was still important, and social workers had to register the aid they distributed. Most white-collar employees could confirm their status by presenting proof of former employment, avoiding the long and intrusive visits of social workers. Although no public works projects existed for *empleados*, price controls and other protections for consumers, as well as the expansion of the state, discussed in chapter 5, became important benefits and a source of work.

The economic and social drama of white-collar employees during the Depression, as well as growing political consensus on the distinctive needs of *empleados*, paved the way for protective legislation in the late 1930s.[88] In 1937, the National Congress approved Law 6,020 to "improve the economic situation" of white-collar employees in the private sector. The law established a minimum wage to guarantee the well-being of private employees. It also provided a family allowance for the spouse, legitimate children, and widowed mother of unemployed private sector employees and created an unemployment fund. While many argued that the law reinforced the status of *empleados* as a "privileged" sector and widened the gap between blue-collar and white-collar workers, the unemployment benefits were more symbolic than real. First, only employees contributed to the fund (1 percent of the salary). To qualify for the fund, the employee must have lost work "through no fault of their own," have been unemployed for at least ten days, and have no additional source of income. Furthermore, not all unemployed employees qualified to receive a subsidy. Instead, only those who social workers considered in need received benefits. The law required unemployed white-collar workers to look for a job, register at the placement office, and accept a similar job offer, as the unemployment fund was limited to sixty days. In 1937, the daily unemployment subsidy was ten pesos, plus an additional three pesos per each child younger than sixteen years old.[89] Despite these limits, white-collar workers were the only workers to gain unemployment insurance in twentieth-century Chile.

THE SERVICIOS DE CESANTÍA AND THE NEW INDIGENT

As part of a larger effort to reorganize unemployment services and increase efficiency and control over the distribution of aid, the second Alessandri administration (1932–1938) focused on reducing unemployment and separating the unemployed from the indigent. In November 1932, the Departamento de Cesantía replaced the old Dirección General de Cesantía, and all unemployment services were placed under the Ministry of Labor. The new department conducted a census of the unemployed population and inspected all unemployment services. As explained in chapter 3, President Alessandri worried that the uncontrolled distribution of aid had increased idleness and vagrancy among working-class men. While government officials believed that men had to return to work and that the state should suspend aid to compel men to accept low-paying jobs, they were unsure how to help women and children.

In 1931–1932, the state had distributed relief to unemployed families. Men, women, and children had arrived in public shelters to receive food and clothes. Given the massive social and economic consequences of the Depression, the lines between the unemployed and the indigent had blurred. Not only had both groups sought help from shelters and soup kitchens but the crisis had displaced families and left many people without labor and social protections. In 1933, when economic conditions began to improve, the state attempted to redraw the line between the unemployed and the indigent. In 1934, the Unemployment Department explained that while unemployment had "disappeared," the nation now faced the "problem of destitute children, women abandoned by their husbands, and those unfit for employment."[90] For example, the crisis had increased the problem of abandoned children, as well as "vagrancy and begging."[91] The indigent, then, were not only unemployable, but also had no formal relationship with a worker and no source of income. Working-class children and mothers were unemployable, but they were not indigent unless the male breadwinner had walked out. Because their needs were urgent, the Department did not only assist unemployed men and their families, but also provided "relief to the indigent."[92]

The indigent required shelter, food, clothing, and medical attention. The question of child welfare attracted special attention from both public and private institutions. In 1933, the government created a special commission to address the problem of indigent children. The commission argued that the economic crisis had "increased, in an alarming way, children's poverty." While the government's economic policies had reduced unemployment, the commission explained, new job opportunities usually required men to move to isolated mining camps or agricultural sites and leave their families behind. The commission, then, identified three types of impoverished children: 1) vagrant, homeless, and abandoned children; 2) children living in poor homes; 3) school children. The commission proposed to institutionalize abandoned children and place them in orphanages, create settlements and day service for poor ones, and provide healthy meals at school.[93] In many cases, the commission worked with philanthropic organizations, showing the intricate relationship between public and private agencies (including religious ones). In Antofagasta, for example, the state subsidized, with food or funding, the Junta de Defensa del Niño, the Red Cross, and other small charities that assisted children. Philanthropic organizations had a long history assisting mothers and children. Wealthy individuals often donated money, properties, and goods to orphanages and other programs that assisted children, and many served on the boards of these institutions.[94]

Despite efforts to distinguish between the unemployed and the indigent and between the employable and the unemployable, the 1936 annual report of the Servicio de Cesantía stated that the office assisted all people without work. As unemployment rates declined, the report explained, the service had "gradually become an institution of social welfare." The Servicio maintained four food distribution centers (*centros de racionamiento*) in Santiago and seven in the provinces of Tarapacá and Antofagasta. In 1936, the centers distributed a total of 170,918 meals, most of them to children and women (about 85 percent). Similarly, the service subsidized rent and provided medical attention. The government had closed all public shelters, but maintained one, the Asilo ex-Cazadores, in Santiago. The shelter's population was between 400 and 500 people and included a mix of unemployed men, vagrants, old people, women, and children. Like in the case of the rationing centers, most of the residents at the ex-Cazadores (about 80 percent) were women, children, and unemployable men (old, sick, disabled).[95]

In the end, the unemployment service could not resolve the tensions created by assisting different groups of people, and the Chilean state did not develop protections for the unemployed, nor the indigent. In contrast, in the United States, social security legislation included both social assistance (Aid to Dependent Children) as well as unemployment insurance.[96] In Chile, lack of unemployment insurance for blue-collar workers left working families vulnerable to changes in the labor market. In addition, Chile's social security legislation only allocated benefits to formal workers and immediate family members, leaving many women and children, but also informal workers, unprotected. In the late 1930s, the unemployment office provided social assistance, but funds were limited and many indigents continued to rely on philanthropic and religious institutions.[97] If Chile did not design a wider system of social welfare and provide protection for the unemployed and unemployable, it did promote the male-headed family as the fundamental unit for the delivery of social welfare and, as explained in chapter 5, gradually adopted a series of protections for consumers and renters (e.g., price control, housing subsidies) after the late 1930s.

CHAPTER 5

PROTECTING CONSUMERS

On June 11, 1932, President Carlos Dávila and the minister of labor decreed the "immediate" return of some of the items pawned at the Caja de Crédito Prendario. People could recover—for free—clothing, domestic items such as blankets and furniture, sewing machines, and tools valued under 300 pesos.[1] A diverse crowd of people immediately responded to the government's announcement and assembled at the main office of the public pawnshop in Santiago. Among them were Juan David González and Marta Krammer, an unemployed couple, and Carmen Sepúlveda, a housewife and occasional seamstress. González, the magazine *Sucesos* explained, had arrived in Santiago after losing his job in the nitrate fields. Unable to find work, he had pawned most of his belongings, including the family's bed linens. Sepúlveda, who had pawned her sewing machine, managed to recover it from the pawnshop.[2] The economic crisis had devastated working families, and many survived unemployment by pawning their most basic belongings.

The return of pawned items was a popular and symbolic measure that touched the heart and daily circumstances of working-class homes at the time. Like other policies of the Socialist Republic, the gesture represented an emotional and populist, rather than comprehensive, response to the economic crisis.[3] Nevertheless, it did provide immediate and concrete benefits to the working poor. The measure also highlighted an enduring problem of the Chilean economy: working families were unable to meet their most basic needs, wages were low, and the increase in the cost of living undermined workers' purchasing power. Since the early twentieth century, social reformers, progressive political parties, and labor activists had denounced the high price of rent and basic foods, such as bread and sugar in relation to wages. Food shortages and price increases had sparked strikes and demonstrations and remained a central issue in labor conflicts throughout the twentieth century.[4]

At the beginning of the Great Depression, 1930–1931, the price of consumer goods declined, but then skyrocketed for the rest of the decade.[5] The economic crisis, this chapter demonstrates, threatened consumers' rights ("*los derechos del pueblo consumidor*") and created a growing demand for state intervention and price controls.[6] Tenement leagues organized against evictions, and consumers rallied against the increase in the cost of living and the abuses of speculators and foreign commercial houses. In response to the economic instability of the 1930s, the state enacted price ceilings, rent control, and minimum wages in efforts to protect working-class and middle-class consumers. The Juntas de Habitación Popular, formed in May 1931, controlled rent and supported the construction of low-income housing. In August 1932, the Socialist Republic established the General Commissariat of Subsistence and Price Controls (Comisariato General de Precios y Subsistencia) to "control the quality and price of articles of prime necessity."[7]

Chile's price controls reflected a growing international concern about the politics of consumption and food, as well as people's demand to balance wages and the cost of living. In the United States, a new "consumer citizen" emerged in the first decades of the twentieth century, a symbol of mass consumption and rapid urbanization. The state and labor movements expanded workers' purchasing power, while housewives found themselves at the center of consumer activism and led boycotts against the increase in the cost of basic food products.[8] Throughout the capitalist world, price ceilings and rationing of consumer goods became common in times of war but also as a response to economic crises, inflation, natural disasters, and business abuses and monopolies.[9] In Latin America, workers spent nearly all their income on food and demanded that the state regulate the price of food, rent, public transportation, and utilities. They negotiated wage increases to keep up with the rise in the cost of living, framing their struggle as part of a larger fight for industrialization, development, and economic nationalism.[10] While consumption practices rapidly changed throughout the twentieth century, until at least World War II, workers' consumption in Latin America was about the struggle for subsistence, including food and rent, rather than a movement toward mass consumption.[11]

THE LABOR DEPARTMENT: WORKERS' SUBSISTENCE

In the 1930s, Chilean workers spent most of their income on food and rent, with little left for other needs. Urban families shopped at neighborhood stores, where shopkeepers offered credit and developed long-term commercial relationships with customers.[12] In some cities, depending on municipal regulations, people purchased vegetables and fruits at street markets (*ferias libres*) and municipal markets.[13] Most working families had limited access to fresh meat, fish, or dairy products. Peddlers canvassed working-class neighborhoods, as well as workplaces and factories during paydays; they also hawked their wares at bars, restaurants, and brothels.[14] More affluent working-class and white-collar families had access to established credit institutions and purchased tools, sewing machines, and household items, which they pawned or resold in times of need.[15] All of these commercial relations, both formal and informal, relied on intermediaries, from wholesalers to peddlers. The long chain of intermediaries considerably increased the price of basic products. This was especially true in northern cities, such as Iquique and Antofagasta, where dependence on imported goods resulted in a higher cost of living.

Like in other parts of Latin America, Chile's Labor Department started researching working families' income and expenses in the early twentieth century. By the 1920s, the Labor Department had become the main public institution that oversaw workers' access to food and housing.[16] The company store, a microcosm of workers' consumption habits, first attracted the attention of labor reformers and the Labor Department. Miners and construction workers, as well as agricultural laborers, worked in isolated places with only limited access to shops. They usually purchased food at company stores or received food rations and lodging from their employers. In these cases, access to food and other essential products caused permanent labor conflicts. Labor organizations accused company stores of charging exorbitant prices, retained workers' salaries, and exploited the working class. In 1924, the employment contract law (law 4053) decreed the freedom to trade and price ceilings at labor camps. Prices at company stores, the law stipulated, could not exceed the cost of transportation plus 10 percent for administration costs.[17]

After the 1924 law, labor inspectors started visiting labor camps and inspecting prices at company stores on a regular basis. In many cases, they found that shopkeepers and employers preyed on workers' isolation and dependence, charging higher prices than in the open market, and cheating on products' quality and weight. In 1928, the minister of social welfare recognized that despite the law and the work of inspectors, problems and abuses continued. In the nitrate province of Antofagasta, the minister explained, "some *oficinas* [nitrate complexes] have closed their towns and only allowed some merchants to trade and sell in their camps."[18] In Copiapó, a labor inspector found that landowners sold their workforce basic products at a higher price than in urban areas.[19] A few months later, the same inspector visited mining camps, where he reduced prices in company stores about 20 percent and requested that police officers supervise the weights and measures.[20] In La Serena, another inspector denounced that landowners had adulterated workers' food rations, mixing butter with horse fat.[21]

The conflict between construction workers and the company store in Vilcuya, Los Andes, illustrates the controversial practices of shopkeepers

TABLE 5.1 ADOLFO ALVEAR'S REPORT

PRODUCT	WORKER 1		WORKER 2	
	BOUGHT	MISSING	BOUGHT	MISSING
Sugar	8 kg	800 g		
Rice	3 kg	400 g	2 kg	300 g
Beans	1 kg	150 g	4 kg	350 g
Yerba Mate	500 g	170 g		
Tea	250 g	120 g		
Lard	1 kg	300 g	1 kg	190 g
Meat	8 kg	600 g		
Noodles	2 kg	170 g	1 kg	180 g
Salt	1 kg	320 g		
Potatoes	12kg	950 g	10 kg	700 g
Cheese			1 kg	290 g

Source: Juan Pezoa Arredondo (Mayor y Prefecto), Los Andes, September 1, 1930; Inspección del Trabajo, Los Andes, September 9, 1930. Both documents in ARNAD, DT, volume 220.

and the efforts of the Labor Department to stop these abuses. In Vilcuya, located eleven miles from Los Andes, a company store (*pulpería*) supplied food and goods for about 300 people working on the construction of an irrigation canal. On August 29, 1930, a group of workers informed the police that the "prices and weight" at the local store were "high and illegitimate." When police officers visited the company store, they confirmed workers' claims that prices were higher than normal and weights were inaccurate. For example, the police explained, the store sold meat at 3.70 pesos per kilo, while its price should be no more than 2.60 pesos per kilo. On September 9, Adolfo Alvear, the labor inspector of Los Andes, visited the camp. Alvear also sided with workers and demonstrated that prices at the company store were between 20 cents and 4 pesos higher than on the open market. When he weighed the food purchased by some of the workers, he discovered that the weight was inaccurate (see table 5.1) and that prepacked food was missing about one-third of the marked weight.

Because Chilean workers spent most of their income on food, high prices and inaccurate weight undermined their daily budget; they felt exploited and mistreated. Workers accused shopkeepers of stealing and cheating, denouncing their illegitimate practices.[22] By curtailing shopkeepers' abuses and protecting workers, the labor inspector legitimated the role of the Labor Department and the Ministry of Social Welfare as "the true defenders of the working, honorable, and hard-working classes." In Vilcuya, workers cheered when the inspector weighed products inside the store and confronted the shopkeeper. Unfortunately, there is no more information on this case. The inspector emphasized that the company and the shopkeeper should be held accountable, while the governor decided to file the case at a civil court, which would have led to a long legal process.[23] Labor inspectors continued visiting company stores and enforcing labor laws in labor and mining camps, but long distances and poor transportation limited their work. Even in places reached by inspectors, abuses were common, and the centrality of the price and quality of food on workers' lives made the company store a permanent source of grievances and conflicts.[24]

Along with inspecting company stores, the Labor Department looked at the larger problem of workers' subsistence and the relationship between salaries and the cost of living. Within its many functions, the Labor Department was responsible for studying and devising mechanisms to decrease the cost of living and increase workers' purchasing power.[25] Since the late 1910s, it had researched family budgets and collected information on salaries, the cost of food, and living conditions. Beginning in 1928, the National Statistic and Census Service (Servicio Nacional de Estadística y Censos) started collecting information on the price of some consumer goods in Santiago, providing the Labor Department with more reliable statistics.[26] In addition, the Ministry of Social Welfare required provincial authorities to submit annual statistical information on the local cost of living, including "food, lodging, clothing, electricity, heat, tobacco."[27] Like in other parts of the world, labor inspectors used surveys and statistics to depict working-class life. They used this information to identify problems, both in the workplace and inside the home, and propose legal reforms. While measuring, counting, and surveying became a symbol of a modern state and labor policy, these research methods also reflected ideas on how working families should live, consume, and work.[28]

International ideas about food consumption and nutrition also influenced how Chile's Labor Department approached the problem of workers' subsistence. Since the 1920s, international organizations, such as the International Labor Organization (ILO), medical doctors, and social reformers had placed food at the center of labor policy and advocated for a minimum salary to fulfill people's basic nutrition requirements.[29] In Chile, the "nutrition lobby," as Thomas Wright calls them, studied food consumption, conducted health surveys, and called attention to the consequences of malnutrition.[30] The Labor Department, as well as the medical doctors of the Social Security Office, believed that the high cost of living undermined workers' access to food and caused larger public health problems. Among the consequences of underconsumption, labor lawyer Moisés Poblete Troncoso argued, were high rates of infant mortality and general morbidity, stunted growth, and alcoholism.[31] The high cost of living, then, was not only about people living in poor conditions and having no access to consumer goods but about the medical and social consequences of undernourishment.

Building on its experience inspecting company stores and studying the social, economic, and medical problem of subsistence, the Labor Department responded to the increase in the cost of living during the Great Depression. In May 1931, Thomas Lawrence, director of the Labor Department, urged labor inspectors to find ways to "lower the price of subsistence products and, above all, stop the abuses in the selling of articles of prime necessity." In mining and construction camps, he asked inspectors to enforce labor laws and guarantee commercial freedom and fair prices. Lawrence also asked his personnel to survey the "problem of subsistence and local conditions of production and consumption" throughout the country. Given the current economic situation, the director urged labor inspectors to act quickly. Lawrence renewed the department's tradition of studying family budgets and home economics, asking inspectors to collect information on working families' incomes and expenses.[32] The sample questionnaire illustrates how the Labor Department investigated the problem of subsistence at the time. Lawrence considered the working family the basic unit of analysis and asked inspectors to list name, age, occupation, income, and personal expenses of each family member (husband, wife, and children) and itemize all family's living expenses such as rent, food, and utilities (water, gas, and electricity).

While Lawrence argued for a balance between the cost of living and salaries, an idea that became the basis of minimum price legislation in the following years, labor inspectors had little power to control the rising cost of living. Prices and social protests increased during the last months of 1931, and the Labor Department and municipal authorities looked for ways to fix the price of basic food and rent.

THE INCREASE IN THE COST OF LIVING AND MUNICIPAL REGULATIONS, 1931–1932

Municipal governments had historically regulated food sales at the local level. Similar to other Latin American countries, these municipal obligations dated from the colonial times and included issues such as sanitation, taxes, alcohol sales, and price controls. Since the late nineteenth century, municipal governments had also sponsored markets (*mercados municipales*) to institutionalize local trade, reduce prices, and lessen the role of intermediaries.[33] By May 1931, according to the sanitary code, municipal governments had to "inspect and regulate" all "establishments that produce, store, or sell foodstuff and beverages," such as slaughterhouses, bakeries, and bars.[34] Municipalities could also set price ceilings for basic products such as oil, tea, and candles and establish mechanisms to prevent abuses in the selling of food.[35]

The capacity of municipal authorities to inspect food sellers and control prices varied throughout the country. In some cases, municipal authorities and labor inspectors collaborated to inspect bakeries and other stores. In Talca, for example, the labor inspector announced a campaign in June 1931 to "reduce the price of food products," and worked with municipal authorities to control and inspect the "selling of products of prime necessity."[36] In Elqui, province of Coquimbo, a commission integrated by a police officer (*subcomisario de carabineros*), a representative of the city council, and the labor inspector studied the price and quality of bread. After inspecting a total of five bakeries and researching the cost and supply of flour, they set the price of bread at one peso per kilo and the weight of a single loaf bread at ten grams.[37] In Victoria, province of Cautín, the mayor established price ceilings for a few products in November 1931; however, a local newspaper denounced the list of products as "primitive and restricted" and neither police officers or city inspectors enforced the law.[38] Despite some efforts, municipalities and labor inspectors failed to lower the price of food and other basic products. Municipalities had few resources and limited personnel, fines were relatively low, and merchants were powerful.

In the last months of 1931, Chileans witnessed a rapid increase in the price of food and a shortage of imported products. In November 1931, the Sociedad de Comerciantes and Industriales de Viña del Mar noticed that the price of rice and other food products had increased during the last weeks.[39] Consumers across the country reacted quickly to the rapid hike in the cost of living.[40] In Temuco, many protested and demanded a rapid solution to the problem of subsistence. On November 8, 1931, a Sunday, a crowd of people from "all social and political trends" rallied to demand that the government "reduce the price of consumer products." At the event, speakers addressed the current economic situation and asked the government to control the price of basic foodstuff as well as rent.[41] A few days later, *El laborista*, the newspaper of the local Democratic Party, denounced the poor quality and high price of bread, the abuses committed by merchants at the municipal market, and the soaring price of electricity.[42] City residents also gathered at the municipal market to protest the increase in the price of wheat on November 27 and, two days later, joined a "hunger demonstration" at the Plaza de Armas.[43] Protests continued in the following months.[44] On March 26, 1932, labor unions marched through downtown Temuco to protest against the increase in the cost of living, unemployment, and poverty. In April 1932, the democratic newspaper asked the mayor to fix the price of milk and other basic foodstuff and use the law to prosecute "speculators." Wholesalers, according to *El laborista*, had become a "gigantic octopus" that threatened the well-being of the population and the "strength of the race."[45]

Throughout the country, protesters blamed President Juan Esteban Montero and his economic and monetary policies, arguing that restrictions on foreign exchange, high tariffs, and import quotas increased the price of imported food, such as sugar and tea.⁴⁶ They criticized tariffs on Argentine meat that protected national producers, because it increased the price of meat for average consumers.⁴⁷ People also accused foreign commercial houses, wholesalers, and shopkeepers of manipulating the market and profiting from workers' meager salaries. *El empleado,* a newspaper published by the Unión de Empleados Particulares de Valparaíso, referred to the problem of the increased cost of living in the last months of 1931, blaming the oil monopoly and "speculators." In December 1931, the paper argued that the government's restrictions on imports had not only increased the price of many basic products, but also foreign and local wholesalers had "hoarded" goods to drive up prices.⁴⁸ In the following months, white-collar employees continued protesting against monopolies, such as the municipal market and mills, asking neighbors to organize and enforce a fair price.⁴⁹

During the first months of 1932, the political and economic crisis worsened. In December 1931, the government had suppressed a communist uprising in Vallenar. Following a wave of strikes and attempted coups, President Montero declared a state of siege (*estado de sitio*) and restricted civil and political liberties in April 1932.⁵⁰ The economic situation deteriorated. Between December 1931 and December 1932, the Central Bank reported, the cost of living increased 27.2 percent, and both imports and exports continued to drop. The 1932 wheat harvest was poor, forcing the country to import wheat to feed the population.⁵¹ In Santiago, the municipal government set ceiling prices for twelve products, including rice, cooking oil, and fuel (*parafina*) in April 1932.⁵² Other municipal governments implemented similar measures. Between March and June 1932, the municipality of Putaendo, Province of Aconcagua, decreed price ceilings for several products, such as meat, wheat, corn, sugar, tea, and coffee. Enforcement of price regulations was uneven, and a local newspaper denounced that "[it] is rare to find in the district (*comuna*) a retail shop that sells the public articles at the price fixed by the municipality." Furthermore, stores did not display prices, as required by the law.⁵³ In the coal town of Coronel, the city council acknowledged the need to fix prices but were still debating the price and list of products in March 1932.⁵⁴ On the eve of the fall of Montero's government, Juan Verdejo, the fictional comic character of the political satire magazine *Topaze,*⁵⁵ lamented the increase in the cost of living:

> In this time of crisis
> That already reaches the nape of the neck
> oil and coffee rise,
> the bread rises, the sugar rises;
> until they get out of your sight,

What a bother! Coal rises
Electricity rises, gas rises
Although the gas has always rise.
The price of milk goes up,
and sometimes she rises alone
and the airplanes go up
and the tumult increases . . . [56]

HOUSING

Like the price of basic foodstuffs, housing shortages, high rents, and substandard living conditions had been long-term problems for working people. Medical doctors and social reformers argued that poor housing conditions spread diseases and increased infant mortality, promiscuity, and alcoholism; they advocated for the regulation of living conditions. Philanthropic organizations, employers, and the Catholic Church had built some model housing, but their efforts remained limited to small neighborhoods. One of the first social laws in the country, the 1906 law of inexpensive housing, regulated housing conditions, limited rent speculations, and encouraged the building of new housing to replace dilapidated tenements. Protections for renters expanded in 1925, and the organization of housing courts provided renters greater means to fight against eviction and high rents and demand that landlords maintain and repair buildings.[57] Despite this legal framework, on the eve of the Great Depression, Chilean working families had few housing alternatives, lived in crowded and unhygienic buildings, and, after food, rent was their second most important expense.[58]

In the 1930s, unemployment, wage reductions, and the increase in the price of food worsened the housing problem. Families fell behind with the rent, eviction cases overran labor courts, and landlords used both legal and extralegal measures to evict tenants.[59] The question of rent mobilized wide sectors of Chilean society including the Labor Department. Ultimately, the housing crisis required state intervention. In Valparaíso, *El empleado* reported that evictions were "commonplace." Most of the families evicted, the voice of the white-collar movement explained, were "honorable workers and employees." In only one week, the newspaper stated, fifty-six families had filed cases in the housing court.[60] In Iquique, the crisis also threatened people's ability to keep their homes, as most working families had fallen behind with rents. While local labor inspectors had tried to prevent evictions in Iquique, they had little power to do so. By the end of the day, the Labor Department lamented, "people were evicted from their homes, according to the law, and were left on the street, and we have to place them in public shelters."[61]

Housing and rent became contentious issues in 1930s Chile. Tenant activism dated back to the economic crisis of 1914, when tenants in Santiago and Valparaíso protested the increase in rent caused by the crisis and migration from the nitrate districts. With ties to the Communist Party, tenant strikes had been instrumental in the passage of housing regulations in 1925.[62] In the early 1930s, like in other countries affected by the crisis, tenant leagues reemerged to resist evictions. Labor and social organizations demanded a moratorium on both housing rents and mortgages, while tenants' leagues protested evictions.

Conflicts and disputes over housing became common in Chilean cities. In Santiago, for example, Ricardo Matte, a landlord, reported to the police that on his properties, which contained several tenement apartments, tenant leagues encouraged residents to resist eviction orders and not to pay rent.[63] According to the tenant leader, the renters belonged to Sub-Comité Bellavista (Población Matte) of the Liga de Arrendatarios de Providencia and had the right to discuss housing issues and organize the neighbors.[64] In Antofagasta, the Liga de Defensa de Antofagasta claimed that landlords disregarded housing regulations and illegally increased rents. Landlords formed a powerful organization, called Unión de Propietarios, and obstructed and delayed court orders. Neighbors filed rent cases at the labor court to demand a reduction of rent and, many times, the court supported their claims, but landlords responded by demanding a reassessment of their properties, delaying the resolution of the case.[65]

Between November 1931 and May 1932, the government approved a general reduction in rent (20 percent) and property taxes (80 percent).[66] The Unemployment Board provided families that qualified, usually white-collar families, with a rent subsidy, but those benefits were always scarce.[67] According to a circular of the Labor Department, the government would provide a house for unemployed families who were either homeless or lived in "unsuitable" buildings. The Department asked families unable to pay rent not to move out, promising that all evictions had been suspended. All housing and rent moratorium applications had to be approved by a social worker, who would conduct a home visit and family survey. As with other social programs, the Department emphasized the need to supervise and control applicants, to "prevent unscrupulous individuals from taking advantage" of this benefit.[68]

Rent subsidies and other measures failed to resolve the housing crisis. Whether landlords illegally increased rents or families were unable to pay, evictions continued. Welfare professionals had few resources to assist those in need. The eviction of a group of impoverished families from a property in Quilicura, on the outskirts of Santiago, illustrates the drama of the housing crisis and the enormous power of landlords. In February 1932, the landlord alleged that his tenants had not paid rent for a long time. Although the tenants were only one month behind on the rent, the landlord asked an off-duty police officer to force them out of their homes. The police and landlord evicted five families, including nineteen children, who, a social worker reported, "remained eight days living in the street." Although the eviction was illegal, the tenants could not return to their homes. A social worker from the relief office helped them find alternative housing, offered a rent subsidy to some, and provided "a relief ID card to each family."[69] Housing remained a central social problem and political demand throughout most of the twentieth century. By 1934, about two-thirds of the population were living in substandard housing, and the country lacked at least three hundred thousand new homes.[70]

PRICE CONTROL, 1932–1933

Between 1931 and 1932, municipalities, the Labor Department, and the unemployment board failed to protect consumers from the increase in the cost of living and the practices of abusive merchants and landlords. The question of subsistence was a large and complex problem. Constantino Macchiavello Varas, a Chilean lawyer and member of the Radical Party, published a thesis about the high cost of living in Chile in 1933.[71] At the University of Chile, he was influenced by the work of international political economists such as Charles Gide and Rene Foiguet, as well as Chilean writers Daniel Martner and Francisco Walker Linares. Based on local studies, statistics, and family budgets and surveys, he analyzed the reasons behind the high cost of living in Chile. Monetary and fiscal problems increased the cost of living, Macchiavello argued, but also the abuses committed by monopolies and intermediaries, poor transportation and infrastructure (e.g., warehouses, slaughterhouses, cold stores), as well as tariffs and international trade agreements.[72] The problem of subsistence was not only about food but also about rent, the price of utilities such as gas and electricity, clothing, and the cost of urban transportation. Like many other progressive writers at the time, Macchiavello believed that the high cost of living was not only a serious economic issue but also a social and political problem.[73]

Despite a growing demand to control the market, little clarity existed on how to best protect both workers and employers, consumers as well as producers. Rather than a coherent economic policy to reduce the cost of living, Macchiavello argued, the state had created a patchwork of many "unconnected" laws and regulations. In their treaties and interventions, politicians and political economists had generated long lists of solutions, but these read more like long-term aspirations, not concrete steps to fight the increase in the cost of living. Enrique Zañartu Prieto, a member of the Liberal Party who briefly served as minister of finance under Alessandri in 1924 and during the Socialist Republic, painted a grim picture of Depression Era Chile: "hunger, misery, and ignorance." As a solution, he proposed to reform the economic, financial, credit, and banking system, as well as increase salaries, build housing for the poor, reorganize social assistance services, and promote rural settlements in the south of the country.[74] Nevertheless, his proposal lacked clear steps for action.

Some political leaders sought to protect agricultural producers and increase the national production of food. In 1930, General Ibáñez had formed the Agricultural Export Board (Junta de Exportación Agrícola), a state agency that protected landowners from falling prices by subsidizing the export of agricultural surplus. The board included members of the Sociedad Nacional de Agricultura, Chile's powerful landowner association, which favored tariffs and restrictions on the import of agricultural and animal products.[75] Because Chilean producers were unable to satisfy national demand, these restrictions clashed with efforts to make food more affordable. While Chile depended on imported sugar, tea, and coffee, the country also had to import wheat, meat, and dairy products to complement national production.[76] In the following decades, the Agricultural Export Board continued protecting landowners, many times, Thomas C. Wright argues, "working at cross purposes" with public agencies protecting consumers.[77]

If the Agricultural Board protected agricultural producers, other agencies protected consumers. Amid the growing debate and protests over the increase in the cost of living, the National Congress approved the formation of a Comisión Nacional de Precios and provincial councils in May 1932. The councils would set prices for basic consumer products, including food, fuel, and transportation, guarantee the supply of basic products, and prevent speculation and hoarding. The national board would supervise and control the work of provincial councils. Both boards included members of the state (the Ministry of Public Welfare at the national level and governors and *intendentes* at the provincial level), representatives of business associations, and representatives of consumers. The councils were a short-term and emergency measure, to be dissolved after one year.[78] In June, the Ministry of Social Welfare approved a list of "articles of prime necessity" subject to price control and established norms for the operation of the councils.[79] The effectiveness of the councils varied from city to city. In Coelemu, province of Concepción, local authorities were still studying prices in mid-July and recognized that "the study of this matter has been a little complicated."[80] In Copiapó, the city council fixed the price of sugar, but merchants considered the price too low and refused to sell sugar at all.[81]

The case of the provincial price council of Antofagasta illustrates the difficulties in fixing prices. In Antofagasta, the council met regularly during the turbulent months of June and July 1932. Led by the *intendente*, the council determined, set, and adjusted price ceilings (both wholesale and retail) for about thirty products. In a city where most products either were imported or came from other parts of the country, setting prices required extensive research on tariffs, transportation costs, and supply chains. One key issue was the price and distribution of sugar. The council struggled to control all the elements of the retail price of sugar. The local refinery sold sugar at 1.35 pesos per kilo. However, after researching the entire supply chain, the council found that the refinery bought sugar at 0.82 per kilo. The costs of administration and washing the sugar, plus a 10 percent profit was 1.14 pesos. The fair price of sugar, then was 1.15 pesos per kilo and not 1.35 pesos. Moreover, the council concluded, the sugar refinery had "profited from the shortage of this product" and had "played with the situation," and, thus, the council imposed a fine on the company.[82]

The price ceilings lasted for a month and were displayed on boards throughout the port of Antofagasta, but complaints from distributors, retailers, or consumers required the council to revisit its decisions. The council also received petitions to add new products to the lists. The Congreso Social Obrero, a labor organization that represented mutual aid societies, addressed the Comité de Control de Precios in Antofagasta to demand the inclusion of animal feed in the price control list. The labor group argued that forage was an essential product for many people in the region, and retailers had "stockpiled (*acaparamiento*)" it and speculated with the price, making it almost inaccessible. The cost of a *fardo* (about fifty-five pounds) of forage and its transportation from Huasco to Antofagasta was 9.90 pesos, the labor group argued, but merchants sold it at fourteen pesos.[83] High prices, excessive transportation costs, and problems of supply were common in the northern port of Antofagasta. The needs of consumers and producers in Antofagasta conflicted with the interests of producers from other parts of the country. For example, the council eliminated protections for national producers, lowered import tariffs, and opened all ports to protect merchants.

Despite efforts, as in the case of Antofagasta, the councils faced many obstacles to reducing prices, including lengthy negotiations and limited authority to enforce them. After unsuccessful efforts to control prices at the local and municipal level, the government, led by Carlos Dávila, created in August 1932 the General Commissariat of Subsistence and Prices (Comisariato General de Subsistencias y Precios), an institution that operated until 1943 under the jurisdiction of the Ministry of Labor. Like the previous councils, the Comisariato aimed to "guarantee the most convenient economic conditions to all the residents of the Republic."[84] To do so, the Comisariato would control the quality and price of basic products (food, clothes, transportation, and heat) and, if necessary, direct the production, distribution, and sales of products. The Comisariato had jurisdiction over a longer list of products than the former Councils and included utilities, transportation, and raw materials; in the 1940s, it distributed products and maintained its own stores (*almacenes*).⁸⁵ As P.T. Ellsworth argued in 1945: "one relatively mild and unworkable law [the law of Price Councils of May 1932] was succeeded by another of most dramatic nature [the Comisariato law of August 1932]."⁸⁶

Conflicts between consumers, intermediaries, and shopkeepers remained at the center of price-control politics at the local level. In the province of Arauco, for example, a leftist group denounced the increase in the price of bread and sugar. The group accused two foreign merchants, named Piché and Pastorini, of hoarding and usury for "hiding flour and other foodstuffs."⁸⁷ In Coelemu, a Spanish merchant, Daniel Soto, claimed that residents and authorities had harassed and attacked him. The story became more complicated because it involved the efforts of the new Commissariat to fix prices. One of Soto's former workers claimed that his boss had moved his merchandise in the middle of the night and did not comply with the regulations of the Comisariato. Other witnesses argued that the town disliked Soto and considered him a "gangster" and "robber." Soto's practices had "caused public outrage," and during a public assembly, members of the community, including the local priest, had spoken against Soto and blamed him for the town's state of misery and widespread hunger. However, the crowd did not hurt Soto and, local authorities argued, all fines and inspections had followed the strict and "legitimate" regulations of the Comisariato.⁸⁸

The Comisariato became one of the most important institutional legacies of the Socialist Republic. In the following years, it fixed prices at company stores, negotiated salary increases, and raised minimum wages. While it did not stop the rise in the cost of living, women, labor, and consumer organizations defended the work of the Comisariato and collaborated with authorities to oversee the enforcement of price controls at the local level.⁸⁹

A MINIMUM WAGE

As Chileans experienced unemployment, work and salary reductions, migration, and rising cost of living, welfare professionals and labor organizations debated how to define minimum employment conditions, wages, and subsistence needs. From public work sites to print shops, labor organizations demanded a minimum wage. In March 1932, the print workers (*trabajadores gráficos*) explained that not only had salaries declined because of the economic crisis but also employers paid women and younger workers less than adult men and had extended piece work. These managerial practices, the union argued, undermined working conditions and salaries. Workers demanded a minimum wage for all print shops, the end of piece work, "equal work, equal salary," and the end of all forms of wage discrimination.⁹⁰ Schoolteachers, who had been at the forefront of the political struggles of the 1930s, also demanded a minimum salary. In October 1932, the National Convention of Teachers presented a long list of demands, including the establishment of a "family salary" that reflected the increase in the cost of living.[91]

Chilean labor laws included provisions to regulate salaries. The Labor Code of 1931 defined the minimum wage for industrial workers as "no less than two-thirds nor higher than three-quarters of a regular salary currently paid in the same class of work, to workers of the same aptitudes or conditions, and in the city or region that is executed." A joint board (*comisión mixta*) integrated by representatives of employers and employees and led by government officials would negotiate and fix the minimum wage. Only in September 1932 did the Department of Labor define the procedures and norms for the election and operation of the board.[92]

Labor inspectors faced many obstacles in applying the law and forming joint boards. The norms remained vague, and each inspector interpreted and adapted to the local conditions. In Talca, the inspector supported regulating "salaries on the basis of justice and equality" because it was a matter of social justice. However, he had not yet formed a joint board in his province and would wait until 1933.[93] In Linares, agricultural workers earned a salary considered "generally derisory." The labor inspector met with the governor and influential landowners to discuss a minimum wage, but he was unable to form a joint board and instead adapted wages to local practices. He did not clarify what these local practices were, but the presence of landowners and no reference to workers' representatives suggests that landowners, as in most of the countryside, refused to increase wages or improve working conditions. The inspector hoped to negotiate a minimum wage for bakery workers, but, he argued, the industry was in crisis, making it impossible to improve conditions at the time.[94]

Chile's efforts to establish a minimum wage intersected with transnational discussions about food and nutrition, ideas of gender and family, and the general debate about workers' subsistence.[95] In fixing a minimum wage, Labor Department officials discussed how to balance wages and the cost of living, measure a living wage, and whether to consider family dependents. In May 1933, the Labor Department asked inspectors across the nation to study the cost of living and determine an "adequate" minimum wage.[96] The exact meaning of an "adequate" wage remained unclear and was left to local interpretation.[97] In Valdivia, the inspector collected statistical data on local wages and the cost of living, differentiating between industrial workers, white-collar employees, domestic workers, and agricultural laborers.[98] Housing and food expenses differed for white-collar employees and industrial workers, reflecting different lifestyles and social status. In the case of domestic workers, the inspector assumed they received lodging and food at the workplace but did not consider whether they supported family dependents not living with them. In determining a living wage, the Labor Department also defined what, how, and how much working families should consume. While the consensus held that wages were too low, labor and social welfare departments also agreed that working men spent too much money on alcohol, while women had poor housekeeping, cooking, and budgeting skills. The Chilean working class, reformers believed, did not plan and did not save.[99]

The history of the minimum wage in the 1930s reflected the differences among workers, showing great disparities across the country and economic sectors. Bakery workers, for example, successfully negotiated a minimum wage. Bakeries, both small family shops (called *amasanderías*) and large and mechanized shops, had been at the center of the debate over labor legislation since the 1910s. In the 1920s, labor inspectors and labor unions had struggled to eradicate night work, improve safety and salaries, and control the labor market and the hiring of workers.[100] Night work had been an especially complicated issue. While the Labor Department had limited resources to inspect bakeries, employers had argued they could not stop bread machines during the night and that workers had to start making the dough as early as 3:00 or 4:00 a.m.[101] Labor unions had long argued that establishing minimum conditions across all bakeries, would improve conditions in an industry in which workers were spread out across small shops and had limited bargaining power.

The work of the joint board in Victoria, Province of Cautín, shows how the system helped bakers. On September 25, 1934, the labor inspector and representatives of employers, the provincial government, and both blue-collar and white-collar labor unions met in Victoria to establish a minimum wage for bakery workers. The board first heard workers' demands. The labor inspector then summarized living and working conditions in the city. Finally, they agreed on a minimum wage of nine pesos for maestros and seven pesos for workers, which would affect all bakeries in the department for one year.[102]

In contrast to bakers, agricultural workers, the worst paid workers in the country, had little power to obtain a minimum wage. In Lontué, a labor union representing workers in the Casa Blanca winery wrote to the Labor Department asking to enforce a minimum wage.[103] The winery was one of the most antiunion agricultural employers in the province, and the owner, Alejandro Dussaillant, had not only opposed rural unionization and demands on his property, but also refused to allow labor inspectors on his land.[104] Employers like Dussaillant successfully lobbied against the expansion of labor rights, including minimum wage laws in the countryside, arguing that labor laws did not apply to rural workers.[105]

Along with the establishment of joint boards, the government approved special wage legislation for nitrate workers. As in the case of the COSACH, working conditions became part of larger efforts to reorganize the nitrate industry. On January 1934, the government created the Corporación de Ventas de Salitre y Yodo en Chile, a corporation that gave the state a monopoly over nitrate exports. The law that created the Corporación de Ventas also established a minimum wage for nitrate workers. Unlike the vague terms of the joint board system, the nitrate minimum wage sought to balance wages and cost of living, as well as workers' family situations. A special joint board for the nitrate industry would fix salaries for a period between six months and one year. Until the formation of the joint boards, the law established a minimum wage of ten pesos for single workers and fifteen pesos for married workers.[106]

While the establishment of a different wage for single and married workers represented an important benefit for workers with large families, it was nonetheless controversial. Before the approval of the law, the Labor Department had collected data on the cost of living throughout the nitrate districts and created sample budgets that corresponded to the size of families. While a single worker in the Oficina Chacabuco would spend 178 pesos per month in food and other expenses, a family of five (husband, wife, and three children under the age of twelve) would spend 496 pesos per month.[107] These calculations were not merely simple statistics of the cost of living; they reflected how the state viewed and defined families as male-headed.[108] In addition, the law furthered inequality between married and single workers. During a meeting between the inspector and representatives of the labor movement in Iquique, a nitrate union leader stated that employers were less likely to hire married workers because they were more expensive. For example, he continued, nitrate companies hired married workers "only for some specific jobs" and "fired them for the most minimal reasons."[109] For the Partido Radical Independiente de Iquique, the minimum wage for nitrate workers created divisions within the working class. As a result, the party asked that "all employees and workers in general benefit with the implementation of a minimum wage."[110]

In 1936, the Chilean government acknowledged the importance of a minimum wage during the First International Conference of American states that were members of the ILO. The conference, held in Santiago in January 1936, brought together delegations from nineteen American countries. Following the ILO tripartite structure, most delegations included members of the state, employers' organizations, and workers. At the conference, the delegates discussed the ILO's conventions, proposing a series of resolutions, such as the one on indigenous workers that reflected the unique reality of the continent. One of the resolutions, presented by Chile's labor lawyer and functionary of the Labor Department Héctor Escribar Mandiola, proposed to guarantee a minimum salary to provide "an adequate standard of living." Although the meanings of "adequate" remained elusive, Escribar Mandiola introduced the concept of a "minimum family wage." This wage, he argued, would allow workers and their families to "satisfy basic needs" such as "food, clothing, housing, general and professional education, rest, and culture."[111] Nevertheless, most of the conference resolutions reflected larger policy goals rather than practical measures.

Despite workers' demands and Chile's international commitment to fix a minimum wage, only some groups of industrial workers (e.g., construction, bakery, print), the nitrate workers, and, after 1937, white-collar employees in the private sector obtained this benefit (analyzed in the previous chapter). In November 1939, Bernardo Ibáñez Águila, a leader of the teachers' union, member of the Socialist Party, and vice-president of Chile's national labor organization (CTCH) attended the second regional ILO conference in Havana. He reflected on the progress and limits of social legislation in the last decade. On the one hand, the Popular Front (elected in 1938) had improved the lives of working people, "limiting the rise in price of articles of first necessity by setting up free markets for the distribution of food to the population and restricting speculation through a Committee on Consumption and Prices." However, Ibáñez Águila concluded, "workers' wages are still insufficient in relation to the high cost of living."[112] Low wages, the increase in the cost of living, and job instability remained central problems in the lives of Chilean workers.

PART III

THE ROAD TO FULL EMPLOYMENT

CHAPTER 6

INCOMPLETE REFORMS

In 1938, the national congress of the Metal Workers Industrial Federation (FIOM) discussed job insecurity and unemployment in their trade. The economic depression was over, the international market was recovering, and the country's industrial, mining, and building sectors were growing.[1] While overall employment in manufacturing was also increasing, metal plants remained small and outdated. Indeed, FIOM's leader Eduardo Saraos argued, metal entrepreneurs had failed to modernize the industry and guarantee basic working conditions, jeopardizing the future of more than 35,000 metal workers. Saraos and other union leaders demanded the government to "promote production and prioritize the development and progress of the metal industry."[2] In 1939, they joined the Defense Committee of the National Metal Industry (Comité de Defensa de la Industria Metalúrgica Nacional), a board integrated by representatives of the state, workers, and metal businesses, and lobbied for special protections for the industry. To defend their jobs, metal workers also supported the development of industrial education and training.[3]

As other Latin Americans at the time, Chilean metal workers believed that the process of industrialization would increase and improve employment opportunities, bringing economic prosperity. This view was emblematic of the model of state industrialization and import substitution that characterized Latin America during the 1930s–1960s. In Chile, supported by the national state, the process of industrialization accelerated from the late 1930s to the 1960s, transforming not only the national economy but also workers' everyday lives. Despite considerable advances, such as the installation of the first steel plant (Huachipato) in 1948, industrial growth did not lead to development, and the national economy remained unstable during the entire period. While a backward agricultural sector increased dependence on food imports and accelerated rural-urban migration, the country continued to depend on export revenues and foreign loans, and the manufacturing sector relied on a complex web of state protections and subsidies.

By the mid-1950s, the industrial sector faced several bottlenecks, including a small domestic market and poor investment; inflation threatened economic stability; and urban unemployment and underemployment increased.[4]

The demands of the metal workers illustrate a new political and economic era in Chile. In 1938, the electoral victory of Pedro Aguirre Cerda, the leader of the Popular Front coalition, inaugurated a time of state-directed development and economic and expansion of social infrastructure.[5] Supported by the national state, the process of industrialization accelerated, transforming not only the national economy but also workers' everyday life. The Front also expanded the social role of the state, modernized public services such as the Labor Department, and supported workers' unionization. At the local level, it consolidated the model of industrial relations established in the late 1920s but limited those rights to industrial workers and white-collar employees.[6]

These economic, political, and institutional shifts changed perceptions and definitions of work and unemployment and legitimated the role of the state in regulating the labor market. During the 1910s–1930s, the characteristics of the export sector and the political and social identity of nitrate workers had influenced the fight against unemployment. In the 1940s, attention shifted to urban areas. Labor and social reforms targeted industrial and urban workers, while the system of social security reinforced the influence of wage workers and male-headed families. Indeed, people who could not work and were not part of a legally recognized family had a hard time finding aid. In the 1950s, the rise of international technical assistance and discussions about full employment provided a technical language and tools to analyze the labor market. Like other Latin American countries, Chile modernized employment services and the collection of labor statistics, reformed the system of social security, and expanded technical education. Most reforms fell short. Bureaucratic hurdles, poor funding, and centralization made services such as the Unemployment Board and the National Placement Service ineffective. Economic instability and inflation undermined workers' jobs, salaries, and pensions, and employers could easily ignore and violate labor protections. These shortcomings paved the way for the radical reforms of the long 1960s.

THE NATIONAL PLACEMENT SERVICE

The need to regulate the labor market, prevent unemployment, and satisfy employers' needs resurfaced during the years of World War II. At the international level, these economic worries parallel the rise of the concept of full employment. Before the end of the war, European countries started planning for the consequences of the postwar and demobilization, especially as they "desire to avoid the sharp recession that followed demobilization after the first world war."[7] William Beveridge, the mastermind of the British social security system, argued that the postwar should not only guarantee a lasting peace but also "freedom from want" and "freedom from idleness." Social security would provide people with the means for a "healthy subsistence," while full employment—"defined as a state of affairs in which there are always more vacant jobs than unemployed men"—would end idleness. Beveridge also emphasized the responsibility of the state to "protect its citizens against mass unemployment."[8] If John Keynes had demonstrated in the 1930s that involuntary unemployment existed in the capitalist world, Beveridge highlighted the social and political importance of guaranteeing full employment in a free and democratic society.[9]

In the 1940s, full employment—when everyone able and willing to work has a job—was not only an economic question, but the basis of social and political stability around the world. In 1944, at the ILO meeting in Philadelphia, delegates committed to achieving "full employment and raising the standard of living."[10] Four years later, the Economic and Social Councils of the United Nations reinstated the global importance of full employment and surveyed countries' different strategies to maintain or achieve this goal. Among these strategies, a UN survey highlighted the establishment of specialized agencies to study employment, support for private investors to maintain and increase jobs, and development of emergency measures to prevent unemployment.[11] While discussions about demobilization and full employment mostly involved industrialized countries, the principle that the state had to create institutions and set up mechanisms to create jobs and prevent unemployment also reached Latin America.

During the war years, Latin American governments feared the economic and social consequences of market disruptions.[12] The war had created opportunities for the expansion of industrial production, but also restricted international trade, affecting Latin America's exports and access to foreign exchange and imports.[13] In 1941, during the International Labor Organization (ILO) conference in New York, Chilean delegate and senator Isauro Torres expressed concern about the dangers of "unemployment and misery" that the war and the postwar could bring to the continent.[14] He was not mistaken. The economic and trade policies of the United States, especially a price ceiling on copper, had a negative impact on the Chilean economy.[15] The country also suffered a severe shortage of oil and other essential products that affected the manufacturing sector. By the end of 1941, the cost of living was rising again, and industrial plants reduced production and employment. In January 1942, the Chilean government recognized that the war had caused economic "instability and disorder, as well as growing unemployment, aggravating a serious social-economic problem, one that the state must answer and preferably resolve."[16]

Chile's reform of employment policies took place during the critical economic conjuncture of World War II and the transnational discussion about full employment. To combat unemployment, President Juan Antonio Ríos turned to an old friend: placement services. The establishment of public employment agencies had been the country's first public responses to unemployment and a widely accepted international recommendation. Along with labor statistics, it was on the agenda of the First International Conference on Unemployment in 1910 and a topic of several ILO recommendations (see chapter 1). By the end of the Great Depression, western countries agreed that an efficient system to place workers could regulate the labor market and reduce unemployment. They also believed that the state should help people find work, inspect private employment agencies, and eliminate all for-profit agencies. Latin American countries generally recognized the benefits of regulating the labor market, yet services were still rudimentary in the 1930s. Lack of funding undermined the capacity of labor departments to organize efficient placement offices and regulate private agencies, while the characteristics of the labor force and its geographical distribution complicated extending services to all workers seeking employment.[17]

Placement services in Chile dated from 1914. During the Great Depression, the office had gained new visibility and become a permanent service of the Labor Department, but it remained small and only placed a limited number of unemployed workers. In 1940, the government had restructured the entire Labor Department and increased its budget and the number of personnel. This reform also reorganized placement services, creating a special subdepartment called the National Placement Service (Servicio Nacional de Colocaciones).[18] In 1942, the National Placement Service passed from the Department of Labor to the Ministry of Labor, and the office gained more administrative autonomy and wider responsibilities.[19] That same year, President Juan Antonio Ríos formed an advisory board to study unemployment (Comité Relacionador de Cesantía). In Chile, advisory boards coordinated activities and policies across ministries and administrative divisions and, sometimes, incorporate nonstate agents. In this case, the board included representatives of social, labor, and economic departments and was charged with "studying, preventing, and absorbing unemployment."[20] Although the board accomplished little and rarely met, it was the country's first effort to set up an agency that could craft a national employment policy.

Political leaders regularly mentioned unemployment as a national problem, but policies changed little during the 1940s–1950s. In 1943, during his annual address to the National Congress and the nation, President Ríos praised the National Placement Service and the board for contributing to

TABLE 6.1. PLACEMENT OFFICE, 1933–1950, YEAR AVERAGE

YEAR	BLUE-COLLAR WORKERS REGISTERED	BLUE-COLLAR WORKERS PLACED	WHITE-COLLAR EMPLOYEES REGISTERED	WHITE-COLLAR EMPLOYEES PLACED	DOMESTIC WORKERS REGISTERED	DOMESTIC WORKERS PLACED	TOTAL REGISTERED	TOTAL PLACED	PERCENTAGE OF WORKERS PLACED
1933	51,957	5,001	14,392	180	5,456	220	71,805	5,401	7.5
1934	20,510	3,078	7,988	211	1,577	206	30,075	3,495	11.6
1935	7,181	1,014	3,058	30	434	156	10,673	1,200	11.2
1936	4,836	1,279	1,374	110	264	150	6,474	1,539	23.7
1937	2,455	740	520	39	228	121	3,203	900	28
1938	2,233	918	1,968	18	377	164	4,578	1,100	24
1939	4,951	692	4,246	285	219	116	9,416	1,093	11.6
1940	4,876	745	3,289	434	386	64	8,551	1,243	14.5
1941	2,193	514	1,598	320	326	72	4,117	906	22
1942	1,011	321	1,189	255	323	89	2,523	665	26.3
1943	1,462	420	1,791	342	367	105	3,620	867	23.9
1944	1,478	456	2,632	548	247	91	4,357	1,095	25.1
1945	1,252	515	3,273	566	101	39	4,626	1,120	24.2
1946	1,003	326	3,303	608	94	33	4,400	967	21.9
1947	1,391	477	3,441	717	105	43	4,937	1,237	25.0
1948	1,106	381	3,156	721	74	31	4,336	1,133	26.1
1949	1,043	400	3,519	768	89	38	4,651	1,206	25.9
1950	724	282	3,345	891	69	29	4,138	1,202	29.0
1951	577	261	2,999	807	79	24	3,655	1,092	29.8

Source: Dirección General de Estadística de Chile, *Estadística Chilena*, Sinópsis.

"the fight against unemployment." In one year (1942–1943), Ríos argued, the employment office had found jobs for 7,982 people, including 3,111 white-collar employees, 3,808 blue-collar workers, and 1,063 domestic workers.[21] The figures of the National Placement Service were less encouraging (table 6.1), confirming the historical trend that only a small portion of the unemployed had access to public employment services, the unregistered population was always more numerous than the registered population, and the office could only place a few of those who asked for help. Between 1941 and 1949, the office placed on average 24.5 percent of those registered. The Labor Department estimated that in the case of blue-collar workers, registered unemployment was only about 20 percent of the total unemployed population in 1948 and less than 10 percent in 1949.[22] In contrast, white-collar employees, because of the requirements of the unemployment fund, usually registered at the National Placement Office; but, few of them found work through the office.

The National Placement Service suffered from many limitations. First, its functions were broad and included activities beyond the mere placement of workers. For example, the agency studied all problems related to employment and unemployment in the country, recommended measures and policies, registered and placed unemployed people, regulated *enganche* contracts, collected employment statistics, and inspected private employment agencies. Second, the office was small and had limited resources and personnel. To handle the registration and placement of unemployed workers, it maintained a specialized service in Santiago; but, in provincial cities, labor inspectors assumed this task as part of their other responsibilities.[23] Third, public placement also coexisted with private institutions such as the placement service of the Sociedad Nacional de Agricultura for agricultural workers, a specialized service for domestic workers maintained by the Catholic Church, and for-profit and unregulated agencies.

Descriptions of the labor exchange office in downtown Santiago evidenced the limits of public placement in the 1940s. Opened from Monday through Friday, the office served blue-collar workers in the morning, from 9:00 a.m. to noon, and white-collar employees in the afternoon, from 3:00 to 4:00 p.m. To register, unemployed workers had to come in person and present their national identification card, proof of previous employment, and, in the case of blue-collar workers, social security card. The registration was valid for ninety days. Along with registering people, a placement section compiled information on available jobs. Four employees met regularly with employers across Santiago, while two female employees compiled data on available jobs for domestic workers. The next step was to match workers and employers. The office employees offered jobs according to classification and skills. First, they approached people waiting at the office and, only then, attempted to contact them at home.[24] In other words, job seekers had to come to the office regularly to increase their chance to find employment, a time-consuming task that limited the opportunities and time to find work through other means. Since there was no linkage between the National Placement Office, social aid departments, and social security offices, blue-collar workers had few reasons to register.

THE REGULATION OF COLLECTIVE LAYOFFS

Public authorities had always been concerned about the layoff of large groups of workers and made efforts to negotiate with employers the timing and terms of dismissal. The reduction and restructuring of production and shutdowns affected large groups of people, but because financial reasons usually motivated these decisions, it was difficult to enforce the labor laws that would protect those groups. In these conditions, as the experience of the Great Depression had shown, securing transportation for workers and their families or guaranteeing that employers paid salaries and benefits were difficult tasks, especially if the Labor Department had no previous information about managers' plans. In the past, the Labor Department and public authorities had also been concerned about the impact of large layoffs on local communities and public order. Therefore, during the Great Depression, the Labor Department had required all employers to communicate to labor inspectors about large layoffs, but this was an emergency measure and not sanctioned by any law.

With memories of massive unemployment still vivid, the Labor Department argued the need to regulate and control large layoffs. In 1943, Law 7747 included several economic, financial, and employment measures, and modified the Labor Code.[25] In response to the "vicissitudes of production in times of war and post-war," the state acquired legal mechanisms to control and limit massive layoff. The new regulations, which became part of the Labor Code (article 86 of the Labor Code), established that the ministers of labor and economics had to authorize the simultaneous dismissal of ten or more workers (*despidos colectivos*), as well as a plant's shutdown (*paralización de faenas*). If the government approved employers' petitions, employers had to provide workers a thirty-day notice; but if the petition was rejected, employers could continue with their plan if they pay workers a lump sum equivalent to fifteen days of salary per year worked. In general terms, this reform provided extra protection for workers affected by shutdowns or large layoffs and increased control over employers' actions.[26]

The Supreme Court referred to this reform as "collective immobility." To limit employers' right to dismiss large groups of workers (more than 10), the Supreme Court explained, was a question of "social interest."[27] As many other Chilean labor laws, the clause of collective layoff did not offer the same protection to all workers. First, the law excluded seasonal agricultural workers and workers whose contracts were under ninety days, and the law did not apply to white-collar employees. Additionally, the president had the right to make exceptions for certain companies or activities. In 1949, President Gabriel González Videla excluded construction workers employed by the State Railroad Company, as well as workers building the smelter in Paipote, Copiapó, and electrical plants. In all these cases, the government argued that the nature of work was "temporary" and not "permanent."[28] In other situations, employers spread out the layoffs over time, avoiding obtaining official authorization or paying compensation. To combat this tactic, the Labor Department stated in 1959 that "the partial dismissal of 10 or less workers, who as a whole exceed that amount, made with the purpose of avoiding the legal procedures required by the ministry and the payment of compensation, constitutes an infraction of Art. 86 of the Labor Code."[29]

The efforts of the Labor Department, labor judges, and the Supreme Court to discern who had and did not have the right to "collective immobility" illustrate the difficulties to protect all workers from the threat of unemployment. When Fábrica Nacional Loza Penco, a large pottery factory located in the Greater Concepción area, fired twenty women working the night shift, the labor court of Concepción ruled that the company had not infringed the law. Although the women claimed that the rules of collective dismissal applied to their case and demanded a compensation equivalent to thirty days of salary, the judged stated that the Labor Code forbade the employment of women in night shifts and, thus, the company's decision to fire the female employees only followed that law.[30] In other words, the law could only protect people if they were legally employed, but in many cases, they were not.

The law was also unclear when companies changed hands and those changes affected workers' employment status. In 1945, the Empresa Nacional de Transportes Colectivos acquired the old Compañía Chilena de Electricidad, stating that it would maintain workers' traditional benefits and rights. The transition, however, reclassified some of its new employees, who passed from blue-collar (*obreros*) to white-collar workers (*empleados particulares*). The company also fired more than ten former employees of the Compañía Chilena de Electricidad, who, in response, filed a claim at the Labor Court demanding the benefits guaranteed in cases of "collective layoff." The case became more complicated when the government gave the company the right to conduct "collective layoffs" without previous authorization, excluding all workers from the protection of Article 86. Although the lower labor court favored workers' demand, the higher labor tribunal dismissed it in favor of the company. In August 1949, the Supreme Court reviewed the case and discussed whether the Empresa Nacional de Transportes Colectivos had violated article 86 of the Labor Code. At the end, the highest court in the country revoked the last ruling and confirmed the ruling of the lower court, arguing that: protections conferred by Article 48 were an "inalienable right," changes in employment status could not mean losing rights, and, more importantly, the layoff had occurred before the government had excepted the company from the obligations of Article 86.[31]

In large unionized plants, labor unions played an important role in regulating large layoffs. In Potrerillos, a copper mine owned by a US company and with a labor force around 5,000 workers in 1941, labor unions struggled to protect their members from the consequences of declining production. The mine had started showing signs of depletion in the early 1940s, and by the end of the decade, management started reducing production and fired about half of the workforce. Chilean authorities considered the company's economic reasons to be legitimate, and the Labor Department carefully supervised the layoffs. Moreover, labor leaders not only successfully negotiated the terms of layoffs and the payment of benefits, but also were able to manage what happened to those who were laid off. For example, some people were reassigned to different jobs, while others decided to leave the company and benefited from the layoff package.[32]

The regulation of collective layoffs protected some workers in very precise situations, in all other cases, workers had almost no protections. In the following decades, efforts to reform social security, provide unemployment compensation, and regulate dismissal would extend protections to other workers.

SHOULD CHILE HAVE UNEMPLOYMENT INSURANCE?

During the postwar era, western democracies consolidated a comprehensive system of social security, the cornerstone of welfare regimes, to maintain social and political stability, as well as redistribute wealth. While social security systems dated back to the first decades of the twentieth century, the Great Depression and World War II reopened the debate about how to organize, finance, and distribute social security benefits. In 1941, British social reformer William Beveridge chaired a national commission on social insurance and allied services such as workers' compensations and health care services. After examining existing services in Britain, he reaffirmed the role of the state to protect the population and provide "against interruption and loss of earning power." A unified system of social security, he argued, was "the way to freedom of want."[33] That same year at the ILO conference in New York, Francis Perkins, US Secretary of Labor, analyzed the social, labor, and economic problems brought by the war and the challenges of rebuilding a free world. Perkins, the architect of social security and minimum wage legislation in the United States, considered social protection as the foundation of democracy. "A free world needs to be a world designed first and last to produce security and comfort to the ordinary man: the wage earner, the farmer, the merchant, the teacher. He must have opportunity to earn his livelihood in useful pursuit. He needs to live in a world which makes provision for the disadvantaged groups of the community: the young, the old, the sick, those without adequate bargaining power, those whose family resources make it impossible for them to develop fully their innate capacities."[34] Although there was a consensus on the social, economic, and political importance of social security, systems differed across the world, ranging from social-democratic model implemented in Scandinavian countries to the United States' post–New Deal liberal system.[35]

While most social security experts recognized unemployment as a social risk, they disagreed on how to protect the unemployed and distribute benefits. Beveridge envisioned a comprehensive system of social security that would protect workers in case of disability, old age, and unemployment, as well as provide medical benefits and cover funeral expenses. However, in the case of unemployment, Beveridge argued, benefits could not be permanent or endless. As described in chapter 1, since the early twentieth century, experts had argued that a solid unemployment insurance system should make the distribution of benefits contingent on a person's ability and desire to work. Unemployment insurance plans had established restrictive eligibility requirements, separated applicants between people able and unable to work, excluded those considered unfit for work, and kept compensation below regular wages. These requirements and practices contributed to stigmatizing unemployment insurance and placement services and driving eligible people out.[36]

In Latin America, the social security movement also reached momentum in the 1940s, symbolized by events such as the Inter-American Conference on Social Security held in Santiago, Chile, in 1942; Mexico Social Security Act of 1943; and Brazil's social security legislation of 1945. In 1945, during the Inter-American conference in Chapultepec, American states committed to improving living and working conditions in their countries, guaranteeing people's access to nutritious food, a safe workplace, health care, housing, and social security.[37] The following year, during the meeting of the American states members of the ILO in Mexico City, ILO Director Edward J. Phelan recognized that American countries had made significant strides in the area of social security and the development of health care protections and services and encouraged them to expand services and "cover all contingencies" and people.[38]

Despite improvements, the Latin American social security system suffered from many problems, and there was a big gap between governments' promises of universalism and people's everyday reality.[39] In the case of unemployment, protections were marginal and, in most cases, nonexistent. In Mexico, the Social Security law of 1943 covered the risk of unemployment only in the case of workers aged 60 or older.[40] Brazil also limited unemployment protections for older workers. In Uruguay, after years of struggles, workers in the meat-processing plants (1944) and wool and hide industry (1945) obtained special protections and compensations in case of unemployment.[41]

The characteristics of Chile's social security system delayed the recognition of unemployment as a risk. Dating back to the 1920s, the system of social security offered retirement, disability, and medical benefits. It was not a unified system but divided in about forty agencies that served different categories of workers from blue-collar workers to white-collar employees to army personnel. Benefits varied widely from group to group, creating a complex, heterogeneous, and unequal system. Social security not only reinforced social stratification, but it was not universal, limiting coverage to formal workers and immediate family members. The largest and most emblematic social security agency was the Caja de Seguro Obrero (CSO) that provided mandatory insurance to blue-collar workers, about 1 million people in the 1940s.[42] Building on the historical influence of medical doctors on social service, the CSO emphasized medical assistance to workers, mothers, and infants, and maintained a network of health care services across the country. In contrast to the rapid expansion of medical services, workers' retirement pensions remained low and irrelevant until the 1950s.[43]

Throughout the 1940s, different sectors of Chilean society voiced concerns over the limits of the system of social security and demanded extensive reform.[44] The system was bureaucratic, mediated by employers, and contingent on the capacity of the state to enforce labor laws. In 1939, Salvador Allende, who served as minister of public health between 1939 and 1942, published his critical analysis of social and medical conditions in Chile. In his description of social security, he argued that social insurance covered only a few of workers' social risks and a fraction of the nonworking and indigent population.[45] The presidential and congressional committees that studied social security in the early 1940s pointed out the lack of medical protections for family members and the "insignificance of the amount of the pensions for the elderly."[46] Similarly, labor organizations complained about the bad quality of medical attention and the meager economic benefits and pensions. In 1946, Bernardo Araya, president of the National Confederation of Chilean Workers (CTCH), argued that while workers paid for insurance, the system had become "an agony for the thousands of workers who had to go and ask for service, because the medicines and pensions provided are a joke for those who get them."[47]

While politicians and welfare professionals failed to reform and expand social security until 1952, labor unions expanded benefits at the local level. Building on the mutual aid tradition of Chile's labor movement, as well as the institutional and financial resources provided by the legalization of labor unions, labor unions offered medical benefits and protected their members and families in case of death, accident, and unemployment.[48] The Sindicato Weiss, a labor union representing workers at a shoe factory in Valdivia, offered members a monetary subsidy in case of sickness, paid for funerary expenses for family members, published a newspaper, and maintained a store (co-op), a night school, and a library.[49]

The CSO did not cover the risk of unemployment until 1953, so the labor movement strove to establish severance payments and workplace protections at the local level. A severance payment was a lump sum paid by employers upon workers' dismissal and calculated based on the length of employment, but it also had restrictions such as the cause of dismissal and employers' financial capacity to pay the indemnity. In some cases, such as railroad, municipal, and sewage workers, severance payments were guaranteed by special legislation.[50] In other cases, labor unions negotiated collective contracts and agreements that included clauses on severance payments. As a result of these collective negotiations, by the late 1940s, the norm in large and unionized plants was a payment equivalent to fifteen days per year employed.[51] In contrast, workers in small plants and in agriculture had almost no bargaining power, were more susceptible to labor abuses and, as a result, only had the limited protection guaranteed by the Labor Code (a six-day notice or the equivalent to one-week payment in cases workers had not broken the terms of the contract).

Proposals to include unemployment insurance for blue-collar workers found little support outside the labor movement and its political allies. In the mid-1940s, the Consejo General del Trabajo, the government's advising board on labor policy, discussed a project of unemployment insurance. Influenced by international insurance plans, the board proposed a program that linked unemployment benefits to registration in placement services, integrating the work of the Department of Social Aid with the National Employment Service.[52] The traditional argument that Chile and Chilean workers were not ready for this kind of benefit resurfaced.[53] Herminia Navarro, a lawyer, argued in 1945 that Chile's economy was not ready to support this type of insurance. As many of her compatriots, she believed that workers' characters would jeopardize the purpose and success of insurance. She explained that "the character of Chilean manual workers, not a great friend of saving and paying contributions" to social security, is "always looking for a way to get around that obligation, but ready to demand all the benefits."[54] Using a similar paternalist tone to social reformers in the early twentieth century, Navarro argued against unemployment insurance for blue-collar workers because workers were "lazy." The solution was not to provide relief, she concluded, but to "reeducate these individuals [unemployed] and force them to work."[55]

If the CSO had left blue-collar workers vulnerable in the face of unemployment, the Caja Nacional de Empleados Particulares (white-collar employees' insurance fund) partially covered the risk of unemployment since 1937 (explained in chapter 4). White-collar employees affiliated with the Caja contributed 1 percent of their salary to an unemployment fund, but without employers or state contributions, the funds were never enough to meet the demand. Additionally, to obtain the *auxilio de cesantía* (unemployment subsidy), employees must meet the following requirements: fired for reasons beyond their control; contributed to the fund for twelve or more months; had not received unemployment payments in the last year; registered at the placement service of the Labor Department; and "lack resources." Therefore, the insurance fund could reject an application for unemployment subsidy if workers had quit their jobs, were fired for "legitimate reasons," or had alternative means of subsistence. If employees met the requirements, they could receive a compensation between 75 and 80 percent of their salary for no more than ninety weeks.[56]

In 1947, Alfredo Gaete, a renowned lawyer and academic expert in labor law, lamented the lack of unemployment insurance for blue-collar workers because they "cruelly suffer the consequences of economic fluctuations."[57] This "cruelty" was visible in the many stories of layoffs. In October 1952, the National Electrical Company (ENDESA) laid off hundreds of workers. Since 1943, ENDESA, a public enterprise, had embarked on an ambitious plan to deliver energy to the country. It promised to create jobs and bring prosperity. While projects attracted thousands of people, construction activities were unstable and seasonal. Migrants labored in harsh conditions and lived in temporary camps. Without job security, they relied on friends, relatives, and contractors to find work. Behind the pompous inauguration of hydroelectric plants hung the uncertainty of unemployment.

Frequent and massive layoffs displayed workers' vulnerability and the contradictions of the economic model. Salvador Ocampo, a Communist Senator with strong ties to the union movement, criticized the layoffs. ENDESA had fired over three hundred workers and planned to discharge seven hundred more in Los Cipreses (Talca). El Abanico, a hydroelectric plant in Los Angeles, expected to lay off nearly three hundred laborers. Layoffs also affected five hundred workers employed by a subcontracting firm and building a water reserve for ENDESA. Labor unions reported that managers fired people overnight and only paid a compensation equal to six days of work. Ocampo declared that in reality, working families "had no other means than the efforts of their hands, muscles, and, sometimes, brain."[58] But the procedure followed the law. Without insurance, unemployed families scrambled for aid and relief, navigating a complex network of private and public institutions.

FINDING SOCIAL AID IN 1940S CHILE

In December 1941, a local judge in the town of Ovalle, province of Coquimbo, found José de la Cruz Miranda guilty of the crime of vagrancy and sentenced him to 180 days in prison. De la Cruz, also known as *"gallina muerta"* (dead chicken), was 35 years old and illiterate, had no job or permanent address, and had been living in the streets of Ovalle for the past two years. The police officers who arrested him testified that he was a vagrant. In light of new evidence, the Court of Appeals of La Serena reopened the case in March 1942. De la Cruz, the judge argued, was "insane" (*enajenado mental*) and physically disabled. Because the culprit was unfit to work, he was not a vagrant or a criminal, but a person in need of assistance. The judge concluded that it "is society that should worry about providing social assistance to this man. Legally, he is not a vagrant because he lacks work skills, and he is forced to ask private individuals for help and sleeps outdoors because he does not have a place."[59] The Court of Appeals absolved De la Cruz, reaffirming the legal distinction between vagrants and people who required social assistance.

The criminal case against José de la Cruz Miranda illustrates Chileans' historical fears about vagrancy, as well as how society decided who deserved social aid. The need to differentiate between the deserving and undeserving poor, workers and vagrants, and between those fit and unfit for work determined the distribution of aid to people out of work in the country. During the Great Depression, previous chapters demonstrated, the Chilean state had established basic services to confront unemployment, distribute aid, regulate the labor market, and assist people to find work. Social workers had organized and professionalized relief and, at the Casa de Socorro in Santiago, tested modern forms of social intervention and assistance. Fearing that the unemployed would become idle and turn into vagrants, the state sent men to public work sites and limited relief to women and children. By 1933, the Unemployment Board (Comisión General de Cesantía) offered food, lodging, and clothing to unemployed families; paid transportation costs for migrant workers; and coordinated the placement of the unemployed in public construction sites, gold panning sites, and the private sector.[60]

Between 1933 and 1940, the Unemployment Board attended the immediate needs of the unemployed as well as the indigent. Along with helping workers to find employment, the Board assisted "children in need, abandoned women, the elderly, and men unfit for work."[61] In 1936, for example, the Board reported the following activities: four food rationing centers in Santiago and eight in the provinces of Tarapacá and Antofagasta; temporary housing and medical attention for about 300 families in collective building (*colectivos*) in Santiago; housing subsidies for families in need in Antofagasta; distribution of clothes; cash subsidies for white-collar employees; and a full-service public shelter in Santiago. The Board had also opened two popular restaurants in Santiago, offering inexpensive and nutritious daily meals to about 1,000 workers.[62] In 1939, the service of workers' restaurants and public shelters became an independent department (Servicio de Restaurantes Populares y Hospederías) and, for a few years, became the flagship program of nutritionists and medical doctors.[63] During the devastating earthquake of 1939, the Board turned to help people affected by the natural catastrophe.[64]

This process was reflected in a series of administrative reforms. In April 1940, President Pedro Aguirre Cerda gave the Unemployment Board the status of a permanent department, the Unemployment Department (Dirección General de Cesantía), and placed it under the direct authority of the Ministry of Interior. Its focus on unemployment faded, and the Department turned almost exclusively to serving the indigent. In 1942, the Ministry of Interior merged the Department with the service of workers' restaurants and shelters (Servicio de Restaurantes Populares y Hospederías) and formed a Department of Social Aid (Dirección General de Auxilio Social). In 1947, the Dirección General de Auxilio Social passed to the presidency, and in 1948 was renamed Servicio Social del Trabajo. In the mid-1950s, following the recommendations of the Klein-Saks mission, the office was relocated to the Ministry of Interior. In 1953, it became the Servicio Nacional de Bienestar y Auxilio Social and, in 1959, the Dirección de Auxilio Social.

Part welfare office for nonworkers, part aid agency for the unemployed, and part relief service for victims of catastrophes (e.g., fires, earthquakes), the responsibilities of the Department of Social Aid (formerly called Unemployment Board) expanded during the Popular Front.[65] In 1943, during his annual address to the nation and the National Congress, President Juan Antonio Ríos praised the work of the Department of Social Aid. At its shelters and workshops, President Ríos explained, indigent men and women lived, worked, and adapted to society. In the last year, Ríos stated, social workers had handled nearly ten thousand social cases or the equivalent of about forty-four thousand people.[66] The Department of Social Aid had also organized summer camps for children from underprivileged families, sent emergency brigades to areas affected by fires and other disasters, and maintained a social service office in Santiago. Despite President Ríos' positive account, the department was underfunded, small, and marginal, and, like other social services, its functions and responsibilities were larger than its physical and material capacity.[67]

By the late 1940s, the office included four divisions: relief (food, clothing, and direct aid); shelter and housing; workshops; and food in restaurants and subsidized stores. It was a top-down approach to social assistance, shaped by gender and class ideas, the everyday practices of welfare professionals, and working families' efforts to obtain benefits. Social workers, for example, institutionalized vagrant children in model orphanages and organized vacations for poor children that included healthy meals, discipline, and physical exercise. They protected and trained women to become better mothers, and "readapted" vagrant men to become active and responsible workers. At the workshops, working women learned to "sew, embroider, and make children toys."[68] In the relief section (the largest section), between ten and twenty social workers helped the needy to find medical care and medicines, provisional shelter, or food; usually directing them to other public offices, as well as private and religious institutions. People in provincial cities had even more limited access to social services. In 1950, the Department of Social Aid was located in the capital city and maintained small offices only in the north of the country (Iquique, Antofagasta, and Coquimbo).[69]

The Department of Social Aid never centralized all public aid, but became part of a network of public and semipublic institutions providing "welfare for non-workers."[70] One of the main problems of Chile's social assistance system, social workers argued in the late 1940s, was the lack of "coordination" among the different institutions helping the poor.[71] By the 1950s, the Departamento de Beneficencia y Asistencia Social (which had evolved from the old Beneficencia described in chapter 4), maintained several programs and activities that, according to the report of the Klein-Saks mission, "had no direct relationship with public health." These services included shelters for the elderly and abandoned children, institutions to control and reeducate juvenile delinquents and indigents, and workshops and small factories, where vagrants, indigents, and abandoned children worked.[72] These services overlapped with those offered by the Department of Social Aid.

Public assistance also coexisted with the work of private and religious organizations. At the local level, parishes offered and distributed direct assistance to the community. In the late 1930s, for example, the Parroquia San Pablo Apóstol, a parish located in a working-class neighborhood in Santiago, included the following social services: medical and dental service three times a week; job placement services for men and women; a shelter for indigent men with 56 beds; and a special shelter for widows with female daughters.[73] Similarly, the Hogar de Cristo, a Jesuit charity institution created in 1944 under the leadership of Alberto Hurtado, offered shelter and food to street children and homeless men and women. Emphasizing traditional gender roles, workshops taught women domestic tasks such as cooking, washing, and sewing. As other religious and charitable organizations serving the poor, Hogar de Cristo also received state subsidies to cover its expenses.[74] The Acción Católica, the movement that brought laypeople into the everyday work of the Catholic Church, expanded in Chile throughout the 1930s–1950s. While their emphasis was to forge spiritual and religious practices, it also reinvigorated apostolic work among the youth and women and channeled donations to support charity organizations and services such as the one offered by San Pablo Apóstol and the Hogar de Cristo.

The Popular Front expanded social assistance and public infrastructure, but it did not build a comprehensive system of social welfare. People could find immediate relief at the Dirección de Asistencia Social, at the Dirección de Beneficencia y Asistencia Social, or at one of the many private and religious institutions that existed in the country.[75] At public schools, children had free food, basic medical and dental care, and some recreational opportunities.[76] An incomplete system of public and private shelters (*hospederías*) offered emergency lodging, but facilities were unclean and imposed restrictions on people's everyday life. Despite the physical limits of social assistance, welfare professionals in public and private institutions sketched an image of the "deserving" poor and attempted to define their material and social needs. To receive social aid, families approached one of these services, completed forms, and demonstrated their needs and eligibility to social workers, nurses, and aid workers. They also faced interviews, home visits, and social workers' intrusion into their family life, and negotiated amid stigmatized views of poverty.[77] At court, people who were physically or mentally impaired like José de la Cruz Miranda had to demonstrate they were not vagrants but indigent and in need of assistance.

THE MODERNIZATION OF EMPLOYMENT SERVICES, 1950S

In 1952, Carlos Ibáñez del Campo, the populist general who had governed the country from 1927 to 1931, returned to power.[78] His electoral campaign, Joaquín Fernández stated, "reflected an anti-oligarchic, anti-imperialist, moralist, and authoritarian populism" and received widespread support from people from all levels of society. Despite the initial enthusiasm, Ibáñez's second term was plagued by economic troubles, rampant inflation, and political instability. Only a few days after he assumed power, his minister of finance, Juan Manuel Rosseti, warned the National Congress that the country was on the verge of financial collapse. He declared that "unless effective measures are adopted to correct the unfavorable economic and financial conditions exposed, Chile will fall into the same disastrous conditions observed in other countries with a loss of not only of the economic structure but also that of democratic institutions and manner of life."[79] He asked Chileans to support the government's economic agenda that included unpopular austerity and stabilization measures. For the rest of the Ibáñez administration, the government would try to implement those measures, while facing growing pressures from below to expand social benefits and rights and protect working-class incomes threatened by uncontrolled inflation.

On the eve of Ibáñez's election, the National Congress had approved a massive reform of the country's system of social security and public health. The Social Security Service (Servicio de Seguro Social, SSS) replaced the CSO and expanded its coverage from blue-collar wage earners to include independent workers. To improve efficiency and service, the administration of medical benefits passed to a new public agency, the Servicio Nacional de Salud (SNS). Benefits increased but not necessarily improved. In addition to the established medical, old age, and disability benefits, social security added medical assistance for family members, extended maternity paid leaves, and distributed pensions for widows and orphans.[80] In 1953, the Ibáñez administration established two additional and compulsory benefits: family compensation (DFL 245, July 31, 1953) and unemployment benefits (DFL 243, August 7, 1953). Contributions also increased. One of the clearest improvements involved retirement pensions. Between 1928 and 1952, the CSO had only given 358 retirement pensions. From 1952 to 1960, that number had increased to 85,900.[81]

The establishment of unemployment benefits in 1953, labor lawyer Alfredo Gaete Berríos argued in 1960, was one of the "most desired workers' conquest, conquest for which the working class has been fighting tirelessly and steadily for many years."[82] The law established two types of subsidies, depending on age and how long workers had contributed to the social security fund. Employed workers over 60 years old and who had contributed to a social security fund for more than 1,560 weeks were eligible to receive their unemployment benefit as a lump sum. The second type of unemployment benefit was a monthly subsidy. Workers dismissed for no legitimate reason and who had contributed to the social security fund for at least 208 weeks (reduced to 156 weeks in 1959), or 104 weeks after receiving the last unemployment subsidy, were eligible for a monthly payment equivalent to 75 percent of their regular wage and for a period of no longer than six months. To obtain the subsidy, dismissed workers had to present proof of unemployment (a certificate provided by their last employer) and register at the National Placement Office. After the initial registration, they had no obligation to return to the placement office, and there were no formal mechanisms for helping the insured unemployed to find work.[83] If employers offered a severance pay higher than the social security's unemployment fund, the former benefit had precedence. In 1959, a legal reform established a partial subsidy in the case of work/salary reduction of 50 percent or less.[84]

While the reform of Social Security increased coverage and benefits including the new unemployment subsidy, workers still faced obstacles procuring those benefits guaranteed by the law. In 1957, the SSS had a total of 1,166,000 workers affiliated (*cotizantes*), and 1,240,000 in 1960.[85] By 1964, it covered about 75 percent of the working population. In 1956, the Klein-Saks Mission pointed out that one of the most serious problems was its expansion without a solid financial foundation and, as a result, its dependence on emergency contributions and loans from the state.[86] A more immediate problem, the Social Security office argued in 1960, was that pensions were still meager because salaries were low. Some employers, the office denounced, did not make regular payments or declared a lower salary to contribute less.[87] In addition, the SSS rejected 29 percent of those who applied to retirement, a total of 2,102 people, in 1960. The main reason for rejection was contributions below eight hundred weeks (men) or five hundred weeks (women). The SSS concluded that given that most people at the age of sixty-five had worked more than eight hundred weeks, "it is purely and simply about breaking the law."[88] Agricultural and domestic workers, the SSS explained, were the most common victims of these abuses.

Foreign advisers also provided the technical tools to reform employment services and labor statistics in the late 1950s, aligning Chile with international norms. In 1955–1956, a technical mission of the International Labor Organization (ILO) studied the country's placement services and recommended multiple reforms. Public placement, both ILO experts and the Chilean government agreed, could improve the labor market, help people without work, and, more importantly, contribute to the "process of economic development." Chile's placement services, the experts reported, had not improved since the Great Depression and covered only a small portion of the working class. While unemployment rate remained relatively low, the ILO experts added, it had increased in the mid-1950s. Seasonal unemployment among construction and agricultural workers had also become a serious problem. The ILO recommended creating a National Employment Service, collecting and systematizing statistical information, and reaching the entire country including the countryside.[89] Following the ILO's mission, the Ministry of Labor modernized its placement services in Santiago, but it did not create a large and nationwide service of employment and placement until the mid-1960s.[90]

Experts agreed that the fight against unemployment not only required a modern labor exchange office but also reliable data on the labor market, something that Chile lacked until at least the late 1950s. Since 1930, national censuses had included information on the size of the labor force (active and nonactive population), distribution of the workforce by economic sector, and unemployment. Data on gender, age, and place (provinces and rural/urban) helped to understand the characteristics of Chile's workforce.[91] But the census, conducted every ten years, only provided a broad overview of the labor market, a picture of the country in a particular time, and could not account for the annual and seasonal fluctuations in the labor market.

The collection of unemployment statistics required a different methodology. Throughout the 1940s–1950s, statisticians around the world argued that measuring unemployment required standard definitions of both employment status and occupational classifications.[92] Statistics should also cover all economic activities and be collected regularly. In 1954, the International Association of Labor Statistics reported that the periodic survey was the "keystone in a broad system of employment, unemployment, and labour force statistic." They also pointed out the need to complement surveys with other sources such as social security and industrial employment records.[93]

Building on international recommendations, the Institute of Economics of the University of Chile, the country's largest public university, conducted the first unemployment survey in greater Santiago in 1957. The survey expanded to other cities in the following years, including Valparaíso and Viña del Mar in 1958, Concepción in 1959, and northern cities such as La Serena, Antofagasta, and Iquique in the 1960s. By 1962, it covered nine cities and eleven thousand households.[94] Cosponsored by the Central Bank, the Institute of Economics received the support and assistance of the Rockefeller Foundation and the United Nations. Roe Goodman, a US census and survey expert who lived in Chile as part of a Food and Agriculture Organization (FAO) technical mission in 1954–1955, designed the first sample survey. The survey included international standards and definitions of the labor force and unemployment. It defined the labor force as people older than fourteen years old and who were either working or were unemployed. It also introduced two categories: a) the unemployed (*cesante*): people who had lost their job and had actively looked for work in the past week; and b) people seeking employment for the first time.

CHAPTER 7

FULL EMPLOYMENT AND LABOR RIGHTS DURING THE LONG 1960S

In October 1966, Jorge Montes, a communist deputy representing the southern district of Concepción, called attention to rising unemployment in the country and, particularly, in his district.[1] In the port of Talcahuano, Montes explained, steel and oil companies had laid off hundreds of people, and, in the coal town of Coronel, there were 2,500 people unemployed. Indeed, more than 16,000 people had registered at the Labor Department, according to a letter from a local unemployment council. Unemployment, he argued, had its roots in a capitalist system based on private property and the "exploitation of man by man," but he also believed that the government should adopt measures such as public works projects and direct relief to help working families.[2] Montes demanded the government to require companies, especially those that received incentives from the state, to protect and create jobs.

Stories about layoffs and unemployment gained new visibility in Chile throughout the 1960s. Like Montes, many other legislators brought the drama of unemployment to the National Congress. From north to south, they painted a gloomy picture that showed the contradictions between the government's promises of industrial development and the everyday reality of working families. For politicians like Manuel Cantero, a communist legislator from Valparaíso who denounced a series of layoffs affecting metal workers in early 1966, the fall in industrial jobs evidenced the shortcomings of the country's development agenda. While private companies received subsidies and credit from state agencies such as CORFO, they did not protect jobs and, instead, reduced employment opportunities to adapt to economic downturns. President Eduardo Frei had promised workers full employment, but Clemente Fuentealba—a member of the Radical Party who represented the mining districts of Copiapó— argued that Chilean citizens were "threatened by unemployment."[3]

These stories reflect not only a time of economic uncertainty in Chile but broader economic, social, and labor tensions. In Chile, as in other parts of Latin America, demographic growth, rural-urban migration, and uneven industrial growth had produced dangerous pockets of poverty and unemployment in larger cities. The promises of industrial growth of the previous decades had not created enough jobs. Experts worried about underemployment, informality, and growing numbers of people employed in nonproductive jobs. At the international level, agencies such as the International Labor Organization (ILO) and the Economic Commission for Latin America and the Caribbean (ECLA), urged Latin American governments to make job creation a priority of development. If local and international experts placed unemployment into the debate about economic development, income inequality, and the fight against poverty, they disagreed on the meaning, scope, and methods to resolve the problem. Workers' rights, especially the right to job security, employers' power, and the role of the state in the labor market became contentious political issues during the Cold War.

This chapter looks at unemployment policies during the governments of Eduardo Frei Montalva (1964–1970) and Salvador Allende (1970–1973). Chile's debates intersected with a growing international concern about development and the labor market in the Global South. During the Frei administration, the government promised full employment, supported the national industry, approved important reforms of the Labor Code, and restructured employment services. Frei's response to unemployment incorporated global and national ideas about economic development, as well as the ongoing debate about urban poverty and marginality, the process of Agrarian Reform, and the transformation of labor relations in the countryside. Important reforms of the Labor Code increased job stability, but economic instability and employers' legal and informal opposition to labor rights undermined many of the gains. On the eve of the election of Salvador Allende, many working families questioned whether an economic model and a legal and political framework would ever protect them from unemployment.

THE INTERNATIONAL LABOR ORGANIZATION AND UNEMPLOYMENT IN THE DEVELOPING WORLD

International agencies called the 1960s the Development Decade, a time when all the United Nation specialized agencies (including the ILO) mobilized and allocated resources "for furthering economic and social development."[4] Regarding unemployment, this shift meant an effort to understand the relationship between economic development and the labor market. In the 1950s, international experts had advised Latin American governments to focus on job creation and recommended countries to modernize production and provide workers the tools to succeed in industrial jobs.[5] As described in the previous chapter, the ILO Manpower Program sponsored seminars and courses and conducted studies throughout the continent to train staff, disseminate knowledge, and develop statistical departments. Despite efforts to increase technical expertise and reinforce state intervention in the workplace, unemployment remained a central but little understood problem on the continent. While the ILO did not abandon its technical approach in the 1960s, it paid increasing attention to economic and social development, central planning, and the need for structural reforms (including Agrarian Reform) in the Global South. By the end of the decade, the ILO and other international agencies recognized unemployment as one of the most challenging issues in the process of social and economic development. Employment policies should be at the heart of any development initiative, they argued.

With the approval of the Employment Policy Convention (C122) in 1964, the ILO reaffirmed its commitment to fight unemployment in the world. Building on the Declaration of Philadelphia (1944) and the Universal Declaration of Human Rights (1948), the ILO declared the "right to work" a fundamental human and social right. The convention, which did not differ much from the postwar idea of full employment, restated that countries should guarantee the following:

(a) There is work for all who are available for and seeking work;
(b) Such work is as productive as possible;
(c) There is freedom of choice of employment. [6]

These ideas were not particularly new, but the approval of a convention, ILO's most important policy instrument, represented a significant achievement.[7] In the following years, Convention 122 sparked a series of studies and discussions throughout the ILO, from the General Assembly to its regional and local offices.[8] At the national level, governments debated whether to approve the Employment Policy Convention and revised their labors laws to comply with international norms. According to the ILO Constitution, governments must report to the ILO Governing Body on the enforcement of ratified conventions. By the end of the 1960s, five Latin American countries had ratified the convention, and many others would do it in the following decade.[9] These reports show how states interpret conventions and resolutions and how they incorporate international recommendations. In 1970, Costa Rica had adopted several measures and programs to comply with the convention, including the creation of the National Human Resource Council, the National Apprenticeship Institute, and a new Employment Office at the Ministry of Labor and Social Welfare.[10] The following year, Chile reported that the creation of the National Employment Service

(SENDE) in 1967 (discussed later in this chapter) aligned with international recommendations.[11]

Throughout the 1960s–1970s, the ILO played a leading role in the global debate about unemployment. But the ILO had also changed. It was more diverse than in the past, and non-European delegates had become a majority in the General Assembly. If ILO experts influenced national debates through resolutions and conventions, reports, and technical missions, their ideas and views also stemmed from a conversation and collaboration with regional experts. In Latin America, Victor Tokman, the ILO regional director in the 1990s, explained, structuralist economists such as Raúl Prebisch and Anibal Pinto and ECLA influenced ILO employment programs. The dialogue among Latin American, Asian, and African regional offices brought new questions, concerns, and analytical tools to the ILO.[12]

In this new context, Latin American nations, which had mostly been spectators in the global debate about unemployment, played an active role. Since 1935, American member countries of the ILO, including the United States and Canada, had met every four years to debate ILO policies and their own labor and economic problems. Three decades later, the ILO regional meeting had become an influential space not only to discuss local issues but to bring new issues and perspectives to the international arena. In 1966, they met in Ottawa, Canada. The meeting took place in a time marked by the challenges of economic development, the radicalization of vast sectors of society, and international tensions. The 1960s, Eric Zolov argues, were a "pivotal moment in the global Cold War, when the possibilities for a reconfiguration of geopolitical alignments and revolutionary transformations in global capitalism seemed real, if not imminent."[13] The presence and intervention of the Cuban delegation also demonstrate how international meetings had become a contested space, shaped by the Cold War and US intervention in the region. At the meeting, the Cuban delegate reminded the audience that "imperialist, colonialist, and neocolonialist exploitation" contributed to Latin America's underdevelopment.[14]

The Ottawa meeting evidenced Latin America's concern and views about unemployment and social protections. After a long debate, delegates approved two resolutions, known as the Ottawa Plan for Human Resources Development for the Americas.

> a. To encourage Latin American countries to integrate "employment and the development of human resources" within more extensive programs of economic and social development. Countries should design a common approach to "employment and manpower planning" across the continent and to carry out studies on employment creation and skill formations.
> b. Task the ILO to design and sponsor programs.

The delegates from the Americas argued the need to integrate employment planning into the larger agenda of economic development and the fight against poverty. As the ILO summarized in 1968, the "basic objective of the Ottawa Plan is therefore to ensure that the development policies of countries of the region are aimed principally at achieving the highest possible levels of productive employment."[15] To advance this agenda, the ILO sponsored technical studies, supported national employment development plans, and recommended policy reform.

Building on the Ottawa Plan and economic development theories, David Morse, a US lawyer and civil servant that directed the ILO between 1948–1970, launched the World Employment Programme (WEP) in 1969.[16] Morse looked back at the 1960s with a bittersweet approach. While he recognized important achievements, the ILO Director was also disappointed at the persistence of poverty around the world. Development and economic growth, Morse argued, had benefited only a few, and unless countries incorporated employment policies into the effort of development, inequality and poverty would persist. He cited the Ottawa Plan as an influential turning point that had brought attention to the need to design effective employment policies throughout the world. In the Global South, Morse explained, WEP would support countries to develop strategies and mechanisms to create productive and industrial jobs, labor-intensive public works projects, and rural development programs. Morse also recognized the importance of vocational and professional training and committed to assisting countries to develop schools and workshops to train the workforce.

The Ottawa Plan and WEP represented significant turning points for how international agencies and experts viewed unemployment. The WEP criticizes the old assumption that employment will automatically grow as a result of capital formation, investment, and export promotion. Instead, they argued that "employment should be seen as a central component of development efforts, not as an eventual result of them."[17] In other words, governments had to make job creation a priority.

WEP ideas resonated with Latin American discussions about development, structural reforms, and poverty. In the late 1960s, the UNDP had formed a small group called PREALC (Employment Programme for Latin America and the Caribbean). PREALC brought together experts working and thinking about employment in the region and collaborated closely with WEP/ILO as well as other international agencies such as ECLA. Through technical assistance to governments, training for experts and government via regional and local seminars and courses, as well as research, PREALC shaped employment policies on the continent.[18] Its most important contribution was in regards to informality. According to Victor Tokman, by shifting to informality, experts changed the emphasis from "unemployment to underemployment."[19]

For the first time, Latin America had become ground zero to observe and discuss unemployment. In 1970, the ILO chose Colombia as the site for the first employment mission. A team of twenty-seven experts went to Colombia to study its "chronic" problem of unemployment, in both rural and urban areas. Its "full employment strategy" was a development plan that included land reform and job creation in the countryside; expansion of manufacturing and construction jobs; and income distribution.[20] The discussions that started during the Eduardo Frei administration in 1964 and continued under Allende reflected the growing consensus that unemployment was a problem of economic and social development.

"THE PEOPLE WANT TO WORK AND HAVE MORE JOBS"

In May 1965, in his first annual account to the National Congress, President Eduardo Frei (1964–1970) declared that "the people voted to increase the pace of economic development as a means to guarantee jobs for all people and to fight against extreme poverty."[21] During his campaign, Frei, a Christian Democrat, promised Chileans a "Revolution in Liberty" and a "profound transformation of Chile" that included the expansion of social and labor rights, redistribution of land, and the solution to the housing needs of urban families. A charismatic, Catholic, and anticommunist leader, he received more than 55 percent of the national vote in 1964 and the backing of the US government and international credit institutions. His sweeping victory did not guarantee long-term electoral and popular support. Between 1967–1970, economic decline, slow industrial growth, and inflation affected working families, who also got frustrated with the pace of social reforms. When social mobilization, including occupations of rural land and urban plots, legal and illegal strikes, and popular demonstrations increased, the government used traditional but controversial repressive tools that further alienated working people and radicalized the youth.[22]

The Frei administration saw unemployment as a problem of economic development and believed that industrial growth, the process of Agrarian Reform, and public investment would create more jobs.[23] In 1966, Frei told the National Congress that "people want to work and have more jobs," but these jobs should be based on "solid economic growth."[24] Influenced by structuralist economists, his views reflected the international consensus that job creation should be at the center of development efforts. Indeed, Jorge Ahumada, the structuralist economist that inspired Frei's economic agenda, had argued in the late 1950s that the slow pace of development combined with rapid demographic growth had caused unemployment and increased inequality in Chile. To resolve these problems, Ahumada proposed, the state would have to modernize agricultural production, control inflation, tackle poverty and social inequality, and promote regional development to avoid the concentration of resources and population in the capital city.[25] Because these issues were interrelated, a comprehensive program of development required state planning and the incorporation of technical experts in the government. Economic and social planning became a distinctive element of the Frei administration. Once in power, he envisioned a specialized technical and planning agency that would oversee and coordinate economic, social, and political reforms, as well as become a bridge with international agencies. The National Planning Agency (Oficina de Planificación Nacional, ODEPLAN), officially created in 1967, became the technical arm of development and incorporated job creation as one of its priorities.[26]

For the "Revolution in Liberty," unemployment was not only an economic problem but had its roots in the social, cultural, and educational aspects of poverty, especially in the growing slums that surrounded Latin American cities. To explain and confront urban poverty, the Christian Democrats turned to the theory of social marginality. By the 1960s, marginality had become a loose concept that could refer to both urban and rural environments. It included a diversity of psychological, economic, political, or cultural elements that prevented people from participating in society.[27] In Chile, Roger Vekemans, a Jesuit priest that influenced the Frei administration, argued that "the fundamental problem of Latin America is the problem of extreme poverty."[28] The poor, Vekemans argued, lived in a state of marginality: limited formal connections to society; no participation in social, economic, cultural, and political institutions; and no formal employment. If exponents of the theory of marginality recognized the economic, political, and cultural obstacles that low-income families confronted, critics argued, they focused exclusively on the "marginal" and not on how society excluded some people.[29]

The theory of marginality inspired Frei's social agenda. Social and cultural organizations, such as urban improvement associations, youth clubs, and women centers in shantytowns, looked to integrate the urban poor into society and economic development, while also fueling the electoral support for the government. Within this view, formal employment would not only provide the financial means for survival but open the door to social security and other benefits.[30] As Frei explained, "their disintegration, the lack of organizations that represent them, the absence of basic resources and education, often low wages and the lack of work constitute the striking marks of their lives."[31] Thus the government would have an active part in "integrating" the poor into the different levels of society. At the same time, economic development and redistribution policies would guarantee that they have a job and a decent salary to support themselves and their families.

Influenced by the global debate on unemployment, the economic development agenda, and views of poverty, the government's employment plan focused on creating jobs and modernizing the workforce.[32] William Thayer, who served as minister of labor under Frei from 1964 to 1968, argued that the government sought to "frame labor policy within the general plan for economic and social development."[33] To do so, the government promoted technical education and training, restructured the Ministry of Labor, the Labor Department, and employment services, and supported the expansion of labor rights. The reform of the labor contract law (1966)—analyzed in the next section—the rural unionization law (1967), and the Occupational Disease and Accidents law (1968) had a significant impact on workers' lives.

Technical education illustrates the confluence of transnational discussions about employment and Chile's quest for industrialization and economic development. In 1962, supported by international agencies such as the United Nations (UN), the United National Development Programme (UNDP), and ILO, as well as bilateral agreements with developed countries, the Chilean state started the construction and building of a public center for technical education (Instituto Nacional de Capacitación, INACAP). The new institute opened its doors in 1966, promising to provide the country with the "sufficient quantity and quality of human resources to make the process [industrial development] more dynamic."[34] It would also enhance workers' skills and, thus, improve their chances of finding better jobs. To accomplish these goals, INACAP offered a wide range of courses from short-term classes to people with no formal education to professional training in areas such as mechanics, electricity, agriculture, and hospitality. By 1968, it had a total enrollment of 25,000 students, maintained technical centers throughout the entire country, and sponsored mobile centers to train workers in situ.

Along with promoting vocational training, labor experts had long debated the need to reform employment services. Although the placement office was one of the oldest services of Chile's Labor Department and a popular employment measure of the ILO, it remained underfunded and small, and its services limited to Santiago. Throughout the 1960s, employment experts argued the need to create a technical department that could address both the study of the labor market and the placement of unemployed people. Additionally, they envisioned an office that could integrate the employment question into development plans. If these ideas influenced the National Employment Service (SENDE), established by President Frei in 1967, the everyday reality of employment and placement services changed little over the following years.

SENDE was a technical and independent administrative unit within the Ministry of Labor and Social Security. It was in charge of designing and coordinating long-term employment policies and organizing placement services.³⁵ Its mission, a study of the ILO-PREALC noted, was "ambitious." Although President Frei praised SENCE for its contribution to battling unemployment, international observers were less optimistic. Two years after its organization, its director noted, small budget and personnel (62 people) and lack of transportation (the office only had one vehicle) considerably limited its ability to tackle unemployment. SENDE had three offices, including the main office in Santiago and two small ones in Valparaiso and Concepcion.³⁶ Although SENDE should have coordinated with other planning offices, the report concluded, it did not have a relationship with ODEPLAN and worked in an isolated manner. Its services did not improve. A decade later, PREALC found, "there is still a significant percentage of the population unaware of its existence and the services it provides." For those who were familiar with SENDE's services, the process of registering and regularly going to the office to learn about job openings was time-consuming, expensive, bureaucratic, and unreliable. Many of the unemployed viewed SENDE "as a place of lengthy processes and little results."³⁷

Despite these institutional reforms, the government failed to design a comprehensive employment policy. In part, there was still little knowledge about the labor market. The National Congress recognized in 1966 that "there are no global statistics, but for certain sectors."³⁸ The National Statistic Office started conducting periodic national employment surveys, but its figures differed significantly from ODEPLAN's numbers, leaving many doubts about Chile's capacity to measure the problem.³⁹ In May 1969, President Frei reported that the country created 75,800 new jobs in 1968, the highest job creation in the history of Chile, and unemployment fell from 6.5 percent in 1960 to 5 percent in January 1967 to 4.4 in 1968. He praised the work of SENDE and INACAP.⁴⁰ But statistical records remained controversial and incomplete. Limited statistics usually hide a reality marked by job instability, regional disparities, disguised unemployment, and underemployment. The economic recession that had started in 1967 had undermined construction and manufacturing jobs, and working families remained unprotected in face of layoffs.⁴¹

LABOR RIGHTS AND WORK SECURITY

In Chile, unemployment was not only the consequence of economic underdevelopment but of unequal power relations in the workplace. Workers had long denounced the inconsistency between a political discourse that emphasized the government commitment to promote industrialization and create jobs and their everyday reality. Employment stability had only benefited a few, and industrial growth and economic development were uneven. Some sectors such as textile labor unions faced the impact of modernization and automation and expressed concern about job loss in their industry. While they did not oppose modernization per se, they asked managers and the state to guarantee that the introduction of new machinery did not "mean unemployment."[42] In the large-scale copper mines, workers faced the rise of subcontracting, a company strategy to erode permanent jobs and benefits.[43] Other trades were disappearing, leaving workers with little hope to find permanent employment. Whale processing plants were closing downs, leaving hundreds of workers in the small fishing towns of Quintay (Valparaíso Province) and Los Molles (province of Tarapacá) without a job.[44] These stories, usually turned invisible by national figures, highlight the existence of pockets of unemployment throughout the country, as well as workers' vulnerability in front of management's production strategies and large economic changes.

To achieve job security, labor unions fought for the reform of the Labor Code and the expansion of unemployment benefits. Since the early twentieth century, the labor movement had demanded the expansion of workplace protections including service indemnity, contract stability, strict limits to unfair firing, and special protections for union leaders. Labor rights and regulations had changed little since the enactment of the Labor Code in 1931, and employers could still fire blue-collar workers without reason if they provided a six-day notice. Arbitrary firing was common, and the labor courts and labor inspectors did not have the resources to protect workers across the country. When, in the mid-1960s, Laura, a textile worker, took an active role in her local union, she was fired. Being a union leader and a pregnant woman granted some legal protection, but the owner had too much power. She became overwhelmed by the "lawsuit, the summons, lawyer, a pile of paperwork, the meetings" and at the end, only received a fraction of the compensation to which to she was entitled.[45] Like Laura, many Chilean workers faced powerful and influential employers, were fired for no reason, and had limited access to labor courts. As Arturo Carvajal, a communist union leader and legislator, noted for the case of the fishing industry's recent layoffs in Tarapacá, employers had "always tried to obtain greater guarantees without giving anything to its workers."[46]

How to reform the work contract to guarantee employment stability became a heated debate at both the international and the national level. In 1962, and again in 1963, ILO delegates addressed the problem of termination of employment and discussed ways to protect workers from "arbitrary action while, at the same time, preserving to the employer the means of the efficient conduct of the undertaking." Standards to regulate dismissal, the report concluded, were especially important for "developing countries."[47] Geijer, a workers' advisor from Sweden, argued that "job security" was the most important demand of the labor movement and that "the principle of the employers' freedom of dismissal has been found obsolete."⁴⁸ Despite a general agreement on the need to guarantee job security, many employers' disagreed. In 1962, Mina, a delegate from Lebanon, suggested that the recommendations were rigid and inflexible. The following year, during the forty-seventh annual conference, Balmaceda Montt, the delegate of employers from Chile, also opposed such regulations because they would affect the "proper functioning of an undertaking" and were difficult to implement. Approved in 1963, the Termination of Employment Recommendation (No. 119) established that "termination of employment should not take place unless there is a valid reason" and workers were entitled to "a reasonable period of notice or compensation." In addition, it encouraged countries to prevent or minimize "reductions of the workforce" and to design instruments and policies, such as employment agencies and unemployment insurance, to help the unemployed.⁴⁹

The ILO resolution influenced labor reforms in Chile. In 1965, deputy Héctor Valenzuela Valderrama, a long-term collaborator of Frei, urged the Congress to protect workers from arbitrary firing and align Chilean legislation with "the principles and resolutions" of the ILO. Valenzuela Valderrama believed that workers could not be left "to the arbitrary decision of employers and *patrones*."⁵⁰ The legal battle to reform the contract law lasted about two years and reflected not only the enormous obstacles to changing the legal framework that regulated the workplace and workers' rights but also the difficulties to enforce labor reforms across the country and economic sectors. As with many of Chile's labor laws, the discussion focused not only on how to protect workers but on who should be excluded as well.

In 1965, the government and the Congress started debating a legal reform to protect workers from arbitrary firing. In April, the National Congress approved a wage increase law. National wage laws had become important mechanisms to redistribute benefits in a country suffering from chronic monetary instability. The law included a new clause (Article 92) that protected workers from arbitrary firing during sixty days before and sixty days after the enactment of the law.⁵¹ While the intention of the law was to prevent employers from firing workers to avoid paying the wage increase, it also became a mechanism to fight unemployment. As Manuel Cantero, a representative of the Communist Party, stated, the law "has brought some stability in the face of growing unemployment."⁵² The Article excluded workers employed less than six months or whose contracts had expired or had a fixed time. Unable to agree on a permanent modification of the Labor Code, legislators continued to renew this temporary measure.⁵³

Every time they debated the renewal of the law, the problem of unemployment resurfaced. Legislators brought along stories of large layoffs and arbitrary firing from around the country, arguing the need for a prompt solution to the problem. On December 14, 1965, President Eduardo Frei and William Thayer, Minister of Labor, submitted to the National Congress a draft project for a permanent modification of the contract law. Labor laws, Frei argued, "must guarantee the worker maximum stability at work, the basis of their economic life and that of their family."[54] The National Congress approved the law in February 1966 (enacted in April 1966).

The employment stability law closed a cycle in the union fight for job security. According to labor lawyer Francisco Tapia, it limited employers' "absolute" control over the terms of employment and was the most important reform of contract conditions since 1924.[55] The main purpose of the law, the Supreme Court stated in 1967, was to "protect employees and workers by granting stability in their jobs, through a regulated dismissal system."[56] The law established that employers could dismiss workers without compensation for justified reasons including dishonesty, imprudence, and absenteeism. After six months, all labor contracts were considered permanent, but employers could dismiss the workforce for economic reasons. In the case of employees in a position of trust such as administrators, school principals, or domestic workers as well as people who had been less than six months in the job, employers could fire them at their own discretion. Unless there was a legally justified reason for dismissal, employers had to provide a thirty-day notice or pay the equivalent to one month's salary. Workers could file a complaint at a labor court, and the court could order employers to reinstate workers or pay the compensation.[57] Employers' opposition, limited government resources (especially within the Labor Department), and legal loopholes would complicate the enforcement of the law.

The law increased job security and limited arbitrary firing, but it also had some limits. According to *Presencia*, a newspaper published by Catholic labor unions, one of the shortcomings of the law was the lack of a penalty fee. If the employer broke the law and unfairly fired a worker with legitimate reason, they could either rehire the worker or pay them the legal compensation. However, the paper lamented, there was not a penalty fee for breaking the law.[58] In addition, while the law had expedited the process to denounce unfair firing, powerful employers could always find legal loopholes to slow down or stop the courts. Between 1966 and 1973, a review of the jurisprudence of Law 16,455 shows that workers, employers, and labor inspectors, as well as the labor judges that oversaw the cases, negotiated the meanings and limits of job security.

While the law and the courts protected workers from unfair firing and increased job stability, legislators did not take away employers' rights to reorganize their industry. When Hucke, a chocolate and cookie factory, sold one of its retail stores in the city of Concepcion in 1966, the company also fired Irma Elena. Irma Elena filed a case at the labor court, arguing that the closure of one store did not end her contract. The local judge ruled in her favor, but the company appealed, and the Supreme Court established that the selling of a store constituted a justified reason to end the contract.[59] The Supreme Court also supported the claims of Shell-Chile S.A. that a reorganization of the company that left Jorge Rafael P. without a job responded to imperious economic needs and was backed by "serious" technical studies. Jorge Rafael P. did not have a case, because, the Supreme Court concluded, "the law gives the power to decide the form of organization of a company to its administrators, from their personal point of view, and they have the exclusive right to modify its structure in a way that, according to them, is more appropriate for the efficiency of their activities."[60]

Because the law did not cover all workers, many employers attempted to reclassify their employees to fire them without compensation or restrictions. This was the strategy followed by the Club de la Unión, an exclusive private club in downtown Santiago that had served the elite since 1864. In 1967, the Club fired Juan V.S., a waiter who had worked at the Club for near 25 years. Juan believed that law 16,455 protected him and filed a case at the local labor court. The judge agreed and ordered the Club to reinstate Juan or pay him the legal compensation. But based on a technicality, the most powerful social Club in the history of Chile appealed to the Supreme Court. The Club's lawyers successfully argued that they were not a regular restaurant because it was not a for-profit institution. They did not serve customers but members, and they were not a business but a "big house." Therefore, their employees were not waiters but domestic workers, and as such, law 16,455 did not apply to them.[61]

During his government, Eduardo Frei restructured unemployment services, reformed labor laws, expanded labor protections, including agricultural workers, and promoted important economic and social reforms. However, his administration was unable to confront the growing problem of job creation, unemployment, and underemployment. On the eve of the victory of the Popular Unity, a report of the ILO/PREALC stated that Chile's "economic growth was insufficient to provide full employment to the workforce and substantially improve the living conditions of all the people." Moreover, the unemployment data did not reveal the extent of the problem and ignored issues such as a large sector of the population considered "nonworkers" (students, stay-at-home women, and disabled people) who were not looking for work but did want to work or worked in the informal sector. Additionally, the report pointed out the existence of underemployment, defined as those who were working only a few hours and earning too little.[62] Unemployment had become a problem of development, but also connected to unequal power relations in the workplace. For many, the solution would be the dismantling of the capitalist system and the incorporation of workers into the production system.

PROTECTING JOBS, EMPOWERING WORKERS

On September 4, 1970, Salvador Allende, the candidate of the Popular Unity coalition (UP), won the presidential election. His victory, he declared the following morning, would "open a new road," a socialist road, and represented "the first authentically democratic, popular, national, and revolutionary government in the history of Chile."[63] During the next three years, the government carried on a radical transformation of the country that included the nationalization of natural resources, expansion of the process of agrarian reform, and massive social programs. The heart of the government agenda was the construction of a "New Economy" that, according to the political right, undermined property rights and created endless legal conflicts. The Popular Unity restructured the economy in three sectors: area of social property (strategic properties owned by the state), area of private property (private capital), and mixed areas (state-private capital). Although the government attempted to control the expropriation process, social, labor, and popular organizations pushed the limits of the revolution. They challenged the legal road to socialism by occupying factories, farms, and the public space, crafting a new meaning, a revolution from below. Amid the Cold War, the socialist revolution faced powerful national and international foes that quickly destabilized the economy and contributed to the polarization of Chilean society.[64]

The experience of the Popular Unity sheds light on the long history of unemployment and underemployment in Chile. From the 1910s into the 1960s, Chile had built institutions to control and regulate the labor market. Influenced by the ILO and global discussions about full employment, the country had developed a national placement service, a modern statistical agency, and vocational training schools. From the late 1930s to the late 1960s, Chilean workers had gained more social benefits than in the past. Although the country lacked a comprehensive system of social security, welfare benefits, and protection in case of unemployment, coverage had expanded. By 1970, most Chilean working families received some form of benefits, especially health care assistance. Reforms of labor laws had made work more stable and had given the Labor Department broader jurisdiction to control and limit layoffs. Despite these gains, this book has shown, chronic economic instability and inflation continued to threaten the well-being of workers, while employers' power and political influence limited workers' rights.

Employment policies and labor laws had failed to empower workers. From the first labor laws of 1924 to the latest reforms of the 1960s, labor laws had not been able to protect all workers. Laws had many exceptions, left entire groups out (e.g., domestic workers, rural workers, informal workers), and the Labor Department lacked the resources to enforce the legislation. Many workers felt powerless and vulnerable in front of managers' decisions. In the late 1960s, the magazine *Presencia* reflected, it was common to "fire a worker because they organized a labor union, blacklist them ... leave parents without work, pay starvation wages, cheat the Social Security Office."[65] Unemployment, job instability, and labor abuses had convinced many of the need not only for structural and revolutionary change but for a profound transformation of labor-management relations. In 1968, after massive layoffs in the textile industry, *Presencia* insisted that employment laws could not protect workers in case of economic restructuring. The only solution was "to participate" and gain a voice within the enterprises and the government.[66]

These experiences and material conditions had radicalized Chilean workers, who voted for the Left and saw in Salvador Allende someone who could understand their demands, defend their rights, and represent their interests. During its first year, the Popular Unity improved material conditions and, for the first time in the history of the country, Chile achieved full employment. It also empowered workers and popular organizations, offering a space that had been historically denied to them. Workers' participation in the new social enterprises, government agencies, and social and popular organizations transformed people's lives. Women-led consumer organizations distributed goods in the neighborhood to battle the black market and international sanctions, workers met in assemblies to discuss production and implementing strategies to resolve everyday problems. Together, they led the battle of production and confronted lockdowns, foreign intervention, and hoarding. While many had a long political affiliation, many others viewed the process as part of workers' historical struggles regardless of their political views.

Workers' incorporation into the company was, then, one of the most radical measures implemented during the UP. In December 1970, Allende and the labor movement agreed on a path that would guarantee workers' participation in the new economy.[67] In both the social property and the mixed economy, workers would join the board of directors and participate in assemblies and production councils. Throughout the country, workers set up committees, organized production, and redefined everyday practices.[68] The changes were enormous. As workers realized during the days of the Popular Unity, only when they were part of the industry, participated in the decision-making process, and understood how their industry worked could they truly protect their jobs. The victories were short-lived; the 1973 military coup and its neoliberal agenda undermined labor rights and job security, ended the state's commitment to create and protect jobs, violently repressed the labor movement, and started an irreversible process of deindustrialization.

EPILOGUE

UNEMPLOYMENT, DICTATORSHIP, AND NEOLIBERALISM (1973-1989)

In 1974, the Chilean military government celebrated its one-year anniversary. In his public address to the nation, General Augusto Pinochet declared he was working toward "a prosperous Chile, [and] to assure the future and welfare of our children."[1] Despite political repression, some people publicly questioned his optimistic account. Jaime Ruiz-Tagle, a sociologist, described the negative impact of the government's economic policies such as the 10 percent unemployment rate and the increasing number of people underemployed or working part-time.[2] Three months later, in December 1974, José Aldunate, a Jesuit priest, argued that people's everyday reality was far away from the government's bright economic account. Working families, Aldunate wrote, could not afford basic consumer products, and their economic situation had deteriorated in the last year. Workers, the Jesuit priest explained, usually said that "we work [to have money] to eat, but we can't even afford that."[3] They had become the first victims of stabilization measures. By 1983, 30 percent of Chilean workers were unemployed or working in emergency programs. On the eve of the transition to democracy, economic conditions had improved, but jobs and employment conditions remained unstable. Dictatorship and neoliberalism had permanently transformed the workplace and eroded job security.

This epilogue provides a brief overview of unemployment during the years of dictatorship (1973–1989). While much more needs to be researched, it offers some ideas on the impact of economic policies, repression, and global changes on job security. By underlining the breaks and continuities in unemployment policy and perceptions of unemployment, I return to the central themes of this book: job security and workers' struggles for labor rights, the historical limits of unemployment assistance, and the relationship between global and local debates on unemployment.

POLITICAL REPRESSION, NEOLIBERALISM, AND UNEMPLOYMENT

In March 1975, Pierre Dubois, a French priest living in one of the most emblematic shanty towns in Santiago (La Victoria), wrote in his diary "unemployment is everywhere. Personnel reduction in public administration. You are dismissed because your [work] is not satisfactory, [and] you are not efficient." Massive layoffs affected workers in the metal industry and local factories. Employers, Dubois explained, "frequently invoke rationalization and modernization" and reasoned that "the free enterprise is the best way to achieve success." Unemployment was worse for those fired for political reasons. They had no possibility to find alternative work and, according to Dubois, were fleeing to Argentina.[4]

Political repression, stabilization policies, trade liberalization, and the erosion of labor protections increased unemployment and job insecurity in the aftermath of the military coup. The military persecuted union leaders, suspended collective bargaining rights and union elections, and outlawed the country's most important labor confederation (Central Única de Trabajadores, CUT).[5] In the case of public servants, including people working in state-owned companies, the Military Junta made all work contracts provisional and fired workers and employees who "endangered" national security.[6] Further legal changes restricted the employment protections guaranteed by the contract stability law of 1966. In 1975, DL 939 allowed employers to fire people if they threatened national security. Joining a strike or discussing working conditions could be considered threats to the country's new political order. Physical and legal repression left workers unprotected from employers' abuses and economic downturns.[7] In 1977, labor organizations argued that the suspension of union rights had deteriorated working conditions and labor relations. Employers, they stated, "had used and abused their privileged position." In other words, "employees' lack of freedom assures the complete freedom of capital holders."[8]

Economic policies also undermined jobs. Between 1973 and 1978, the Junta carried out a stabilization program. By lifting price controls and cutting public expenditures, the government and their economic advisers sought to stabilize the economy and reduce inflation. In their meetings, the Junta proposed to "reduce the size of the public sector" by shutting down social services, eliminating jobs, and "rationalizing" public servants' benefits.[9] They also agreed to lower the number of state-owned enterprises including companies nationalized during the previous socialist government. In response to inflation, orthodox economists prescribed stricter measures. In 1975, Milton Friedman and Arnold C. Harberger visited the county, and Sergio de Castro, the new minister of economy and finances, implemented a "shock treatment." Although the government eventually reduced inflation, the process was slow and painful. Inflation slowly fell from 343 percent in 1975 to 198 percent in 1976 and down to 84 percent in 1977. Moreover, unemployment rates remained high, increasing from 16 percent in 1975 to 19 percent in 1976 and averaging between 18 and 17 percent for the rest of the decade.[10]

The military did not just try to stabilize the economy, Chilean economist Alejandro Foxley argued, but imposed a neoliberal agenda.[11] In Chile, neoliberal ideas had grown from cooperation agreements with the United States and a long relationship between the University of Chicago and Chile's Catholic University that dated back to the mid-1950s. Critical of structuralism and political economic theories associated with ECLA (the UN's Economic Commission for Latin America), a group of experts questioned state intervention in the economy, arguing that the private sector should be the motor of economic growth.[12] Chicago-trained economists Dominique Hachette, Rolf Lüders, and Guillermo Tagle, for example, argued that "growing state intervention in the economy did not produce the economic growth or income distribution anticipated by its defenders." Following the military coup, they led a neoliberal transformation of the Chilean economy that included privatization, trade liberalization, and deregulation of the labor market. In other words, Hachette, Lüders, and Tagle explained, "the new strategy has relied on the restoration of the market as the main economic policy tool and the private sector as the principal agent of development."[13] Although the "Chicago Boys" did not dominate the Junta immediately after the coup, by 1976 they had a solid position within the military government and directed economic and social policies.[14]

Regarding labor, the political right and the business class had traditionally opposed the expansion of union rights and employment protections, arguing that they undermined productivity, increased the cost of labor, and diminished work discipline. Rolf Lüders, who served as Minister for Finance and Economy under Pinochet between 1982 and 1983, believed that state intervention in the labor market distorted the market.[15] These "distortions" included the wage legislation and automatic wage increases that had become popular in the 1950s–1960s to diminish the impact of inflation on working-class and middle-class families. Right-wing economists also criticized employment protections that restricted employers' power to dismiss the workforce and referred to social security payments as an "unfair" tax that artificially increased the cost of labor. Critical of the social and economic role of the state, they argued the need to privatize public companies to reduce the size of the state and increase free competition. As a result, by 1980, more than 350 state enterprises were privatized or, as Hachette, Lüders, and Tagle wrote, returned to their "legitimate owners."[16]

Led by the Chicago Boys, the economic and labor policies of the late 1970s transformed the workplace, workers' rights, and the role of the state in the labor market. Public employees, especially working in the social ministries and departments, were the first to feel the blow of workplace restructuring. From 1975 to 1981, public employment fell by 30 percent.[17] Institutions such as the public health department (Servicio Nacional de Salud) fired nearly 10 percent of its personnel, 5,703 people, between 1973 and 1980. Part of a larger plan to make the public administration more efficient, these personnel reductions became permanent and undermined the economic and employment security traditionally associated with public service.[18]

Neoliberalism also influenced the state's views and responses to unemployment. If throughout the 1960s and especially between 1970–1973, Claudio Llanos argues, the Chilean state considered job creation the cornerstone of economic development, the dictatorship and its neoliberal allies looked at employment policies as political "distortions."[19] Victor Tokman, director of PREALC, explained that in 1973 the Chilean state passed from "creating jobs" and having an "active role" in the job market to having a "subsidiary role."[20] At the international level, this shift reflected the decline of full employment policies, the rise of neoliberalism and monetary approaches to control inflation and fiscal deficit, and a critique of work-welfare programs.[21] While Chile was not the only country to embrace neoliberal and free market approaches, repression and authoritarianism made it possible to impose reforms more quickly.

Between 1973 and 1980, the military government developed a series of mechanisms and institutions to confront unemployment. Although the traditional emphasis on job placement, training, and assistance remained, the role and relationship between employers, the state, and workers shifted. First, new programs and legal reforms considered the business class and the private sector the cornerstone of economic growth and job creation in a free market economy. Second, programs stressed the individual and not the collective, keeping benefits low and marginal. As a result, unemployment benefits did not become rights or permanent policies but stigmatized aid that further increased inequality and marginalization.[22] Third, like with other public institutions, the government decentralized unemployment services and passed many of the responsibilities to municipal governments.[23]

In 1974, the government announced its first measure to battle unemployment: a subsidy for all unemployed workers in the private and public sector. Until 1973, only white-collar employees received a subsidy in case of unemployment (since 1937). Both white-collar and blue-collar workers (since 1953) received a mandatory severance pay equivalent to one month pay per year worked. Social security funds (the Caja de Empleados Particulares and Servicio de Seguro Social) had historically administered and distributed these benefits. In 1974, the Junta created a small subsidy for all salaried employees in the public and private sector. The subsidy was kept to a minimum, always depending on available funds. To receive the subsidy, the person had to meet three criteria: 1) be unemployed "for reasons beyond their control, that have the capacity to work and are willing to do so"; 2) had made continuous payments to social security for at least 52 weeks in 12 months, or discontinued for two years; and 3) had registered as unemployed in their social security fund. However, because the Junta had expanded the rights of employers to fire people (e.g., Decree Law 539 mentioned above), they also restricted the number of people eligible to apply. The subsidy was equivalent to 75 percent of their salary for a maximum of ninety days (and could be renewed in special circumstances). If workers rejected, they could lose unemployment subsidies.[24] The subsidy remained limited, and, in the period 1974–1979, only 15 percent of the unemployed had access to it.

The dictatorship also reformed employment institutions. In 1976, the Junta brought together in a single public institution, called National Service of Employment and Training (Servicio Nacional de Capacitación y Empleo, SENCE), job placement services and job training. While this was part of the long evolution of employment services in Chile, it realigned its mission and work with the economic and labor agenda of the government. As discussed throughout this book, international organizations and unemployment experts had argued the need to establish a system of public placement to assist people to find work. Since the Chilean government had opened its first public placement service in 1914, the service had expanded and institutionalized. During the Great Depression, the Labor Department assumed the responsibility to organize placement, and the placement office became a specialized unit within the department. Throughout the 1940s–1950s, the Ministry of Labor reformed and renamed the placement officer several times. In 1967, President Eduardo Frei created the National Service of Employment (SENDE) as a technical institution within the Ministry of Labor. At the same time, workforce training had become a central issue in labor market policy throughout the world. In 1966, the National Institute of Training (INACAP) opened its doors, offering workshops throughout the country. In addition, urban and rural labor unions had received funding to train their members.

While the new employment institution maintained its commitment to offer free placement services to all unemployed workers, its approach differed from the past. To rationalize and make the service more efficient, the responsibility to administer placement services passed from the Ministry of Labor to municipal governments. Employers became responsible for training the workforce, while the role of the state was now limited to provide a few scholarships to unemployed workers. The law erased references to labor unions or workers, referring to workers as "private individuals" (*particulares*). The government also severely restricted the rights of labor unions to administer their economic resources and organize training workshops. For example, SENDE took over rural unions' educational and extension funds. In addition, INACAP started a process of privatization and cut most of its service to workers.[25]

Along with the modification of unemployment benefits and institutions, the government established a program of minimum work. The new unified system of unemployment subsidy required applicants to register at municipal offices, which would maintain a registry and "assign them assistance work to benefit the community." The characteristics of this "assistance work" were unclear until the end of 1974, when the government announced a national emergency work plan called Minimum Employment Plan (Plan de Empleo Mínimo, PEM). Under the authority of the Ministry of Interior and administered by municipal governments, PEM started in February 1975 and quickly symbolized the social costs of economic reforms, growing from 19,041 registered people in March 1975 to 263,763 in December 1983.[26] The government conceived PEM as an "emergency" and "temporary" program. Like in the 1930s, authorities argued that a low subsidy could provide for some income without competing with the private sector and, thus, PEM's workers were only entitled to a subsidy equivalent to one-third of the minimum wage and were ineligible to receive social benefits. As a result, the employment program lowered salaries and provided cheap labor to municipal governments.[27]

In 1976, two years after the reform of unemployment subsidies, the ILO work program for Latin America (PREALC) conducted a research study on how working people coped with unemployment in Santiago, specifically surveying people's strategies to find work.[28] The interviews and surveys showed that only a small minority of workers who qualified for the unemployment subsidy applied for it. Many eligible workers were unaware of the subsidy, while others found the process too bureaucratic or had no money for transportation. Only 10 percent of interviewed people used the services provided by SENCE. In contrast, people draw upon personal, family, and community networks and resources. For example, the Catholic Church had opened breakfast programs, workshops for unemployed people, and health care centers in poor neighborhoods. The interviews provide a glimpse of the problem of unemployment. One of the interviewed persons was a "man, 33 years old, head of household, three children (11, 9, and 2), unemployed since 1974." He had worked in a plastics manufacturing plant since he was 18 and was fired after 13 years of work. After losing his job, he performed odd and informal jobs including plumbing, electrical work, and construction. He and his family also received help from neighbors, family members, and the Catholic Church. Like him, PREALC argued, many Chilean workers had lost their jobs because of the "structural redefinition of the Chilean economic system." Few received state assistance. Some registered at PEM, but salaries were below the minimum wage.[29]

The national economy started showing signs of recovering by 1978. While neoliberal economists celebrated the beginning of the "economic miracle," the unemployment rate was about 12 to 13 percent. Roberto Kelly, a former naval officer who served between 1973 and 1978 as minister of the Office of Social Development (ODEPLAN), provided the footprint of unemployment and social policy. At ODEPLAN, Kelly and other Chicago Boys such as Miguel Kast tested neoliberal social reforms. They made labor protections the culprit of unemployment. According to Kelly, employers' freedom to make investment decisions including reducing wages and firing people at their own discretion would increase production and create jobs.[30] The existence of regulations and protections in the labor market (especially salary protections), they argued, were inhibiting job creation and causing unemployment.[31] His plan, known as Plan Kelly, looked to eliminate "the rigidity of the labor market and stimulate employment." The main points of his plan included: ending employers' contribution to social security fund; establishing a ceiling to increase in the minimum salary; ending employment security for new hires; and overturning the agrarian reform.[32]

In April 1978, the Junta and its ministers discussed the problem of unemployment and the future reform of the Labor Code. Both issues became entangled. Arturo Merino, navy admiral and member of the Junta, pointed out the need to "generate employment to prevent unemployment." Drawing on Kelly's unemployment plan, Merino wanted to eliminate service indemnity payments and other employment protections. Without these "restrictions," employers would hire more people. Similarly, the minister of finance Sergio de Castro, an economist trained in Chicago, explained that the law of employment stability of 1966 had discouraged employers to hire more people, causing unemployment. The business class, De Castro noted, should not have to incur additional expenses if they need to fire people, but the state should help people out of work. While he supported giving the unemployed a small subsidy, he also believed that deregulating the labor market and work contracts would increase production and eliminate involuntary unemployment, making the subsidy unnecessary.[33]

Although many agreed on the logic of the changing labor regulations, some members of the military, including General Pinochet, worried about the political impact of extreme measures such as eliminating mandatory service indemnity payments. The service indemnity payments survived, but the reform of the labor contract announced on May 1, 1978, increased the number of legal causes to fire people, deregulated the work contract, and made the labor market more flexible. In the following years, the Junta turned to replace the legal framework that had regulated labor relations and workers' rights since the 1920s. Known as the Labor Plan, these reforms included a series of decree laws that transformed workers' rights to form unions and bargain collectively. Together, these reforms imposed an individualist view of work and eroded the basis of collective action and the power of the union movement:

1. Decree-Law 2,200 (May 1, 1978): replaced the first two chapters of the Labor Code. Among its important changes were the incorporation of additional legal reasons to fire workers without compensations and the increase of the work week to 48 hours,
2. Decree-Law 2,756 (July 3, 1979): unionization rights: open shops, more than one union per shop.
3. Decree-Law 2,758 (July 6, 1979): collective bargaining: restricted the matters subject to negotiation, limited the right to strike to 30 days, and allowed employers to hire people during a strike.
4. Decree-Law 3,648 (March 10, 1981): eliminated labor courts and passed their matters to civil courts.
5. Law 18,620 (May 27, 1987): new labor code (codified the previous reforms)

These decrees permanently transformed the labor movement, workers' rights, and jobs. Labor organizations and the Catholic Church openly opposed the reforms. Manuel Bustos, textile union leader and future president of CUT, argued that the plan "shows lack of respect for workers," and the measures proposed were "repressive measures that have nothing to do with employment." Federico Mujica, union leader of white-collar employees, declared that the reforms "disregard people's right to work."[34] In the end, these reforms did not create good jobs but low-paid jobs in the service and new export and agricultural activities, leaving workers completely unprotected to face the worst crisis of the Chilean economy since the Great Depression.

THE CRASH OF 1981–1983

Between 1978 and 1981, Chile experienced a euphoric economic miracle. Throughout the country, the military government reassured people that "vamos bien, mañana mejor" (we are doing well, tomorrow better). Based on external credit, high consumption, rising imports, and speculation, prosperity was short-lived. The deregulation of the national economy and the financial sector made the country especially vulnerable to international shocks. Between 1982 and 1983, the country plunged into economic chaos and a wave of bankruptcies.

The bankruptcy of large companies and factories symbolized the devastating impact of the crisis. In May 1981, CRAV (Compañía de Refinería de Azúcar de Viña del Mar), Chile's largest and oldest sugar refinery, permanently closed its doors. In 1979, changes in import tariffs had affected business, and CRAV bought large quantities of unrefined sugar in advance. When the international price of sugar fell in 1981, the company went bankrupt, laying off between 450 and 500 workers.[35] A large economic group, CRAV's downfall shook the national economy, especially the banking sector. For people critical of the dictatorship, it evidenced "the vulnerability of the current economic model," the irresponsibility of the economic and political leadership, and the consequences of the concentration of capital and wealth in a few hands.[36] For workers, the fall of one of Chile's oldest companies augured the erosion of industrial jobs. The collapse of the textile sector further confirmed people's worst fears. Like CRAV, textile factories had also suffered the consequences of tariff reductions. Unable to compete with cheaper imports, mill owners had closed their factories, reduced personnel, and merged in the late 1970s. The economic and financial crash of 1981–1983 hit hard an industry already weakened by foreign competition and debt.[37] The number of textile workers fell from 39,081 in 1973 to 13,073 in 1982, and while employment increased in the following years, it never recovered its pre-1973 level.[38]

To respond to the crisis, the government devalued the peso and ended wage indexation. On September 11, 1982, the ninth anniversary of the military coup, General Pinochet addressed the nation and explained that "because of the inflexibility to maintain wages and salaries, the fall of expenditures contributed, even more, to the increase in unemployment." To palliate the impact of unemployment, Pinochet explained, the government offered employers a subsidy to hire workers, expanded PEM, gave additional money or funding to municipal governments to build low-income housing, and would eliminate norms that could increase unemployment.[39] The following year, the government intervened in more than 16 banks and finance houses and created a new emergency work program (Programa de Ocupación de Jefes de Hogar). Although real unemployment (including people working in emergency programs) reached 30 percent in 1983, Pinochet was optimistic. On the tenth anniversary of the coup, he said that the flexibility of the work contract, subsidies to employers, SENCE's training programs, and support for municipal governments had reduced unemployment.[40]

Despite the government's promise of fast recovery, high unemployment, poverty, and repression affected working-class families until the late 1980s. In Santiago, a third of the population lived in shantytowns, or *poblaciones*. Building on their long organizing tradition, political networks, and the support of the church, people organized to face the challenge of subsistence, unemployment, and violence.[41] They also mobilized and protested an oppressive legal and economic system, and, between 1983 and 1985, shantytowns became the epicenter of social and political mobilization.[42]

Like in the past, the economic crisis, unemployment, and inflation limited people's access to food. The overall consumption of nutritious food dropped, and malnutrition reached dangerous levels. Subsistence became the most immediate problem for most Chileans, sparking a wide range of community's responses. To eat, residents in shantytowns organized community soup kitchens (*ollas communes*), planted community gardens, and shopped together. The community soup kitchens epitomized the devastating impact of the crisis, the long tradition of community organizing among the urban poor, and the increasing presence of women in the fight against unemployment, poverty, and neoliberalism. Organized by neighborhood, the soup kitchens of the 1980s brought together between fifteen and twenty-five families (feeding about a hundred people). Using a community space (a church, a sports club, a union hall), families contributed money and volunteered to cook, serve food, and clean up. Unlike traditional soup kitchens organized by the Church and charity organizations, these grassroots organizations emphasized class solidarity over top-down social assistance. Like other community organizations, participating at the *olla* transformed women's traditional views of family, gender, and community, offering them a space of socialization, activism, and politicization.[43]

In 1986, from the heart of Chile's industrial suburbs, the soon-to-be one of the country's most acclaimed national rock bands, Los Prisioneros, released their hit *Muevan las industrias* (set the factories in motion). In a direct allusion to the impact of unemployment on Chilean society, the Prisioneros reproduced the sounds of the factory, hoping that the machines would move again. While economic conditions improved in the late 1980s, those factories never moved again.

NOTES

INTRODUCTION

1. The Chilean labor culture incorporated many traditions including the struggles of nitrate workers at the turn of the twentieth century, mutualism, anarchism, socialism, and communism. Beginning in the 1930s, these traditions provided a sense of community and collective memory that would continue to influence the labor movement and infused the new legal labor unions. Thomas Miller Klubock, *Contested Communities: Class, Gender, and Politics in Chile's El Teniente Copper Mine, 1904–1951* (Durham, NC: Duke University Press, 1998).

2. Moisés Poblete Troncoso, *The Rise of the Latin American Labor Movement* (New York: Bookman Associates, 1960).

3. Until the 1960s, unionization rates remained around 9 and 12 percent of the workforce. James O. Morris and Roberto Oyaneder, *Estudio de afiliación y finanzas sindicales en Chile, 1932–1959* (Santiago: INSORA, Universidad de Chile, 1962).

4. Labour Conference of the American States which are Members of the International Labour Organisation, fourth sitting, Saturday, January 3, 1936, ILO-BIT archives, diplomatic series (D), file 1086/1/0.

5. Seminario de Investigaciones Sociales del Instituto de Servicio Social, *Instituciones de asistencia social de Santiago* (Santiago: Editorial Jurídica de Chile, 1966).

6. Carlos Contreras Labarca, *La defensa del proletariado contra el riesgo profesional de la desocupación* (Santiago: Imprenta del Instituto Sordo-Mudos y Ciegos, 1923).

7. Brian Loveman, *Struggle in the Countryside: Politics and Rural Labor in Chile, 1919–1973* (Bloomington: Indiana University Press, 1976); Peter Winn, *Weavers of Revolution: The Yarur Workers and Chile's Road to Socialism* (New York: Oxford University Press, 1986). See also Sebastián Leiva Flores, "Vida y trabajo de la clase obrera chilena. Los trabajadores textiles y metalúrgicos entre las décadas de 1930 y 1960" (PhD diss., Universidad de Santiago, 2018), Klubock, *Contested Communities*; and Jody Pavilack, *Mining for the Nation: The Politics of Chile's Coal Communities from the Popular Front to the Cold War* (University Park: Pennsylvania State University Press, 2011).

8. Lynne Haney in her study of welfare institutions in Hungary examines how the state looked at people in need, defined those needs, and established eligibility criteria. She refers to this process as constructing an "architecture of need." Haney demonstrates that ideas, policies, and practices changed over time, paying attention to the relationship between welfare professionals and citizens and, especially, women and mothers. Her work offers a model to analyze how social categories such as work and non-work influenced policies and practices. Lynne A. Haney, *Inventing the Needy: Gender and the Politics of Welfare in Hungary* (Berkeley: University of California Press, 2002).

9. Brian Loveman and Elizabeth Lira, *Arquitectura política y seguridad interior del estado, Chile 1811–1990* (Santiago: DIBAM, Universidad Alberto Hurtado, 2002) and *Poder Judicial y conflictos políticos. Chile 1925–1958* (Santiago: LOM Ediciones, Universidad Alberto Hurtado, 2014); Brian Loveman, "The Political Architecture of Dictatorship: Chile before 1973," *Radical History Review* 125 (January 2016): 11–42.

10. Raymond Williams, *Keywords: A Vocabulary of Culture and Society* (New York: Oxford University Press, 1985), 325–26.

11. Some of the most influential work on the birth of unemployment in Europe and the United States are: John Burnett, *Idle Hands: The Experience of Unemployment, 1790–1990* (New York: Routledge, 1994); Alexander Keyssar, *Out of Work: The First Century of Unemployment in Massachusetts* (Cambridge: Cambridge University Press, 1986); Robert Salais, Nicolas Baverez, and Bénédicte Reynaud, *L'Invention du chômage: histoire et transformations d'une catégorie en France des années 1890 aux années 1980* (Paris: Presses universitaires de France, 1986); Christian Topalov, *Naissance du chômeur, 1880–1910* (Paris: A. Michel, 1994); and Bénédicte Zimmermann, *La constitution du chômage en Allemagne* (Paris: Éditions de la Maison des sciences de l'homme, 2001).

12. Ingrid Sauthier, "Histoire de la définition du chômage," *Courrier des statistiques* 127 (2009): 5–12.

13. See for example: Francisco E. Balderrama and Raymond Rodriguez, *Decade of Betrayal: Mexican Repatriation in the 1930s*, rev. ed. (Albuquerque: University of New Mexico Press, 2006); Lizabeth Cohen, *Making a New Deal: Industrial Workers in Chicago, 1919–1939*, 2nd ed. (Cambridge: Cambridge University Press, 2008); Cheryl Lynn Greenberg, *To Ask for an Equal Chance: African Americans in the Great Depression* (New York: Rowman and Littlefield, 2009). On Germany, see Richard J. Evans and Dick Geary, *The German Unemployed: Experiences and Consequences of Mass Unemployment from the Weimar Republic to the Third Reich* (New York: St. Martin's, 1987).

14. Kristin O'Brassill-Kulfan, *Vagrants and Vagabonds: Poverty and Mobility in the Early-American Republic* (New York: New York University Press, 2019).

15. Keyssar, *Out of Work*.

16. Topalov, *Naissance du chômeur*.

17. In 1925, the Real Academia Española defined *desocupado* as "sin ocupación, ocioso" (without occupation, idle), *cesante* as a public employee who had lost their job, and *paro* as the interruption of work. Real Academia Española, *mapa de diccionarios* (available online).

18. In 1923, Carlos Contreras Labarca explains that the following terms referred to unemployment: *desocupación professional, paro forzoso,* and *cesantía involuntaria*. Contreras Labarca, *La defensa del proletariado,* 9.

19. Karl Marx, *Capital,* vol. 1 (New York: Vintage, 1977), 784.

20. Burnett, *Idle Hands,* 145.

21. Originally published in Italian in 1909, *Passività economica* was translated into Spanish in 1911 and French in 1912. Santiago Macchiavello Varas, a Chilean political economist, cited the French edition in his work *Política económica nacional: antecedentes y directivas* (Santiago: Establecimientos Gráficos Balcells, 1931), 110.

22. William H. Beveridge, *Unemployment: A Problem of Industry,* 3rd ed. (London: Longmans, Green, 1912), 3.

23. Burnett, *Idle Hands*.

24. On unemployment and statistics, see Claudia Daniel, "De crisis a crisis: la invención de la desocupación en la Argentina," *Revista de Indias* 73, no. 257 (2013): 193–218; Alberti Manfredi, *La 'scoperta' dei disoccupati: Alle origini dell'indagine statistica sulla disoccupazione nell'Italia liberale (1893–1915)* (Florence, Italy: Firenze University Press, 2013).

25. Silvana Patriarca, *Numbers and Nationhood: Writing Statistics in Nineteenth-Century Italy* (Cambridge: Cambridge University Press, 1996), 7.

26. Mara Loveman, *National Colors: Racial Classification and the State in Latin America* (Oxford: Oxford University Press, 2014); James Scott, *Seeing Like a State: How Certain Schemes to Improve the Human Condition Have Failed* (New Haven, CT: Yale University Press, 1998); Mauricio Tenorio, *Mexico at the World's Fairs: Crafting a Modern Nation* (Berkeley: University of California Press, 1996), see chapter 8.

27. Elizabeth Quay Hutchison, "La historia detrás de las cifras: la evolución del censo chileno y la representación del trabajo femenino, 1895–1930," *Historia* (Santiago) 33 (2000): 417–34.

28. Simón Rodríguez, *La estadística del trabajo* (Santiago: Imprenta Cervantes, 1908).

29. W. R. Garside, *The Measurement of Unemployment: Methods and Sources in Great Britain, 1850–1970* (Oxford: Basil Blackwell, 1980).

30. Sauthier, "Histoire de la définition du chômage."

31. Topalov, *Naissance du chômeur,* 407–12.

32. For the case of Latin America, see for example: Ann S. Blum, *Domestic Economies: Family, Work, and Welfare in Mexico City, 1884–1943* (Lincoln: University of Nebraska Press, 2009); Paulo Drinot, *The Allure of Labor: Workers, Race,*

and the Making of the Peruvian State (Durham, NC: Duke University Press, 2011); Donna J. Guy, *Women Build the Welfare State: Performing Charity and Creating Rights in Argentina, 1880–1955* (Durham, NC: Duke University Press, 2009); Enrique Ochoa, *Feeding Mexico: The Political Uses of Food since 1910* (Wilmington, DE: Scholarly Resources, 2000). For the case of Chile, some of the most important work on social welfare has been written by María Angélica Illanes, Juan Carlos Yáñez Andrade, and María Soledad Zárate. See also Karin Alejandra Rosemblatt, *Gendered Compromises: Political Cultures and the State in Chile, 1920–1950* (Chapel Hill: University of North Carolina Press, 2000).

33. Carlos Contreras Labarca (1899–1982) was a lawyer and emblematic leader of the Communist Party in Chile. He served in the National Congress first as deputy (1926–1930, 1937–1941) and later as senator (1941–1949 and 1961–1969). Between 1931 and 1946, he was elected secretary general of the Communist Party.

34. Leon Fink, ed., *Workers across the Americas: The Transnational Turn in Labor History* (New York: Oxford University Press, 2011).

35. Juan Manuel Palacio, *La justicia peronista: la construcción de un nuevo orden legal en la Argentina* (Buenos Aires: Siglo XXI, 2018), 48.

36. Leon Fink and Juan Manuel Palacio, eds., *Labor Justice across the Americas* (Urbana: University of Illinois Press, 2018).

37. Daniel T. Rodgers, *Atlantic Crossings: Social Politics in a Progressive Age* (Cambridge, MA: Belknap Press of Harvard University Press, 1998).

38. Davide Rodogno, Bernhard Struck Vogel, and Jakob Vogel, eds., *Shaping the Transnational Sphere: Experts, Networks, and Issues from the 1840s to the 1930s* (New York: Berghahn Books, 2015); Pierre-Yves Saunier, "Circulations, connexions et espaces transnationaux," *Genèses* 4, no. 57 (2004): 110–26.

39. Sandrine Kott and Joëlle Droux, eds., *Globalizing Social Rights: The International Labour Organization and Beyond* (New York: Palgrave Macmillan, 2013). For a case study on the influence of international standards on a group of workers, see Leon Fink, *Sweatshops at Sea: Merchant Seamen in the World's First Globalized Industry, from 1812 to the Present* (Chapel Hill: University of North Carolina Press, 2011).

40. Juan Carlos Yáñez Andrade, *La OIT en América del sur: El comunismo y los trabajadores chilenos (1922–1932)* (Santiago: Ediciones Universidad Alberto Hurtado, 2016).

41. In 1919, the ILO approved six conventions including: hours of work (industry), unemployment, maternity protection, night work (women), minimum age (industry), and night work of young persons (industry). For an overview of the history of the ILO, see Gerry Rodgers et al., *The International Labour Organization and the Quest for Social Justice, 1919–2009* (Geneva: International Labour Office, 2009).

42. Palacio, *La justicia peronista,* see chapter 1.

43. Drinot, *Allure of Labor,* 32.

44. Similarly, William Suárez-Potts has shown the strong influence of European currents in Mexico's first labor laws. European legal theorists and political

economists as well as the social critique coming from Leon XIII's *Rerum Novarum* shaped the Mexican event. However, Suárez-Potts also argues the need to consider the influence of local political and labor conditions. William J. Suárez-Potts, *The Making of Law: The Supreme Court and Labor Legislation in Mexico, 1875–1931* (Stanford, CA: Stanford University Press, 2012).

45. Manuel Gálvez, "La inseguridad de la vida obrera (informe sobre el paro forzoso)," *Boletín del Departamento Nacional del Trabajo*, no. 22 (1913): 4–433.

46. Yáñez, *La OIT en América del Sur*.

47. Statistics recorded the number of people unemployed but did not calculate unemployment rate. According to the 1930 census, the economically active population in the 1920s was about 1.2 million people.

48. Yves Zoberman, *Une histoire du chômage: de l'antiquité a nos jours* (Paris: Perrin, 2011).

49. Gabriel González Videla, *Discurso pronunciado por el presidente de la república Excmo. Sr. Gabriel González Videla, en la ceremonia de inauguración de la planta de Huachipato, 25 de noviembre de 1950* (Santiago: Artes y Letras, 1950).

50. Founded in 1907, the department was initially called Oficina de Estadística del Trabajo.

51. See for example the work of Ricardo Ffrench-Davis, Markos Mamalakis, Mario Matus, Patricio Meller, Gabriel Palma, and Barbara Stallings.

52. "Zapateros a tus zapatos," in David Benavente, *A medio morir cantantando: rastrojos de la memoria chilena 1978–1998* (Santiago: Catalonia, 2007), 79–85.

CHAPTER 1. THE GLOBAL DEBATE ON UNEMPLOYMENT

1. Charles Gide was known for his work on cooperatives and solidarity. As a political economist, he criticized liberalism and looked for a middle point between individualism and communism. His *Principle d'économie politique* was first published in French in 1884 and was translated into multiple languages including Spanish. For an overview of Gide's work, see Marc Pénin, *Charles Gide, 1847–1932: l'esprit critique* (Paris: L'Harmattan, 1997).

2. "Discours de M. Léon Bourgeois," in Conference International du chômage, *Compte rendue de la conference international du chômage*, (Paris: Secrétariat général de la conference du chômage and Librairies de science politiques et sociales, 1911), 1:76.

3. Luis Malaquías Concha Stuardo (1883–1961) was the son of Luis Malaquías Concha Ortiz. Concha Ortiz was a prominent lawyer, politician, and leader of the Democratic Party who served in the House between 1897 and 1918 and in the Senate, between 1918 and 1924. Throughout his political career, Concha Ortiz advocated for a progressive labor and social legislation. Concha Stuardo did not have the political influence of his father. He served in the House between 1915 and 1918. Between 1939 and 1940, he was Chile's ambassador in Panamá and Costa Rica. After that, he left politics.

4. Juan Manuel Palacio, "From Social Legislation to Labor Justice: The Common Background in the Americas," in *Labor Justice across the Americas*, ed. Leon Fink and Juan Manuel Palacio (Urbana-Champaign: University of Illinois Press, 2018), 16–43; Davide Rodogno, Bernhard Struck, and Jakob Vogel, eds., *Shaping the Transnational Sphere: Experts, Networks, and Issues from the 1840s to the 1930s* (New York: Berghahn Books, 2015); William J. Suárez-Potts, *The Making of Law: The Supreme Court and Labor Legislation in Mexico, 1875–1931* (Stanford, CA: Stanford University Press, 2012).

5. Paulo Drinot, *The Allure of Labor: Workers, Race, and the Making of the Peruvian State* (Durham, NC: Duke University Press, 2011), 32.

6. Daniel T. Rodgers, *Atlantic Crossings: Social Politics in a Progressive Age* (Cambridge, MA: Belknap Press of Harvard University Press, 1998), 31.

7. Rodogno, Struck, and Vogel, *Shaping the Transnational Sphere*.

8. "La disoccupazione. Relazioni e discussioni del 1° Congresso internazionale per la lotta contro la disoccupazione 2–3 ottobre 1906," Società Umanitaria, Milano 1906, p. IX. Cited in Manfredi Alberti, *La 'scoperta' dei disoccupati: Alle origini dell'indagine statistica sulla disoccupazione nell' Italia liberale (1893–1915)* (Florence: Firenze University Press, 2013), 160.

9. Alberti, *La 'scorpeta' dei disoccupati*, 162.

10. Éric Lecerf, "Les Conférences internationales pour la lutte contre le chômage au début du siècle," *Mil neuf cent*, no. 7 (1989): 99–126.

11. Alberti, *La 'scoperta' dei disoccupati;* Silvana Patriarca, *Numbers and Nationhood: Writing Statistics in Nineteenth-Century Italy* (New York: Cambridge University Press, 1996).

12. Harald Westergaard, "Rapport général sur la statistique du chômage," in Conference International du chômage, *Compte rendue*, vol. 3.

13. Westergaard, "Rapport général sur la statistique du chômage."

14. The category of unemployment is never fixed and reflects the changing ideas about work. For example, even in the most obvious case, age, society continues to debate when people should start and stop working. In revolutionary Mexico, Ann Blum demonstrates, working families contested the definition of who was and who was not a legal worker, challenging the state efforts to impose restrictions on child labor. Ann S. Blum, "Speaking of Work and Family: Reciprocity, Child Labor, and Social Reproduction, Mexico City, 1920–1940," *Hispanic American Historical Review* 91, no. 1 (2011): 63–95.

15. Manlio Andrea D'Ambrossio, *La passivité économique* (Paris: M. Giard & E. Brière, 1912).

16. Sigrid Wadauer, Thomas Buchner, and Alexander Mejstrik, eds., *The History of Labour Intermediation: Institutions and Finding Employment in the Nineteenth and Early Twentieth Centuries* (New York: Berghahn Books, 2015).

17. Alexandre Schiavi, "Rapport général sur la question du placement," in Conference International du chômage, *Compte rendue*, vol. 3.

18. M. Dominicus (adjoint au maire du Strasbourg), in Conference International du chômage, *Compte rendue*, 1:100–101.

19. On the development of unemployment insurance see: Miriam Cohen and Michael Hanagan, "Politics, Industrialization and Citizenship: Unemployment Policy in England, France, and the United States, 1890–1950," *International Review of Social History* 40, no. 3 (1995): 91–129; Ingrid Sauthier, "Modern Unemployment: From the Creation of the Concept to the International Labour Office's First Standards," in *Globalizing Social Rights: The International Labour Organization and Beyond*, ed. Sandrine Kott and Joëlle Droux (New York: Palgrave Macmillan, 2013), 67–84.

20. Raoul Jay was a prominent French law professor and author of numerous legal treaties such as *La protection légale des travailleurs* (Paris: Sirey, 1910).

21. Ph. Falkenburg, "Rapport général sur la question du controle des chômeurs dans les caisses d'assurance," in Conference International du chômage, *Compte rendue*, vol. 3.

22. Intervention of Pissarjevsky, in Conference International du chômage, *Compte rendue*, 1:131–32.

23. Intervention of Marguerie, in Conference International du chômage, *Compte rendue*, 1:149–50.

24. *Boletín de la Oficina del Trabajo* (Santiago), no. 3 (1911), 117–19.

25. Eric Hobsbawm, *The Age of Extremes: A History of the World, 1914–1919* (New York: Vintage, 1996).

26. David Crew, *Germans on Welfare: From Weimar to Hitler* (New York: Oxford University Press, 2001); Young-Sun Hong, *Welfare, Modernity, and the Weimar State, 1919–1933* (Princeton, NJ: Princeton University Press, 1998).

27. Albert Thomas's speech at the ILO conference in 1932, quoted in H. B. Butler, "Albert Thomas, the First Director," *International Labour Review*, 26, no. 1 (1932): 1–7.

28. League of Nations, *Report on Unemployment: Prepared by the Organising Committee for the International Labour Conference, Washington, 1919* (London: Harisson & Sons, n.d.), 29.

29. This effort was consistent with the tradition of drafting special legislation for sea workers, who, as Leon Fink explains, were "often regarded as a breed apart and thus in need of special legislative or other legal administration" from other workers. Leon Fink, *Sweatshops at Sea: Merchants Seamen in the World's First Globalized Industry, 1812 to the Present* (Chapel Hill: University of North Carolina Press, 2014), 2. ILO, "C002—Unemployment Convention, 1919 (No. 2)" and "C008—Unemployment Indemnity (Shipwreck) Convention, 1920 (No. 8)."

30. ILO, "R011—Unemployment (Agriculture) Recommendation, 1921 (No. 11)."

31. ILO, "C044—Unemployment Provision Convention, 1934 (No. 44)."

32. Olivier Feiertag, "Réguler la mondialisation: Albert Thomas, les débuts du BIT et la crise économique mondiale de 1920–1923," *Les cahiers Irice*, no. 2 (2008): 127–55.

33. International Labour Organisation, *Remedies for Unemployment* (Geneva: ILO, 1923).

34. International Labour Organisation, *Methods of Compiling Statistics of Unemployment. Replies of the Governments* (Geneva: ILO, 1922).

35. ILO, *Methods of Compiling Statistics*.

36. Fabián Herrera León, Patricio Herrera González, and Juan Carlos Yáñez Andrade, eds., *América Latina y La Organización Internacional del Trabajo: redes, cooperación técnica e institucionalidad social (1919–1950)* (Morelia, Michoacán, México: Instituto de Investigaciones Históricas, Universidad Michoacana de San Nicolás de Hidalgo, 2013); Juan Carlos Yáñez Andrade, *La OIT en América del Sur: el comunismo y los trabajadores chilenos (1922–1932)* (Santiago: Ediciones Universidad Alberto Hurtado, 2016).

37. In the case of the ILO Unemployment Convention, 1919 (C08), Argentina, Chile, and Uruguay ratified it in 1933, Nicaragua in 1934, Venezuela in 1944, and Ecuador in 1962. In 1938, the ILO "called the attention of the American countries which are Members of the Organization to the necessity for developing a complete system of free public employment agencies, as provided for the Unemployment Convention 1919, and to the necessity for strict supervision of the activities of fee-charging employment agencies." "Report by the International Labour Office on the Action taken to give Effect to the Resolutions adopted by the Santiago Conference, Geneva, 1938," ILO-BIT Archives, Diplomatic Series (D), file 2086/000.

38. Hilda Sábato y Luis Alberto Romero, *Los trabajadores de Buenos Aires. La experiencia del mercado* (Buenos Aires: Editorial Sudamericana, 1992).

39. Juan Pablo Pérez Sáinz, *Mercados y bárbaros: la persistencia de las desigualdades de excedente en América Latina* (San José, Costa Rica: FLACSO, Sede Costa Rica, 2014).

40. On vagrancy and social control, see: Alejandra Araya Espinoza, "Guerra, intolerancia a la ociosidad y resistencia: los discursos ocultos tras la vagancia, Ciudad de México, 1821–1860," *Boletín Americanista*., no. 52 (2002): 23–55; Edwin Monsalvo Mendoza and Roberto González Arana, "Contra la moral i las buenas costumbres: el control de la vagancia y la prostitución en la frontera sur de Antioquia, Manizales, Colombia, 1850–1870," *Caravelle*., no. 104 (2015): 153–75; Adriana Sánchez Lovell, "El problema de la vagancia: una propuesta de enfoque teórico desde la historia del trabajo, a partir del caso de Costa Rica en el siglo XIX," *Diálogos* 17, no. 2 (2016): 161–90; Ricardo Salvatore, *Wandering Paysanos: State Order and Subaltern Experience in Buenos Aires during the Rosas Era* (Durham, NC: Duke University Press, 2003); and Ronny Viales Hurtado and Emmanuel Barrantes Zamora, "Mercado laboral y mecanismos de control de mano de obra en la cafilcultura centroamerica: Guatemala y Costa Rica en el período 1850–1930," *Revista de Historia*, no. 55–56 (2007): 15–36.

41. Drinot, *Allure of Labor*, 33.

42. Rosemary Thorp, *Progress, Poverty, and Exclusion: An Economic History of Latin America in the 20th Century* (Washington, DC: Inter American Development Bank, 1998), chapter 4.

43. Ricardo Salvatore, *Disciplinary Conquest: U.S. Scholars in South America, 1900–1945* (Durham, NC: Duke University Press, 2016).

44. L. S. Rowe, *Early Effects of the European War upon the Finance, Commerce and Industry of Chile* (New York: Oxford University Press, 1918), 37.

45. L.S. Rowe, *Early Effects of the War upon the Finance, Commerce, and Industry of Peru* (New York: Oxford University Press, 1920), 14.

46. Rowe, *Early Effects of the European War*, 47.

47. See, for example, Julia Rodríguez, *Civilizing Argentina: Science, Medicine, and the Modern State* (Chapel Hill: University of North Carolina Press, 2006); Kristin Ruggiero, *Modernity in the Flesh: Medicine, Law, and Society in Turn-of-the-Century Argentina* (Stanford, CA: Stanford University Press, 2004).

48. "Rapport du membre de la délégation argentine," in Conference International du chômage, *Compte rendue*, 1:177.

49. Manuel Gálvez, "La inseguridad de la vida obrera (informe sobre el paro forzoso)," *Boletín del Departamento Nacional del Trabajo,* no 22 (1913): 10.

50. For a discussion on problem of unemployment in Argentina, see José Panettieri, *Ayer y hoy: desocupación y subocupación en la Argentina* (Buenos Aires, Argentina: Grupo Editor Universitario, 1997).

51. *Boletín del Departamento Nacional del Trabajo* (Buenos Aires), no. 36 (1918), 22.

52. Eduardo Zimmermann, *Los liberales reformistas: la cuestión social en la Argentina, 1890–1916* (Buenos Aires: Editorial Sudamericana, 1995), 202.

53. Claudia Daniel, "De crisis a crisis: la invención de la desocupación en la Argentina," *Revista de Indias*, 73, no. 257 (2013): 193–218.

54. Manuel Gálvez, "La inseguridad," 8; Zimmermann, *Los liberales reformistas*, 202–9.

55. *Boletín de la Oficina del Trabajo* (Santiago), no. 8 (1914), 254–65.

56. "Alejandro E. Bunge is an eminent Argentine economist whose opinions and whose published works are today the subject of discussion in all the principal universities and particularly in those of the United Sates." He wrote extensively about Argentina's industrial and economic problems. *The Pan American Magazine*, vol. 33, no. 5 (October 1921), 243.

57. Alejandro Bunge, "Desocupación obrera en Buenos Aires," *Boletin del Departamento Nacional del Trabajo* (Buenos Aires), no. 25 (1913): 949–60.

58. "Memoria del Departamento Nacional del Trabajo correspondiende a 1916," *Boletin del Departamento Nacional del Trabajo* (Buenos Aires), no. 33 (1916), 12.

59. Maricel Bertolo, "Estado y trabajadores en Argentina. El Departamento Nacional del Trabajo ante el fenómeno de la desocupación, 1907–1934" (PhD

diss., Facultad de Filosofía y Letras, Universidad de Buenos Aires, Argentina, 2008).

60. *Boletin del Departamento Nacional del Trabajo* (Buenos Aires), no. 24 (1913), 502.

61. *Boletin del Departamento Nacional del Trabajo* (Buenos Aires), no. 27 (1914), 12.

62. México, Departamento del Trabajo, "Reglamento de Agencias de Colocaciones," *Diario Oficial* (Mexico), April 14, 1934.

63. Conferencia de Trabajo de los Estados de América miembros de la Organización Internacional del Trabajo, "Examen de los Convenios internacionales del trabajo con respecto a: 2) paro forzoso y colocación. Santiago, Chile, enero de 1936," ILO-BIT Archives, Diplomatic Series (D), file 1086/105/3.

64. I have compared these policies in more detail in Ángela Vergara, "Cuando los obreros no trabajan: una aproximación a la historia del desempleo en América Latina," in *Trabajadores y sindicatos en Latinoamérica: conceptos, problemas y escalas de análisis*, ed. Silvia Simonassi and Daniel Dicósimo (San Martín, Argentina: Imago Mundi, 2017).

65. Alejandro Serani Burgos, January 2, 1936, "Labour Conference of the American States which are Members of the International Labour Organization. Second sitting, January 2, 1936," ILO-BIT Archives, Diplomatic series (D), file 1086/401.

CHAPTER 2. UNEMPLOYMENT IN EARLY TWENTIETH-CENTURY CHILE

1. E. P. Thompson, *The Making of the English Working Class* (New York: Vintage, 1963), 776.

2. The historiography on the nitrate industry is very extensive and rich. For an overview on the economic history of nitrate see Harold Blakemore, *British Nitrates and Chilean Politics, 1886–1896: Balmaceda and North* (London: Athlone Press for the Institute of Latin American Studies, 1974); Michael Monteón, *Chile in the Nitrate Era: The Evolution of Economic Dependence, 1880–1930* (Madison: University of Wisconsin Press, 1983); Thomas O'Brien, *The Nitrate Industry and Chile's Crucial Transition, 1870–1891* (New York: New York University Press, 1982); Carol Cariola Sutter and Osvaldo Sunkel, *Un siglo de historia económica de Chile, 1830–1930* (Santiago: Editorial Universitaria, 1990).

3. Sergio González Miranda, *Hombres y mujeres de la pampa. Tarapacá en el ciclo del salitre* (Santiago: LOM Ediciones, 2002), 311.

4. For a labor and social history of nitrate see González Miranda, *Hombres y mujeres de la pampa*; Michael Monteón, "The *Enganche* in the Chilean Nitrate Sector, 1880–1930," *Latin American Perspectives* 6, no. 3 (1979): 66–79; Julio Pinto Vallejos, *Trabajos y rebeldías en la pampa salitrera: El ciclo del salitre y la reconfiguración de las identidades populares (1850–1900)* (Santiago: Universidad de Santiago, 1998).

5. Floreal Recabarren, *La matanza de San Gregorio 1921: crisis y tragedia* (Santiago: LOM Ediciones, 2003), 11.

6. *Boletín de la Oficina del Trabajo*, no. 9 (1914), 57.

7. *Boletín de la Oficina del Trabajo*, no. 9 (1914), 56.

8. Ministro de Relaciones Exteriores, Peru, *Memoria del Ministro de Relaciones Exteriores* (Lima, Peru: Imprenta Americana, 1914), 78.

9. L. S. Rowe, *Early Effects of the European War upon the Finance, Commerce, and Industry of Chile* (New York: Oxford University Press, 1918), 45.

10. Ministerio del Interior, Law 2,923 (August 24, 1914) and Law 2,946 (November 21, 1914).

11. For an overview of the impact of the 1913–1914 crisis on industrial workers see Peter DeShazo, *Urban Workers and Labor Unions in Chile, 1902–1927* (Madison: University of Wisconsin Press, 1983); Mario Matus, and Isabel Jara Hinojosa, eds., *Hombres del metal: trabajadores ferroviarios y metalúrgicos chilenos en el ciclo salitrero, 1880–1930* (Santiago: Universidad de Chile, 2009).

12. *Boletín de la Oficina del Trabajo*, no. 9 (1914), 78–80.

13. Ministerio de Industria y Obras Públicas, "Servicio de Colocación," August 18, 1914, in Moisés Poblete Troncoso and Oscar Álvarez Andrews, *Legislación social obrera chilena (Recopilación de leyes vigentes sobre el trabajo y la previsión social)* (Santiago: Imprenta Santiago, 1924), 182–83.

14. Boletín de la Oficina del Trabajo, nos. 8 and 9 (1914). For an overview of the placement system in Chile, see Juan Carlos Yáñez Andrade, "Las bolsas de trabajo: modernización y control del mercado laboral en Chile (1914–1921)," *Cuadernos de Historia* no. 26 (2007): 107–34.

15. DeShazo, *Urban Workers*, 24 and 46.

16. *Boletín de la Oficina del Trabajo*, no. 9 (1914), 78.

17. *Boletín de la Oficina del Trabajo*, no. 9 (1914), 92–93.

18. Mario Matus, *Crecimiento sin desarrollo. Precios y salarios reales durante el ciclo salitrero en Chile (1880–1930)* (Santiago: Editorial Universitaria, 2012); 277–89.

19. Brian Loveman, *Chile: The Legacy of Hispanic Capitalism*, 3rd ed. (New York: Oxford University Press, 2001), 170.

20. Law 3516 (July 21, 1919); Law 3812 (November 29, 1921); and Law 3890 (October 19, 1922).

21. República de Chile, Dirección General de Estadística, *Resultados del X censo de la población efectuado el 27 de noviembre de 1930* (Santiago: Imprenta Universo, 1931), 1:12.

22. Médico del cuerpo, Santiago, April 7, 1922, Archivo Nacional (hereafter AN), Intendencia de Santiago, vol. 524.

23. Matus, *Crecimiento sin desarrollo*, 279–83.

24. Arthur Stickell, "Migration and Mining: Labor in Northern Chile in the Nitrate Era, 1880–1930" (PhD diss. Indiana University, 1979), see especially chapter 4.

25. In his speech, Alessandri indistinctly referred to unemployed workers and unemployed men, women, and children. Thus, it is unclear whether he referred to the person without a job or to the family affected by the job loss. *Mensaje leído por S.E. el Presidente de la República en la apertura de sesiones ordinarias del Congreso Nacional* (Santiago: Imprenta fiscal de la penitenciaría de Santiago, 1922), 34–35.

26. On the economic crisis and social mobilization see Sergio Grez Toso, *Historia del comunismo en Chile. La era de Recabarren (1912-1924)* (Santiago: LOM Ediciones, 2011), 194–204; Julio Pinto Vallejos, *Desgarros y utopías en la pampa salitrera: La consolidación de la identidad obrera en tiempos de la cuestión social (1890–1923)* (Santiago: LOM Ediciones, 2007), chapter 5; and Juan Carlos Yáñez Andrade, *La intervención social en Chile, 1907–1932* (Santiago: RIL Editores, 2008).

27. Bustamante, Santiago, April 22, 1922. AN, Intendencia de Santiago, vol. 524.

28. In 1917, a decree from the Ministry of Interior authorized regional authorities (*gobernadores* and *intendentes*) to mediate in labor conflicts. Ministerio del Interior, Decree 4353, December 14, 1917. In: Poblete Troncoso and Álvarez Andrews, *Legislación social obrera chilena*, 188–90.

29. Ministro del Interior, *Memoria del Ministro del Interior* (Santiago: Imprenta Nacional, 1921), 13.

30. Stickell, "Migration and Mining." He argues that by 1921, most nitrate companies were paying the fifteen-day indemnity, which had become the norm in the nitrate mines.

31. Floreal Recabarren, *La matanza de San Gregorio 1921: crisis y tragedia* (Santiago: LOM Ediciones, 2003), 13.

32. In the early 1920s, the Chilean labor movement had evolved from mutual aid organizations to trade unions and national labor organizations, including anarchist, communist, and Catholic groups. Founded in 1909, the Federación Obrera de Chile (FOCH) became one of the largest workers' organization and included labor councils from around the country. In 1912, the foundation of the Partido Obrero Socialista (later to become the Communist Party) gave a political voice to the labor movement. In 1919, the FOCH turned to the left and built a strong support among nitrate workers and in 1921 became affiliated with the Profintern.

33. Luis Emilio Recabarren, "La masacre de San Gregorio," *La Comuna*, February 12, 1921, in *Recabarren: Escritos de prensa*, vol. 4, *1919–1924*, ed. Ximena Cruzat and Eduardo Devés (Santiago: Nuestra América y Terranova Editores, 1987), 130–31.

34. Recabarren, *La matanza de San Gregorio 1921.*

35. On port and maritime unions see Camilo Santibáñez Rebolledo, "Los trabajadores portuarios chilenos y la experiencia de la eventualidad: Los conflictos por la redondilla en los muelles salitreros (1916–1923)," *Historia* 50, no. 2 (2017): 699–728, and "Huelgas y lockouts portuarios por la redondilla: Los conflictos por

el control de la contratación en los muelles chilenos (1916–1923)" (MA thesis, Universidad de Santiago de Chile, 2016).

36. "Talcahuano—La redondilla," *La voz del mar* (Valparaíso), March 24, 1925, p. 5.

37. "Decreto sobre inscripción y distribución de los trabajadores de los puertos de la zona salitrera," Santiago, April 28, 1922. Previous decrees included: "Forma de solucionar los conflictos en las faenas marítimas de los puertos" (Santiago, October 24, 1921) and "Disposiciones sobre la redondilla," (Santiago, October 24, 1921).

38. José Santos González Vera, "Concepto de la Libertad de Trabajo," *Claridad*, Santiago, November 12, 1921, in *Letras anarquistas: José Santos González Vera, Manuel Rojas*, ed. Carmen Soria (Santiago: Planeta, 2005), 82–83.

39. On bakers see Juan Carlos Yáñez Andrade, "Por una legislación social en Chile. El movimiento de los panaderos (1888–1930)," *Historia* 41 (2008): 495–532.

40. Juan Enrique Couyoumdjian, *Chile y Gran Bretaña: durante la Primera Guerra Mundial y la postguerra, 1914–1921* (Santiago: Editorial Andrés Bello), chapter 9.

41. Federación Obrera de Chile, August 24, 1921, cited in Recabarren, *La matanza de San Gregorio 1921*, 13.

42. José Santos González Vera, "Medidas para aumentar la desocupación," *Claridad* (Santiago), October 29, 1921, in Soria, *Letras anarquistas*, 75–76.

43. Rolando Álvarez Vallejos, "'¡Viva la revolución y la patria!': Partido Comunista de Chile y nacionalismo, 1921–1926," *Revista de historia social y de las mentalidades*, no. 7 (2003): 25–44.

44. Juan Manuel Palacio, "From Social Legislation to Labor Justice: The Common Background in the Americas," in *Labor Justice across the Americas*, ed. Leon Fink and Juan Manuel Palacio (Urbana: University of Illinois Press, 2018).

45. For an overview of social laws, see Juan Carlos Yáñez Andrade, *La intervención social en Chile, 1907–1932* (Santiago: RIL Editores, 2008).

46. James Morris called this the "conservative project." He underscored the influence of *Rerum Novarum* but also the local roots of the project. He argued that "in other words, the Conservative bill was not original in the creative sense. It was original, however, in the selective and adaptive sense, in the kind of ideas that were borrowed and the way they were put together." James O. Morris, *Élites, Intellectuals, and Consensus: A Study of the Social Question and the Industrial Relations System in Chile* (Ithaca, NY: School of Industrial and Labor Relations, Cornell University, 1966), 135.

47. The following senators of the Conservative Party presented the project: Carlos Aldunate Solar, Alfredo Barros Errázuriz, Joaquín Echeñique, Rafael Urrejola, Pedro Correa Ovalle, Rafael Ariztía Lyon, and Silvestre Ochagavía. Chile, Cámara de Senadores, sesión ordinaria, *Diario de sesiones*, June 2, 1919, 40–44.

48. Francisco Walker Linares, *Panorama del derecho social chileno* (Santiago: Editorial Jurídica, 1947), 53.

49. On Moisés Poblete Troncoso and his relationship with the ILO, see, Juan Carlos Yáñez Andrade, "La OIT y la red sudamericana de corresponsales. El caso de Moisés Poblete, 1922–1946," in *América Latina y la Organización Internacional del Trabajo: redes, cooperación técnica e institucionalidad social (1919–1950),* ed. Fabián Herrera León, Patricio Herrera González, and Juan Carlos Yáñez Andrade (Morelia, Michoacán, Mexico: Instituto de Investigaciones Históricas, Universidad Michoacana de San Nicolás de Hidalgo, 2013), 25–61.

50. Walker Linares, *Panorama del derecho social chileno*, 54.

51. In January 1921, Jorge Errázuriz Tagle had proposed to regulate placement agencies and established some form of unemployment benefits. He called for social insurance modeled along the lines of the Ghent system. His project did not pass. Chile, Cámara de Diputados, *Diario de sesiones*, January 5, 1921, 1210–12.

52. Poblete Troncoso's proposal for unemployment insurance is discussed in J. Toribio Lira Vergara, *El seguro contra el paro forzoso* (Santiago: Talleres Gráficos La Aurora, 1938), 141–45.

53. In the midst of political conflict, the military demanded that President Alessandri and the National Congress approve social reforms and introduced political changes in the government. The Congress approved the laws, but the crisis continued. Few days later, Alessandri fled the country, and a military junta took control of the government until his return in March 1925. Loveman, *Chile*, 180–82.

54. Ministerio del Interior, Ley 4053 (del contrato de trabajo), September 29, 1924.

55. República de Chile, *Código del Trabajo* (Santiago: Editorial Nascimento, 1932).

56. Fábrica Nacional de Sombreros, Cintolesi Hns. Ltda, *Libreta de asistencia al trabajo* (Santiago: Imprenta Gutenberg, n.d).

57. Fundición y Fábrica de José Robinovitch, *Reglamento interno* (Santiago: Imprenta Universidad, n.d).

58. Copiapó, July 31, 1930. Archivo Nacional de la Administración del Estado (hereafter ARNAD), Dirección del Trabajo (hereafter DT), vol. 218.

59. "La mentira de la ley," *Boletín Oficial de la Unión Industrial de Obreros de Gath y Chaves*, April 8, 1926, no. 2, p. 4.

60. Diego Ortúzar and Ángela Vergara, "Bringing Justice to the Workplace: Labor Courts and Labor Laws in Chile, 1930s–1980s," in Fink and Palacio, *Labor Justice across the Americas.*

61. Secretaría de Bienestar Social, Intendencia de Bío Bío, n.d., ARNAD, DT, vol. 215.

62. Thomas Miller Klubock, *Contested Communities Class, Gender, and Politics in Chile's El Teniente Copper Mine, 1904–1951* (Durham, NC: Duke University

Press, 1998); Enzo Videla Bravo, Hernán Venegas Valdevenito and Milton Godoy Orellana, *El orden fabril: paternalismo industrial en la minería chilena 1900–1950* (Valparaíso: América en Movimiento, 2016).

63. María Angélica Illanes, *Cuerpo y sangre de la política: la construcción histórica de las visitadoras sociales, Chile 1887–1940* (Santiago: LOM Ediciones, 2007).

64. Jorge Baraona Puelma, *El paro forzoso* (Santiago: Imprenta Cervantes, 1923), 107.

65. Carlos Cañas O'Ryan, *Seguros sociales* (Santiago: Imprenta y Litografía La Ilustración, 1922), 62.

66. Santiago Wilson Hernández, "Nuestra crisis económica y la desocupación obrera" (thesis, Universidad de Chile, Santiago, 1933).

CHAPTER 3. FIGHTING UNEMPLOYMENT

Epigraph: "Circular de S.E. el Presidente de la República a los Intendentes del país," *Boletín del Ministerio de Bienestar Social* 4, nos. 32–36 (January–April 1931), 1–2.

1. Guillermo del Fierro to the Labor Department, Copiapó, July 15, 1930, ARNAD DT, vol. 218.

2. The job placement service (*servicio de colocación*) was first organized in 1914. Offices were usually located near a railroad station and collected information from both job seekers and employers. Labor inspectors used this information to place unemployed workers and manage the labor market. See chapter 2 for a larger discussion on the organization of the job placement office.

3. I use the generic term "Labor Department," but the office changed names several times throughout this period. It was first called Oficina de Estadística del Trabajo and was under the authority of the Ministerio de Industria y Obras Públicas. In 1919, the Oficina del Trabajo was organized in different subdepartments, including statistics and inspection. Between 1924 and 1927, it became the Dirección General del Trabajo and passed to the new Ministerio de Higiene, Asistencia, y Previsión Social. Between 1928 and 1932, it was renamed Inspección General del Trabajo and the ministry was renamed Ministerio de Bienestar Social. After 1932, it became again the Dirección General del Trabajo and was placed under the new Ministerio del Trabajo.

4. The personnel of the Labor Department increased from only 19 employees in 1924 to 343 in 1930. Ministerio de Bienestar Social, Decreto 1331, August 5, 1930. See also Dirección General del Trabajo, *La Inspección General del Trabajo. El surgimiento de la fiscalización laboral, 1924–1934* (Santiago: Dirección del Trabajo, 2010), 225. For an overview of the early history of the Labor Department, see Juan Carlos Yáñez Andrade, *La intervención social en Chile y el nacimiento de la sociedad salarial, 1907–1932* (Santiago: RIL Editores, 2008).

5. Ernesto Ortíz Wormald, Santiago, January 1930, ARNAD, DT, vol. 213.

6. Brian Loveman, *Chile: The Legacy of Hispanic Capitalism*, 3rd ed. (New York: Oxford University Press, 2001), 170.

7. Ernesto Ortíz Wormald to Inspector General, Santiago, February 1930, ARNAD, DT, vol. 213.

8. Departamento de Asociaciones, "Resumen estadístico de la paralización, movilización y ocupación de los obreros de la región salitrera," Santiago, February 18, 1931, ARNAD, DT, informes varios.

9. "Los obreros cesantes de las salitreras," *Revista del Trabajo*, August 1931.

10. Banco Central de Chile, *Séptima memoria anual presentada a la Superintendencia de Bancos, año 1932* (Santiago: Dirección General de Prisiones, 1933), 20.

11. Ministerio del Interior, Ley 4053 (del contrato de trabajo), September 29, 1924. This law was later incorporated into the Labor Code of 1931.

12. "Circular," Santiago, August 19, 1929, ARNAD, DT, vol. 213.

13. Intendente de Tarapacá to Inspector General del Trabajo, Iquique, January 23, 1930, ARNAD, DT, vol. 213.

14. Robinson Paredes (Secretario Bienestar Social) to Inspector General del Trabajo, Iquique, May 20, 1931, ARNAD, DT, vol. 244.

15. Igor Goicovic, "Crisis económica y respuesta social: Choapa 1929–1931," *Notas históricas y geográficas* no. 4 (1993): 119–153 and "La crisis económica de 1929 y el retorno de los salitreros: efectos politicos y sociales en el Valle del Choapa (1929–1938)," *Espacio Regional* 1, no. 8 (2001): 51–68.

16. Gobernación de Tocopilla to Gerente Compañía Chilena de Vapores, Tocopilla, June 23, 1931, ARNAD, DT vol. 246.

17. David Méndez Alvear (Inspector del Trabajo) to Secretario Bienestar Social, Coquimbo, January 28, 1931, ARNAD, DT, vol. 242.

18. Ambrosio Viaux to Minister of Interior, Santiago, March 14, 1931, ARNAD, DT, vol. 240.

19. To intendente de Santiago, Santiago, December 3, 1930, ARNAD, DT vol. 224.

20. Dirección General del Trabajo, *La inspección general del trabajo*, 225.

21. Santiago Wilson Hernández, "Nuestra crisis económica y la desocupación obrera," thesis, Universidad de Chile, 1933, 51.

22. Eduardo Lavanderos (Governor of Traiguén) to Inspector General del Trabajo, Traiguén, October 15, 1931, ARNAD, DT, vol. 255.

23. Dirección General del Trabajo to Ministro de Bienestar Social, Santiago, February 27, 1931, ARNAD, DT, Informes Varios, 1931.

24. Manuel Marfán, "Políticas reactivadoras y recesión externa, 1929–1938," *Estudios Cieplan* 12 (1984): 89–119; Banco Central de Chile, *Séptima memoria anual*.

25. Dirección General del Trabajo to Ministro de Bienestar Social, Santiago, February 27, 1931, ARNAD, DT, Informes Varios, 1931.

26. Lizabeth Cohen argues that "the Great Depression replayed this dynamic of employers promises and worker disillusionment in even greater intensity and left worker surer than ever that employers only valued welfare capitalism when it was convenient and cheap." Lizabeth Cohen, *Making a New Deal: Industrial Workers in Chicago, 1919–1939* (Cambridge: Cambridge University Press, 2008), 238. See also Ronald W. Schatz, *Electrical Workers: A History of Labor at General Electric and Westinghouse, 1923–60* (Urbana: University of Illinois Press, 1983).

27. Since the 1910s, large mining and industrial companies had developed social programs such as company housing and recreation programs, hired social workers, formed welfare departments, and granted benefits for families. In doing so, they influenced, controlled, trained, and retained the workforce. On corporate social welfare in early twentieth-century Chile see María Angélica Illanes, "Ella en Lota-Coronel: poder y domesticación. El primer servicio social industrial de América Latina," *Mapocho* 49 (2001): 141–48; Thomas M. Klubock, *Contested Communities: Class, Gender, and Politics in Chile's El Teniente Copper Mines, 1904–1951* (Durham, NC: Duke University Press, 1998); Enzo Videla Bravo, Hernán Venegas Valdevenito, and Milton Godoy Orellana, eds., *El orden fabril. Paternalismo industrial en la minería chilena, 1900–1950* (Valparaiso: América en Movimiento, 2016).

28. Markos Mamalakis and Clark Winton Reynolds, *Essays on the Chilean Economy* (Homewood, IL: Richard D. Irwin, Inc, 1965), 230.

29. By the late 1920s copper represented 38 percent of Chile's exports. Juan Brown et al., "Economía chilena 1810–1995: estadísticas históricas," *Documento de Trabajo* (Facultad de Economía, Universidad Católica), no. 187 (2000): 130; Norman Gorvan, "Las corporaciones multinacionales del cobre en Chile," in *El cobre en el desarrollo nacional*, ed. Ricardo Ffrench-Davis and Ernesto Tironi (Santiago: Ediciones Nueva Universidad, 1974), 115; Gabriel Palma, "Chile 1914–1935: de economía exportadora a substitutiva de exportaciones," *Estudios CIEPLAN* no. 12 (1984): 61–88.

30. Carlos Hurtado Ruiz-Tagle, *Concentración de población y desarrollo económico. El caso chileno* (Santiago: Universidad de Chile, Instituto de Economía, 1966), 195; and Eduardo Ortiz, *La gran depresión, 1929. Impacto en Chile* (Santiago: Liberalia, 2014), 53–55.

31. Klubock, *Contested Communities*, 81–82.

32. Secretario General de Bienestar to Inspector General del Trabajo, Rancagua, July 9, 1931, ARNAD, DT, vol. 246.

33. "La Cía Andes rebaja sus sueldos," *El Progreso* (Chañaral), December 31, 1931; Carlos Souper (governor of El Loa) to Intendente, Calama, April 30, 1932, Archivo Histórico Nacional (herafeter AHN), Intendencia de Antofagasta, vol. 115.

34. "La Cía Andes rebaja sus sueldos," *El Progreso* (Chañaral), December 31, 1931.

35. Secretario Bienestar to Inspector General del Trabajo, Concepción, June 9, 1931, ARNAD, DT, vol. 245.

36. "Informe de datos recopilados y observaciones hechas en jira ordenada por el señor Ministro del Trabajo a la zona carbonífera," September 21, 1932, ARNAD, DT, vol. 306. For a history of coal mining communities and labor conflicts in the area, see Jody Pavilack, *Mining for the Nation: The Politics of Chile's Coal Communities from the Popular Front to the Cold War* (University Park: Pennsylvania State University Press, 2011).

37. Goicovic, "Crisis económica y repuesta social. Choapa 1929–1935," 128.

38. Intendente de Atacama to Ministro Bienestar Social, Copiapó, May 9, 1931 and "Acta de Visita," May 12, 1931, ARNAD, DT, vol. 244.

39. Brown et al., "Economía chilena 1810–1995."

40. Teodoro Schmidt, *Los trabajos públicos y la cesantía 1931–1934* (Santiago: Imprenta Nascimento, 1934).

41. Ernesto Neira Salas to Governor of La Unión, La Unión, May 2, 1931, ARNAD, DT, vol. 245.

42. Teodoro Schmidt, Santiago, May 2, 1931, ARNAD, DT, vol. 243.

43. Ernesto Neira Salas to Governor of La Unión, La Unión, May 2, 1931, ARNAD, DT, vol. 245.

44. Guillermo Cruz (Secretario de Bienestar Social) to Inspector General, Valdivia, May 25, 1931, DT, vol. 243.

45. Ministerio del Interior, Santiago, May 12, 1931, ARNAD, DT, vol. 245.

46. Chile, Cámara de Diputados, *Diario de sesiones*, September 1, 1931, 1835–36.

47. Ernesto Manríquez (Inspector del Trabajo), Osorno, May 31, 1931, ARNAD, DT, vol. 245.

48. Dirección General del Trabajo, Santiago, May 1931, ARNAD, DT, Informe Varios, 1931.

49. Fernando Ullmann (Secretario Bienestar Social) to Intendente, Puerto Montt, April 24, 1931, ARNAD, DT, vol. 243.

50. For an overview on the fall of Ibáñez, see Enrique Brahm García, "La visión de la diplomacia alemana sobre un momento de crisis del régimen de gobierno chileno: la caída del presidente Carlos Ibáñez del Campo en julio de 1931." *Revista de estudios histórico-jurídicos* no. 33 (2011): 487–510.

51. Intendente de Concepción, August 22, 1931, ARNAD, DT, vol. 251.

52. Chile, Cámara de Diputados, *Diario de sesiones*, August 31, 1931, 1793.

53. Leo de Bray, *Asistencia social y cesantía* (Santiago: Imprenta Universitaria, 1934), 15.

54. Loveman, *Chile*, 186–89.

55. Work relief programs were not new. In 1848, the French Second Republic established the *ateliers nationaux* to provide work to the unemployed in Paris and "guarantee work for all citizens." The French experiment lasted only a few months, but it provided an antecedent on how to organize work, register, place, and distrib-

ute the unemployed, and establish methods of control. Émile Thomas, *Histoire des ateliers nationaux* (Paris: M. Lévy frères, 1848), 19.

56. Bureau International du Travail, *Une politique des travaux publics*, Études et Documents, série C (chômage), no. 19 (1935), 155.

57. David F. Crew, *Germans on Welfare: From Weimar to Hitler* (New York: Oxford University Press, 1998), 191.

58. Edwin Amenta, *Bold Relief: Institutional Politics and the Origins of Modern American Social Policy* (Princeton, NJ: Princeton University Press, 1998).

59. Crew, *Germans in Welfare*, 195–97.

60. Schmidt, *Los trabajos públicos*.

61. Carlos Castillo (Secretario de Bienestar) to Inspección General del Trabajo, Valparaíso, June 23, 1931, ARNAD, DT, vol. 246.

62. "Chile Studies Plan to Aid Unemployment," *New York Times*, July 30, 1931, 9.

63. Schmidt, *Los trabajos públicos*, 7 and 14.

64. Schmidt, *Los trabajos públicos*, 7.

65. Before the crisis, at its peak in 1928–1929, public works projects employed about twenty-six thousand people. Schmidt, *Los trabajos públicos*.

66. Teodoro Schmidt to Macchiavello Varas, Santiago, January 3, 1932, ILO-BIT Archives (Geneva), Unemployment U 15/01/12.

67. Alcalde to Intendente, Isla de Maipo, December 15, 1932, AHN, Intendencia Santiago, vol. 837.

68. Manuel Concha Pedregal (Director General de Carabineros) to Minister of Interior, Santiago, October 30, 1931, ARNAD, DT, vol. 254.

69. Alfredo Espinoza Valenzuela to Minister of Interior, June 25, 1932, AHN, Intendencia Chiloé, vol. 118.

70. Chile, Cámara de Diputados, *Diario de sesiones*, August 31, 1931, 1792.

71. Chile, Cámara de Diputados, *Diario de sesiones*, September 15, 1931, 2146.

72. Secretaría Bienestar to Inspector General del Trabajo, Temuco, November 21, 1931, ARNAD, DT, vol. 256.

73. Chile, Cámara de Diputados, *Diario de sesiones*, January 12, 1931, 2791.

74. On rural workers and labor conditions in the countryside, see Brian Loveman, *Struggle in the Countryside: Politics and Rural Labor in Chile, 1919–1973* (Bloomington: Indiana University Press, 1976).

75. Chile, Cámara de Diputados, *Diario de sesiones*, January 12, 1932, 2790.

76. In December 1932, the Ministry of Interior (circular no. 79, December 1932) ordered all local authorities to inspect public works sites, classify the workforce according to occupation, and fire agricultural workers. Fearing a labor shortage during the harvest season, local landowners joined local authorities and visited worksites in their regions. This movement from the countryside to low-pay construction work also suggest how appalling working conditions in rural areas were at the time. See documents regarding "clasificación de obreros" in AHN, Intendencia Santiago, vol. 837.

77. Vicente Doren Arrate (Inspector) to Director Inspección del Trabajo, San Antonio, August 24, 1931, ARNAD, DT, vol. 251.

78. J. Melo Moreno (Inspector) to Secretario Bienestar Social, Illapel, October 7, 1931, ARNAD, DT, vol. 256.

79. Guillermo Cruz (Secretario Bienestar) to Ministerio de Bienestar Socail, Santiago, October 15, 1931, ARAND, DT, vol. 252.

80. Secretaría Bienestar, Temuco, November 21, 1931, ARNAD, DT, vol. 256.

81. Humberto Sotomayor to Inspector General del Trabajo, Calera, November 11, 1931, ARNAD, DT, vol. 255.

82. "Tesis del Buró Sudamericano de la Internacional Comunista sobre las grandes luchas revolucionarias del proletariado chileno," December 4, 1931, in *Chile en los Archivos Soviéticos 1922–1991*, vol. 2, ed. Olga Ulianova and Alfredo Riquelme (Santiago: Centro de Investigaciones Barros Arana, LOM Ediciones, 2005), 114–44.

83. On nitrate workers' politics, labor tradition, and migration, see Julio Pinto Vallejos, *Desgarros y utopías en la pampa salitrera: La consolidación de la identidad obrera en tiempos de la cuestión social, 1890–1923* (Santiago: LOM Ediciones, 2007).

84. Klubock, *Contested Communities*, 87.

85. Jaime Flores, "Un episodio de historia social de Chile 1934, Ranquil. Una revuelta campesina" (MA thesis, Universidad de Santiago de Chile, 1993).

86. Ernesto Boholavsky argues that while many of the conflicts that took place in the south of Chile at the time were local acts of resistance, they were also part of political and intellectual traditions. Ernesto Bohoslavsky, "Casa tomada. Pobreza, desempleo y asaltos populares en el sur de Chile en los '30," *Entrepasados. Revista de Historia*, no. 23 (2002): 101–22.

87. "Conclusiones del Comicio celebrado hoy en la Plaza Condell por la Federación Obrera de Chile," ARNAD, DT, vol. 252.

88. In July 1930, Ibáñez had formed the COSACH, a joint venture between the state and the largest and most modern nitrate companies. The COSACH planned to enhance nitrate's competitiveness in a volatile international market by modernizing the industry and incorporating new technology. Along with the rationalization of production, it established welfare departments to ensure fair working conditions. Although advertised as a solution to the nitrate crisis, the COSACH was unpopular and, for those who opposed General Ibáñez, a symbol of the government's corruption and "starvation policy." Tax cuts benefited foreign companies, and the new production methods required fewer workers, a controversial move in a time of economic crisis. In August 1931, the National Congress organized a commission to investigate the Ibáñez administration and its political and economic "crimes," including the formation of the COSACH. The commission accomplished little and ended in December 1931. Elizabeth Lira and Brian Loveman, *Los actos de la dictadura. Comisión investigadora 1931* (Santiago: DIBAM, 2006). On the COSACH,

see also Alfredo Houston, "Presentación hecha a la comisión investigadora de los actos de la dictadura por la compañía de salitre de Chile," Santiago, September 4, 1931; Cámara de Diputados, *Compañia de Salitre de Chile* (COSACH) (Santiago: El Imparcial, 1933); Julio Pérez Canto, "La industria salitrera y la intervención del Estado," *Revista universitaria* 5–6 (September 1933): 571–76.

89. Chile, Cámara de Diputados, *Diario de sesiones*, October 13, 1931, 209–15.

90. For a longer discussion of the project, see Chile, Cámara de Diputados, *Diario de sesiones*, January 20, 1932.

91. Ministerio de Hacienda, Law 5105, April 18, 1932.

92. Roberto Yunge to Minister of Social Welfare, Santiago, March 16, 1932, ARNAD, DT, vol. 297.

93. *Barómetro Económico*, no. 39, July 26, 1933, 1.

94. Chile, Cámara de Diputados, *Diaro de sesiones*, April 12, 1932, 5188.

95. Manuel Dinamarca, *La República Socialista: orígenes legítimos del Partido Socialista* (Santiago: Documentas/Estudio, 1987).

96. "Programa de acción económica inmediata," June 1932, in Julio César Jobet, *Historia del Partido Socialista* (Santiago: Documentas/Estudio, 1987), 69–74.

97. Paul Drake, *Socialism and Populism in Chile, 1932–52* (Urbana: University of Illinois Press, 1978), 76.

98. Carlos Dávila, "Chile no está arruinado. Plan de gobierno socialista de Dn. Carlos Dávila," in *El Presidente Dávila y la revolución de junio* (Santiago: Imprenta Socialista, n.d.).

99. Ministerio de Fomento, DL 228, "Crea la Dirección de Cesantía," *Boletín de leyes y decretos*, July 1932, 1656–59.

100. Ministerio de Fomento, DL 521, "Crea el Consejo de Economía Nacional," *Boletín de Leyes y decretos*, September 1931, 2811–23.

101. For a longer analysis of gold panning see Ángela Vergara, "'Busquemos oro': trabajo, lavaderos de oro y ayuda fiscal durante tiempos de crisis, Chile 1930–1936," *Revista Tiempo Histórico*, 6, no. 11 (2015): 75–92.

102. *Oro*, August 1932, 1.

103. "El Estado da amplias facilidades a los que se interesen por explotar lavaderos de oro." *Oro*, no. 1, August 1932, 6.

104. Víctor M. Navarrete, "Industrialización de los lavaderos de oro," *Boletín Minero* 54, no. 464 (December 1938), 1096–99.

105. Banco Central de Chile, *Séptima memoria anual*, 22; "40,000 hombres absorverá el trabajo de los lavaderos," *Oro*, no. 1, August 1932, 4.

106. Santiago, September 15, 1932, ARNAD, DT, vol. 309.

107. Vergara, "'Busquemos oro,'" 75–92.

108. Schmidt, *Los trabajos públicos*.

109. Jorge Rojas Flores, Alfonso Murua Olguín, and Gonzalo Rojas Flores, *La historia de los obreros de la construcción* (Santiago: Programa de Economía del Trabajo, 1993), 38–40.

110. Oelckers to Ministro Interior, Puerto Montt, September 10, 1932, AN, Intendencia Chiloé, vol. 118.

111. The total population of the province of Chiloé, which included the departments of Llanquihue, Ancud, and Castro, was 183,499 people.

112. Oelckers to Ministro Interior, Puerto Montt, November 24, 1932, AN, Intendencia Chiloé, vol. 118.

113. Oelckers to Ministro Interior, Puerto Montt, November 28, 1932, AN, Intendencia Chiloé, vol. 118.

114. Albert O. Hirschman, *Journeys toward Progress: Studies of Economic Policy-Making in Latin America* (Garden City, NY: Doubleday, 1965), 242.

115. Arturo Alessandri, October 5, 1932, in Ricardo Donoso, *Alessandri, agitador y demoledor. Cincuenta años de historia política de Chile*, vol. 2 (Santiago: Editorial Tierra Firme, 1954), 116 and 123.

116. There is a rich historiography on this period. Some scholars have focused on the civil-military relations, exploring how the Alessandri government strengthened the milicias republicanas, reshuffled military leaders, and reduced the military budget. Social and labor historians have highlighted the differences between the first and the second Alessandri administrations, paying attention to the repression of social, peasant, and labor movements and cases such as Ranquil (1934). Some important work on this period is the following: Carlos Maldonado, *La Milicia Republicana: historia de un ejército civil en Chile, 1932–1936* (Santiago: WUS, 1988); Jaime Rosenblitt, "El ministerio de Gustavo Ross y la configuración del estado nacional desarrollista," *Historia* 25 (1995–1996): 405–21; Verónica Valdivia Ortiz de Zárate, *Las Milicias Republicanas. Los civiles en armas, 1932–1936* (Santiago: Centro de Investigaciones Diego Barros Arana, 1992).

117. The Dirección General de Cesantía (created under the Socialist Republic) became the Departmento de Cesantía in November 1932.

118. In 1932, Argentina had also ordered a national census of the unemployed, making special emphasis on identifying Argentine and foreign workers. Claudia Daniel argues that Argentina's emphasis on nationality influenced how the government understood unemployment and viewed immigrant workers. Claudia Daniel, "De crisis a crisis: la invención de la desocupación en la Argentina," *Revista de Indias* 73, no. 257 (2013): 193–218.

119. Decreto Supremo 117, February 2, 1933, in *Revista del Trabajo*, nos. 2–3, February–March 1933, 27–29.

120. On the controversy over the irregularity see *El Mercurio*, "Sobre irregularidades denunciadas en el Departamento de Cesantía," March 21, 1933, and "Servicio de Cesantía," March 23, 1933.

121. Arturo Alessandri and Horacio Hevia, Decree 257, Santiago, March 22, 1932, ILO, Geneva.

122. Schmidt, *Trabajos públicos*, 15.

123. Ministerio del Trabajo, Decreto 257, ARNAD, Ministerio del Trabajo, Decretos, vol. 60, 1933.

124. Inspector Provincial del Trabajo to Inspector General, Temuco, May 18, 1933, AN, Intendencia de Cautín.

125. Amanda Labarca, "La reeducación del cesante," *El Mercurio*, March 21, 1933.

126. Mercedes Pinto, "Apuntes de viajes: el panorama de Santiago de Chile," *En viaje*, April 1933, 10–11.

127. "Memorial anual y general de los servicios de cesantía de Chile, durante el año 1936," ILO-BIT Archives (Geneva), Unemployment, U 10/01/12.

128. "Memorial anual y general de los servicios de cesantía de Chile, durante el año 1936," ILO-BIT Archives (Geneva), Unemployment, U 10/01/12.

129. Servicio de Cesantía, "Organizacion y funcionamentiento de los servicios de cesantía en Chile," c. 1938, ILO Archives, Geneva.

CHAPTER 4. SOCIAL ASSISTANCE AND THE RATIONALIZATION OF AID

1. In Argentina, government officials also used the term indistinctly, which, Claudia Daniel argues, reflected that they did not yet distinguish between the economically active and the not economically active population. Claudia Daniel, "De crisis a crisis: la invención de la desocupación en la Argentina," *Revista de Indias* 73, no. 257 (2013): 193–218.

2. República de Chile, Dirección General de Estadística, *Resultados del X censo de la población efectuado el 27 de noviembre de 1930* (Santiago: Dirección General de Estadística, 1931), XXXI.

3. Karin Alejandra Rosemblatt, *Gendered Compromises: Political Cultures and the State in Chile, 1920–1950* (Chapel Hill: University of North Carolina Press, 2000). In the case of Mexico, historians have also demonstrated the strong influence of ideas of family on state policy. Ann S. Blum, *Domestic Economies: Family, Work, and Welfare in Mexico City, 1884–1943* (Lincoln: University of Nebraska Press, 2009); Nichole Sanders, *Gender and Welfare in Mexico: The Consolidation of a Postrevolutionary State* (University Park: Pennsylvania State University Press, 2012).

4. Lizabeth Cohen, *Making a New Deal: Industrial Workers in Chicago, 1919–1939*, 2nd ed., (Cambridge: Cambridge University Press, 2008), 222.

5. Eric Strikwerda, *The Wages of Relief: Cities and the Unemployed in Prairie Canada, 1929–39* (Edmonton, Canada: Athabasca University Press, 2013).

6. On the impact of the crisis on the Province of Coquimbo, see Igor Goicovic, "Crisis económica y respuesta social. Choapa 1929–1935," *Notas históricas y geográficas* no. 4 (1993): 119–153.

7. Nicasio Greek Gross (Intendente), April 16, 1931, ARNAD, DT, vol. 242.

8. Nicasio Greek Gross (Intendente), April 22, 1931, ARNAD, DT, vol. 242.

9. La Serena, April 22, 1931, ARNAD, DT, vol. 242.

10. On the history of charity in Chile, see Macarena Ponce de León Atria, *Gobernar la pobreza. Prácticas de caridad y beneficencia en la ciudad de Santiago, 1830–1890* (Santiago: Editorial Universitaria, Centro de Investigaciones Diego Barros Arana, 2011).

11. Alcaldía, Coquimbo, April 17, 1931, ARNAD, DT, vol. 242.

12. Paul W. Drake, *The Money Doctor in the Andes: The Kemmerer Missions, 1923–1933* (Durham, NC: Duke University Press, 1989), see chapter 3.

13. Gabriel Palma, "Chile 1914–1935: de economía exportadora a substitutiva de exportaciones," *Estudios CIEPLAN* no. 12 (1984): 61–88.

14. Drake, *Money Doctor*, 82.

15. "Decreto que crea el Comité de Ayuda a los Cesantes," Decreto 640, August 19, 1931, *Revista del Trabajo* 1, no. 3 (September 1931).

16. Adriana Izquierdo, "Como se organizó la ayuda a los cesantes y la participación que a ella le corresponde a la escuela de servicio social Elvira Matte de Cruchaga" (thesis, Escuela de Servicio Social Elvira Matte de Cruchaga, July 1932), 4.

17. Intendencia, Valdivia, May 1932, ARNAD, DT, vol. 309 (1932).

18. Juan Carlos Gómez Leyton, "Crisis, hambre y socialismo: Chile 1931–1932," *Andes* no. 5 (1987): 132.

19. Izquierdo, "Como se organizó la ayuda," 4.

20. On the eve of the Great Depression, the Catholic Church was one of the most important and largest providers of social assistance. Since the late nineteenth century, the influence of social Catholicism and the papal encyclicals *Rerum Novarum* (1891) and *Quadragesimo Anno* (1931) had inspired some sectors of the church to expand social services such as orphanages, housing programs, and clinics. See Patricio Valdivieso, *Dignidad humana y justicia: la historia de Chile, la política social y el cristianismo, 1880–1920* (Santiago: Ediciones Universidad Católica, 2006).

21. Izquierdo, "Como se organizó la ayuda," 5.

22. Sociedad San Vicente de Paul, *Memoria de la Sociedad San Vicente de Paul, año 1931* (Santiago: Dirección General de Prisiones, 1932).

23. Donna J. Guy, *Women Build the Welfare State: Performing Charity and Creating Rights in Argentina, 1880–1955* (Durham, NC: Duke University Press, 2009).

24. Esteban Ivovich and Isauro Torres, *Orígenes y desarrollo de la beneficencia pública en Chile* (Santiago: Imprenta Universitaria, 1933); Rosemblatt, *Gendered Compromises*, 126.

25. "The Hospital and the Hospital System of Chile," *Modern Hospital* 11, no. 6 (December 1918): 440–44.

26. In 1932, the social workers employed outside Santiago were at Hospital Van Buren (Valparaíso), Juzgado de Menores (Valparaíso), Cía de Refinería de Azúcar (Viña del Mar), Departamento de Cesantía (Valparaíso), Municipalidad (Viña del Mar), and the offices of the Seguro Obligatorio in Iquique, Antofagasta, Concepción, and Valdivia. "Crónica," *Servicio Social* 4 (1932): 317–19.

27. For an overview of Santiago at the time, see Armando de Ramón, *Santiago de Chile. Historia de una sociedad urbana* (Santiago: Catalonia, 2015).

28. A former military man, Roberto Yunge had directed the Labor Department during the first years of the Ibáñez administration. In 1927, President Carlos Ibáñez del Campo fired the Ministry of Social Welfare and former collaborator José Santos Salas and purged the ranks of the ministry and the Labor Department. In 1928, Ibáñez accused Roberto Yunge of helping Santos to flee to Argentina and conspiring against the government, imprisoned and tortured him, and sent him to internal exile in Easter Island. Yunge returned to the Labor Department after the fall of Ibáñez in 1931. Arturo Olavarría Bravo, *Durante la tiranía* (Santiago: La Alianza, 1931), 8–9.

29. The information on the school is based on "El desarrollo del servicio social en Chile," *Revista del Trabajo*, July 1931; and Leo Cordemans (de Bray), "La escuela de servicio social de Santiago de Chile," *Servicio Social* 1–2 (1928): 8–41.

30. On the history of social work in Chile see María Angélica Illanes, *Cuerpo y sangre de la política: La construcción histórica de las visitadoras sociales, Chile 1887–1940* (Santiago: LOM, 2007).

31. Alice O'Connor, *Poverty Knowledge: Social Science, Social Policy, and the Poor in Twentieth-Century U.S. History* (Princeton, NJ: Princeton University Press, 2001).

32. Daniel J. Walkowitz, *Working with Class: Social Workers and the Politics of Middle-Class Identity* (Chapel Hill: University of North Carolina Press, 1999), 57–62.

33. Illanes, *Cuerpo y sangre*.

34. "Las visitadoras sociales y el problema de la cesantía," *Servicio Social* 3–4 (1931): 236–38.

35. "Las visitadoras sociales," 236–39.

36. I have analyzed the history of this identification practice in Ángela Vergara, "Identifying the Unemployed: Social Categories and Relief in Depression-Era Chile (1930–1934)," *Labor* 15, no. 3 (2018): 9–30.

37. "Las visitadoras sociales," 236–39.

38. Izquierdo, "Como se organizó la ayuda."

39. Leo de Bray, "El servicio social y los cesantes," *Servicio Social* 1 (1932): 106–7.

40. Inés Oliveira, "El servicio social en un centro de racionamiento," *Servicio Social* 4 (1932): 312–14.

41. Ministerio Bienestar Social Santiago, December 30, 1931, AN, Intendencia Concepción, vol. 1951.

42. Gobernador, "Memoria correspondiente al 3er trimester del año 1931," Lebu, October 1931, AN, Intendencia de Concepción, vol. 1950.

43. Constitución, April 8, 1932, ARNAD, DT vol. 300.

44. Gómez Leyton, "Crisis, hambre y socialismo," 131–32.

45. Santiago Wilson Hernández, "Nuestra crisis económica y la desocupación obrera" (thesis, Universidad de Chile, Santiago, 1933).

46. Izquierdo, "Como se organizó la ayuda."

47. María Benavides de la Cruz, "Psicología de los albergados," *Servicio Social* 3–4 (1931): 240–44.

48. Ministerio de la Propiedad Austral, Decreto con Fuerza de Ley no 68, March 24, 1931, AN, Intendencia de Concepción, vol. 1945.

49. Secretaría de Bienestar, April 25, 1931, ARNAD, DT, vol. 242.

50. Inspección General del Trabajo, December 24, 1931, ARNAD, DT, vol. 254.

51. To locate the shelters, I am using the *Plano completo de Santiago con todas la calles, pasajes, citées, etc. [material cartográfico]: confeccionado por orden del Sr. Prefecto de Policía Don Rafael Toledo Tagle* (Santiago: Sociedad Imprenta-Litografía Barcelona, n.d.).

52. Inspección General del Trabajo, October 1, 1931, ARNAD, DT, vol. 254. The list of Santiago's shelters and their population is also included in Gómez Leyton, "Crisis, hambre y socialismo," 132.

53. "Las visitadoras sociales y el problema de la cesantía," *Servicio Social* 3–4 (1931): 236–40.

54. María Benavides de la Cruz, "Psicología de los albergados," *Servicio Social* 3–4 (1931): 240–44.

55. In 1931, the society collected 8,130 pesos and purchased 410 blankets, 240 shirts, and 408 handkerchiefs. Sociedad San Vicente de Paul, *Memoria*, 6–7.

56. On maternity, childhood, and health care, see Jadwiga E. Pieper Mooney, *The Politics of Motherhood: Maternity and Women's Rights in Twentieth-Century Chile* (Pittsburgh: University of Pittsburgh Press, 2009) and María Soledad Zárate, *Dar a luz en Chile, s. XIX: de la ciencia de hembra a la ciencia obstétrica* (Santiago: DIBAM, Universidad Alberto Hurtado, 2007).

57. Blum, *Domestic Economies*, see chapters 4 and 5.

58. "Las visitadoras sociales y el problema de la cesantía," *Servicio Social* 3–4 (1931): 236–40.

59. Santiago, August 17, 1931, ARNAD, DT, vol. 248.

60. Luisa Pfau became one of the most emblematic advocates of maternal education and, in the 1950s, of family planning. María Soledad Zárate, "Al cuidado femenino. Mujeres y profesiones sanitarias, Chile, 1889–1950," in *Historia de las mujeres en Chile*, vol. 2, ed. Ana María Stuven and Joaquín Fermandois (Santiago: Taurus, 2014).

61. The Red Cross described the conflict in its letters to the Labor Department on December 4, 15, and 17 of 1931. A newspaper clip is included with the letter from December 15, ARNAD, DT, vol. 258.

62. Guillermo Bravo Acevedo, "La crisis de 1929 y los problemas de la sociedad urbana de Valparaíso," in *Valparaíso 1536–1985*, edited by Instituto de Historia (Valparaíso: Universidad Católica de Valparaíso, 1987), 171–83.

63. Carlos Castillo (Secretario Bienestar Social) to Intendente, Valparaíso, July 4, 1931, ARNAD, DT, vol. 246.

64. Inspector del Trabajo, Valparaíso, April 27, 1932, ARNAD, DT, vol. 300.

65. Inspección del Trabajo, Santiago, August 13, 1931, ARNAD, DT, vol. 252.

66. Inspector del Trabajo, Iquique, February 28, 1931, ARNAD, DT, vol. 302.

67. Temuco, August 27, 1931, ARNAD, DT, vol. 250.

68. Talca, September 17, 1931, ARNAD, DT, vol. 250.

69. Valdivia, June 5, 1931, ARNAD, DT, vol. 245.

70. Carabineros de Chile, Prefectura Concepción, Concepción, June 11, 1932, AN, Intendencia Concepción, vol. 1954.

71. Rufino Letelier Aravena (capitán) Santiago, September 28, 1931, ARNAD, DT, vol. 251.

72. "Tesis del Buró Sudamericano de la Internacional Comunista sobre las grandes luchas revolucionarias del proletariado chileno," December 4, 1931, in Olga Ulianova and Alfredo Riquelme, *Chile en los Archivos Soviéticos, 1922–1991*, vol. 2, *Komintern y Chile entre julio de 1931 y febrero de 1935 crisis e ilusión revolucionaria* (Santiago: Centro de Investigaciones Barros Arana, LOM Ediciones, 2005), 121.

73. Julio Bustamante (Intendente Santiago), Santiago, October 31, 1931, ARNAD, DT, vol. 254.

74. Julio Pinto argues that in the 1920s, public shelters became a space of radicalization and meeting point between nitrate workers and other Chilean workers. Julio Pinto Vallejos, *Desgarros y utopías en la pampa salitrera: La consolidación de la identidad obrera en tiempos de la cuestión social (1890–1923)* (Santiago: LOM Ediciones, 2007), chapter V.

75. Santiago, July 20, 1931, ARNAD, DT, vol. 246.

76. Temuco, December 21, 1931, ARNAD, DT 292.

77. Temuco, January 13, 1932, ARNAD, DT, vol. 292.

78. Valparaíso, July 5, 1930, ARNAD, DT, vol. 218.

79. Newspaper clip, n.d., AN, Intendencia de Cautín, vol. 417.

80. República de Chile, Dirección General de Estadística, *Resultados del X censo de la población efectuado el 27 de noviembre de 1930,* 2 vols. (Santiago: Imprenta Universo, 1931), volume *ocupaciones*, xi.

81. República de Chile, *Código del Trabajo* (Santiago: Editorial Nascimento, 1932), art. 2, p. 6.

82. Historians of the Latin American middle class have demonstrated the importance of status among white-collar employees and their efforts to maintain and reinforce their own class identity and differences from blue-collar workers. This distinction was also reinforced by labor legislation, which in places like Chile and Peru separated blue-collar from white-collar unions, creating two parallel systems of unionization, bargaining, social security, and rights. These differences did not prevent political alliances and collaborations, and in many places white-collar and blue-collar workers joined national labor movements. See David S. Parker, *The*

Idea of the Middle Class: White-Collar Workers and Peruvian Society, 1900–1950 (University Park: Pennsylvania State University Press, 1998); David S. Parker and Louise E. Walker, eds., *Latin America's Middle Class: Unsettled Debates and New Histories* (Lanham MD: Lexington Books, 2013). On Chile's middle-class and white-collar employees see Patrick Barr-Melej, *Reforming Chile: Cultural Politics, Nationalism, and the Rise of the Middle Class* (Chapel Hill: University of North Carolina Press, 2001); Azún Candina Polomer, *Clase media, estado y sacrificio: La Agrupación Nacional de Empleados Fiscales en Chile contemporáneo (1943–1983)* (Santiago: LOM Ediciones, 2013); and J. Pablo Silva, "The Origins of White-Collar Privilege in Chile: Arturo Alessandri, Law 6020, and the Pursuit of a Corporatist Consensus, 1933–1938," *Labor* 3, no. 1 (2006): 87–112.

83. Gobernación de Vallenar to Ministro Bienestar Social, Vallenar, November 15, 1931, ARNAD, DT, vol. 258.

84. Luis Miranda to Juan E. Montero, Santiago, November 18, 1931, ARNAD, DT, vol. 259.

85. Manuel to Ministerio Bienestar Social, November 1931, ARNAD, DT, vol. 257.

86. To the Intendente, Iquique, September 1931, ARNAD, DT, vol. 252

87. Unión de Empleados Públicos Cesantes o Ministro Bienestar Social from, December 1931, ARNAD, DT, vol. 257.

88. J. Pablo Silva argues that the approval of special legislation was a result of Alessandri's political and labor agenda. Silva, "Origins of White-Collar Privilege in Chile." For a legal discussion, see Benito de la Fuente Lillo, *Tema: Ley No 6020 que mejora la situacion económica de los empleados particulares* (Santiago: Dirección General de Prisiones, 1939).

89. Ministerio del Trabajo, Decreto 738, "Reglamento de Fondo Especial de Cesantía de la Ley número 6020," November 25, 1937. *Boletin de leyes y decretos*, vol. 107, November 1937.

90. Decreto 551, June 27, 1934, "Determina las funciones que corresponde a los Servicios de Cesantía," *Boletín de leyes y decretos*, vol. 103, June 1934.

91. "Comunicación del Ministro del Interior a los Intendentes y gobernadores," originally in *La Nación*, June 24, 1933, cited in *Boletín Médico de la Caja de Seguro Obligatorio* 19 (1935): 34.

92. Decreto 551, June 27, 1934, "Determina las funciones que corresponde a los Servicios de Cesantía," *Boletín de leyes y decretos*, vol. 103, June 1934.

93. "Informe final de la Comisión Asistencia del Niño al Supremo Gobierno, 1933," *Boletín Médico de la Caja de Seguro Obligatorio* 19 (1935): 36–40.

94. Jorge Rojas Flores, *Historia de la infancia en el Chile republicano: 1810–2010* (Santiago: Junta Nacional de Jardines Infantiles, 2010).

95. Chile, Servicios de Cesantía, "Memoria annual y general de los servicios de cesantía de Chile durante el año 1936," Santiago, January 1937, ILO archives, Unemployment (U) 10/01/12.

96. On the US social security legislation see Edwin Amenta, *Bold Relief: Institutional Politics and the Origins of Modern Social Policy* (Princeton, NJ: Princeton University Press, 1998); Jill Quadagno, *The Color of Welfare: How Racism Undermined the War on Poverty* (New York: Oxford University Press, 1995), chapter 1 on the New Deal.

97. The Servicio became the Dirección General de Auxilio Social under Pedro Aguirre Cerda, but despite his initial support, it had little power or influence. Rosemblatt, *Gendered Compromises*, chapter 4.

CHAPTER 5. PROTECTING CONSUMERS

1. Ministerio del Trabajo, Decreto Ley 15, June 11, 1932, *Boletín de leyes y decretos*, vol. CI, June 1932, 1220–22.

2. "Devolución de prendas en la Caja de Crédito Popular," *Sucesos*, June 1932.

3. Paul W. Drake, *Socialism and Populism in Chile, 1932–52* (Urbana: University of Illinois Press, 1978), 74–82.

4. Peter DeShazo, *Urban Workers and Labor Unions in Chile, 1902–1927* (Madison: University of Wisconsin Press, 1983), 64–67; Thomas C. Wright, "The Politics of Urban Provisioning in Latin American History," in *Food Politics and Society in Latin America*, ed. John C. Super and Thomas C. Wright (Lincoln: Nebraska University Press, 1985), 24–45.

5. Based on the *Sinópsis Estadística* and the *Anuario Estadístico* of the Dirección General de Estadística, Thomas Wright calculated that the index of the general cost of living increased from 100 in 1913 to 202 in 1925, and from 115.6 in 1928 to 244.8 in 1940 (with an index of 107 in 1930–1931). In Santiago, P.T. Ellsworth calculated that the average index of cost of living (March 1928=100) was 108 in 1930, 104 in 1931, 113 in 1932, and 140 in 1933. P. T. Ellsworth, *Chile: An Economy in Transition* (New York: Macmillan, 1945), 165; Thomas C. Wright, *Landowners and Reform in Chile: Landowners and Reform in Chile: The Sociedad Nacional de Agricultura, 1919–1940* (Urbana: University of Illinois Press, 1982), 106 and 112.

6. The sentence is taken from the Presidente del Comisariato de Concepción, November 2, 1932, AN, Intendencia de Concepción, vol. 1954.

7. Ministerio del Trabajo, Decreto Ley 520, August 30, 1932.

8. On consumer politics in the United States see Lizabeth Cohen, *A Consumers' Republic: The Politics of Mass Consumption in Postwar America* (New York: Vintage Books, 2003); Meg Jacobs, *Pocketbook Politics: Economic Citizenship in Twentieth-Century America* (Princeton, NJ: Princeton University Press, 2007); Emily LaBarbera-Twarog, *Politics of the Pantry: Housewives, Food, and Consumer Protest in Twentieth-Century America* (New York: Oxford University Press, 2017). On workers' consumption in Latin America, see Eduardo Elena, *Dignifying Argentina: Peronism, Citizenship, and Mass Consumption* (Pittsburgh: University of Pittsburgh Press, 2011); Natalia Milanesio, *Workers Go Shopping in Argentina: The Rise of Popular Consumer Culture* (Albuquerque: University of New Mexico Press, 2015).

There is a growing literature on food and consumption; see, for example, Enrique C. Ochoa, *Feeding Mexico: The Political Uses of Food since 1910* (Wilmington, DE: Scholarly Resources, 2000). For the case of Chile, see Rodrigo Henríquez, *En "estado sólido": políticas y politización en la construcción estatal. Chile, 1920–1950* (Santiago: Pontificia Universidad Católica de Chile, 2014).

9. "Price Control and Rationing in Foreign Countries during the War," *Monthly Labor Review* 61 (November 1945): 882–89.

10. Rafael Ioris, "'Fifty Years in Five' and What's in it for Us?' Development Promotion, Populism, Industrial Workers and Carestia in 1950s Brazil," *Journal of Latin American Studies* 44, no. 2 (2012): 261–84.

11. Moisés Poblete Troncoso, *El subconsumo en América del Sur, alimentos, vestuario y vivienda* (Santiago: Editorial Nascimento, 1946).

12. In 1935, the League of Nations and the Chilean government conducted the first nationwide investigation on nutrition. A group of nurses and social workers conducted 593 family surveys, a total of 3,383 people, from Iquique to Magallanes and from both rural and urban communities. They concluded that working families spent about 78 percent of their income on food. They also argued that most interviewed families had credit lines and debts with shopkeepers and were behind rents. Carlo Dragoni and Etienne Burnet, "L'Alimentation populaire au Chili: première enquête générale de 1935," *Apartado de la Revista chilena de higiene y medicina preventive* 1, no. 10–12 (1938): 407–611.

13. Gabriel Salazar, *Ferias libres: espacio residual de soberanía ciudadana* (Santiago: Ediciones Sur, 2003).

14. Nicomedes Guzmán, one of the most important literary voices of the 1938 generation, depicts the busy commercial life during pay day that included a myriad of street peddlers selling fruits, pastries, and candies as well as many opened bars, restaurants, music halls, and brothels. Nicomedes Guzmán, *La sangre y la esperanza* (Santiago: Orbe, 1943).

15. Mario Matus, *Crecimiento sin desarrollo. Precios y salarios reales durante el ciclo salitrero en Chile (1880–1930)* (Santiago: Editorial Universitaria, 2012), 281.

16. The situation was similar in other Latin American countries. In early twentieth-century Argentina, working families spent most of their income in food and rent, and even those basic needs were not always met. In Mexico, the Labor Department also studied and collected information on the cost of living. Milanesio, *Workers Go Shopping*; Ochoa, *Feeding Mexico*, 32.

17. Ministerio del Interior, Ley 4053 (del contrato de trabajo), September 29, 1924

18. Ministerio de Bienestar Social, *Memoria del Ministerio de Bienestar Social correspondiente al año 1929* (Santiago: La Ilustración, 1930), 236.

19. Guillermo del Fierro, Copiapó, March 14, 1930, ARNAD, DT, vol. 215.

20. Guillermo del Fierro, Copiapó, July 15, 1930, ARNAD, DT, vol. 218.

21. Inspección del Trabajo, La Serena, February 13, 1930, ARNAD, DT, vol. 214.

22. Like the crown in the English markets of the eighteenth century, workers demanded a fair price that could satisfy people's necessities. However, in the twentieth century, demands were not only about food but also about wages and social protections. E. P. Thompson, "The Moral Economy of the English Crowd in the Eighteenth Century," *Past and Present* 50 (1971): 76–136.

23. Juan Pezoa Arredondo (Mayor y Prefecto), Los Andes, September 1, 1930; Inspección del Trabajo, Los Andes, September 9, 1930, both documents in ARNAD, DT, vol. 220.

24. Ángela Vergara, "Precios y raciones: La Anaconda Copper Company en Chile entre 1932 y 1958," *Investigaciones de historia económica* 3 (2012): 135–43.

25. Ministerio Bienestar Social, Decreto 369, April 2, 1932, "Reglamento orgánico de la Inspección General del Trabajo," *Boletin de leyes y decretos*, April 1932, vol. 101, 862–92.

26. Henríquez, *En "estado sólido"*, 168–69.

27. Ministerio de Bienestar Social, Chile, *Memoria del Ministerio de Bienestar Social correspondiente al año 1928* (Santiago: La Ilustración, 1929), 282.

28. On the influence of social surveys and statistics on labor policy in the United States, see Alice O'Connor, *Poverty Knowledge: Social Science, Social Policy, and the Poor in Twentieth-Century U.S. History* (Princeton, NJ: Princeton University Press, 2001), chapter 1; Thomas A. Stapleford, *The Cost of Living in America: A Political History of Economic Statistics, 1880–2000* (New York: Cambridge University Press, 2009), see part I. In Latin America, Paulo Drinot has shown the influence of ideas of race on Peru's labor police, while Karin Rosemblatt has demonstrated how ideas of gender and class influenced Chile's Labor Department. Paulo Drinot, *The Allure of Labor: Workers, Race, and the Making of the Peruvian State* (Durham, NC: Duke University Press, 2011); Karin Alejandra Rosemblatt, *Gendered Compromises: Political Cultures and the State in Chile, 1920–1950* (Chapel Hill: University of North Carolina Press, 2000).

29. Corinne A. Pernet, "L'OIT et la question de l'alimentation en Amérique latine (1930–1950). Les problémes poses par la definition internationale des norms de niveau de vie," in *L'Organisation Internationale du Travail: origines, développment, avenir*, ed. Isabelle Lespinet-Moret and Vincent Viet (Rennes: Presses Universitaires, 2011), 167–78.

30. Wright, *Landowners and Reform in Chile*, 113–17. On food and nutrition policies in Chile, see Juan Carlos Yáñez Andrade,"Alimentación abundante, sana y barata: los restaurantes populares en Santiago (1936–1942)," *Cuadernos de Historia* no 45 (2016): 117–42.

31. Poblete Troncoso, *El subconsumo*, 187.

32. Thomas Lawrence, ARNAD, DT, Informe Varios [no vol.], 1931.

33. Gabriel Salazar, *Ferias libres: espacio residual de soberanía ciudadana* (Santiago: Ediciones Sur, 2003), 75–81; Richard Walter, *Politics and Urban Growth in Santiago, Chile 1891–1941* (Stanford, CA: Stanford University Press, 2005), 20 and 109–10.

34. Ministerio de Bienestar Social, DFL 226, May 15, 1931.

35. Ministerio Interior, D.F.L. 195, May 15, 1931.

36. Inspector del Trabajo, Talca, June 17, 1931, ARNAD, DT, vol. 245.

37. "Elqui, Informan sobre control expendio artículos alimenticios primera necesidad comercio local," 1931, ARNAD, DT, vol. 246.

38. "Artículos alimenticios," *El ideal* (Victoria), November 24, 1931, 2.

39. "La situación del mercado interno," *El comercio* (Viña del Mar), November 14, 1931, 4.

40. The increase in the cost of living was a permanent argument in most labor demands, both at the bargaining table and at the national level. Sentences such as "aumento de jornales basándose en la carestía de la vida" became standard in collective bargaining and demands for wage increase. The sentence is from Conciliación fábrica Paños Bío-Bío, April 1934, ARNAD, DT, vol. 456.

41. "El comicio público del domingo," *El laborista* (Temuco), November 11, 1931, 3.

42. "Nuestro pan cotidiano," *El laborista* (Temuco), November 14, 1931, 2; "El comercio del pueblo y el trust del Mercado," *El laborista* (Temuco), November 14, 1931, 3; "Sobre la carestía de la luz," *El laborista* (Temuco), November 18, 1931, 4; "Hambre," *El laborista* (Temuco), November 21, 1931, 1.

43. "Artículos de consumo," *El laborista* (Temuco), November 28, 1931, 1; "Comisio del hambre," *El laborista* (Temuco), November 28, 1931, 4.

44. "Comisio obrero en la Plaza Brasil," *El laborista* (Temuco), March 28, 1932, 3.

45. "El alza del precio de la leche," *El laborista* (Temuco), April 2, 1932, 3 and "Honradez en el comercio, castigo para el especulador," *El laborista* (Temuco), April 6, 1932, 2.

46. On foreign trade controls during the Depression, see Ellsworth, *Chile*, chapter IV.

47. "El abaratamiento de la carne," *El comercio* (Viña del Mar), November 26, 1931. Labor and social movements had historically opposed and mobilized against the tax on Argentine meat, seeing as one of the main factors increasing the price. See Sergio Grez Toso, "Una mirada al movimiento popular desde dos asonadas callejeras (Santiago, 1888–1905)," *Revista de Estudios Históricos*, vol. 3, no. 1 (2006): 158–93.

48. "Las subsistencias encarecen," *El empleado* (Valparaíso), no. 9, December 4, 1931, 1.

49. "Abajo los monopolios," *El empleado* (Valparaíso), December 23, 1931, 7; "Alerta con los monopolios," *El empleado* (Valparaíso), January 8, 1932, 5; "Los

especuladores" and "Debería fusilarse," *El empleado* (Valparaíso), April 1, 1932, 1; "La UECH protesta de la odiosa especulación," *El empleado* (Valparaíso), April 8, 1932, 8.

50. Elizabeth Lira and Brian Loveman, *Poder judicial y conflictos políticos (Chile-1925–1958)* (Santiago: LOM Editores, 2014), chapter 1; Eduardo Ortiz, *La gran depresión, 1929. Impacto en Chile* (Santiago: Liberalia, 2014), see chapter III.

51. Banco Central de Chile, *Séptima memoria anual presentada a la superintendencia de bancos. Año 1932* (Santiago: Dirección General de Prisiones, 1933), 17 and 23; Manuel Marfán, "Políticas reactivadoras y recesión externa: Chile, 1929–1938," *Estudios CIEPLAN*, no. 12 (1984): 89–119.

52. Decree 1,167 (Ministerio de Hacienda) authorized Santiago's city government to set the price for six imported products (rice, oil, coffee, tea, yerba mate, and paraffin) and four national products (oatmeal, noodles, lard, candles). Ministerio de Hacienda, Decreto 1,167, Santiago, April 15, 1932, *Boletín de leyes y decretos*, April 1932, book 101, 780–81.

53. "Un decreto que no se cumple," *La opinión* (Putaendo), April 10, 1932, 1.

54. Alcalde Municipal, Coronel, March 21, 1932, AN, Intendencia Concepción, vol. 1954.

55. Verdejo spoke from the perspective of a lower-class Chilean. He had no stable job, lived in a tenement house, and his cousin Policarpo was working in the gold panning industry.

56. "En estos tiempos de crise / que ya los llega a la nuca / sube el aceite, el café, / sube el pan, sube el azuca; / hasta pederse de vista, / ¡que embromar! Sube el molío / sube la luz, sube el gas, / aunque el gas siempre ha subío. / Suben de precio la leche, / y a veces se sube sola, / y suben los aeroplanos / y sube la batahola." "Cosas de Verdejo," *Topaze* (Santiago) May 11, 1932, no. 40, n.p.

57. The first housing law was from 1906 (Ley de Habitaciones para obreros, Law 1,838). The Congress introduced modifications to the law in 1909, 1912, and 1916. In 1925, Decreto Ley 308 created a Consejo de Habitación Barata). See Moisés Poblete Troncoso and Oscar Álvarez Andrews, *Legislación social obrera chilena. (recopilación de leyes y disposiciones vigentes sobre el trabajo y la previsión social)* (Santiago: Imprenta Santiago, 1924), 27–50.

58. Rodrigo Hidalgo, *La vivienda social en Chile y la construcción del espacio urbano en el Santiago del siglo XX* (Santiago: DIBAM, 2005).

59. In 1925, Housing Tribunales (Tribunales de la Vivienda) were established to handle tenants' disputes in regards to rent and housing conditions. In 1927, as part of a larger reform of labor courts, these housing tribunals merged with labor courts. Hidalgo, *la vivienda social*.

60. "Propietarios sin corazón," *El empleado* (Valparaíso), October 30, 1931. See also "Los cánones de arrendamiento," *El empleado* (Valparaíso), October 16, 1931, 6.

61. Santiago, December 24, 1931, ARNAD, DT, vol. 305.

62. Nicky Antonio Cerón Blau, "Por una vivienda digna de ser ocupada por seres humanos: Movimiento Social Arrendatario: dinámicas asociativas y de politización popular (1914–1925)" (thesis, Universidad de Chile, 2017).

63. Santiago, October 2, 1931, ARNAD, DT, vol. 251.

64. Santiago, September 11, 1931, ARNAD, DT, vol. 251.

65. Liga de Defensa de Arrendatarios, Antofagasta 1932, ARNAD, DT, vol. 251.

66. Ministerio de Bienestar Social, DF 290, "Reglamento de la Ley 5,001," *Boletín de Leyes y Decretos*, May 1932, vol. 101, 1046–55.

67. Héctor Behm Rosas, *El problema de la habitación mínima* (Santiago: Leblanc, Stanley y Urzúa, 1939), 20.

68. Roberto Yunge, "Sobre habitaciones de cesantes," *Revista del Trabajo*, May–June 1932, 48.

69. Santiago, February 17, 1932, ARNAD, DT, vol. 295.

70. Poblete Troncoso, *El subconsumo*, 252.

71. Constantino was the older brother of Santiago Macchiavello Varas, also a lawyer, a prolific writer, and member of the Radical Party. Santiago was an elected congressman between 1930 and 1934.

72. Constantino Macchiavello Varas, *Contribución al estudio de nuestro problema de la carestía de la vida frente al problema de la subsistencia* (Santiago: Imprenta Walter Gnadt, 1933).

73. Macchiavello, *Contribución al estudio*, 79.

74. Enrique Zañartu Prieto, *Hambre, miseria e ignorancia* (Santiago: Editorial Ercilla, 1933). See also Cesar Fuenzalida, *¿Hemos vencido la crisis?* (Santiago: Editorial Nascimento, 1934); Gregorio Guerra, *Desocupación y miseria* (Santiago: Editorial Problemas, 1937).

75. Wright, *Landowners and Reform in Chile*, 109–11.

76. Poblete Troncoso, *El subconsumo*, 382.

77. Wright, *Landowners and Reform in Chile*, 111.

78. Ministerio de Bienestar Social, Ley 5,125, May 17, 1932.

79. Ministerio de Bienestar Social, Decreto 621, June 1, 1932. See also Ministerio de Bienestar Social, "Normas generales para los consejos departamentales y sub-consejos," June 1, 1932, AN, Intendencia de Concepción, vol. 1951.

80. Roberto Fuentes, gobernador de Tomé, AN, Intendencia Concepción, vol. 1943.

81. "La especulación del azúcar," *Adelante* (Copiapó), June 11, 1932, 3.

82. "Sesión del consejo departamental de precios," June 14, 1932, AN, Intendencia Antofagasta, vol. 88 (1930).

83. Congreso Obrero to Consejo Departamental de Precios, Antofagasta, June 19, 1932, AN, Intendencia Antofagasta, vol. 88.

84. Decreto Ley 520: "Crea el comisariato general de subsistencias y precios." *Diario Oficial de la República de Chile*, August 31, 1932, 2485–87.

85. Henríquez, *En "estado sólido,"* 213–24.

86. Ellsworth, *Chile*, 81.

87. There is not much information on who was behind this pamphlet. The police arrested the principal of the local school. El Comité Provisiorio, "A los trabajadores de Arauco," reported by the police on December 18, 1932, AN, Intendencia Concepción, vol. 1964.

88. Following Daniel Soto's complaints, the Intendencia of Concepción ordered a complete investigation and interviewed several witnesses. Coelemu, October 15, 1932, AN, IC, vol. 1954.

89. For an overview of consumer groups, see Jorge Guisti, "Participación popular en Chile: antecedentes para su estudio, las JAP," *Revista Mexicana de Sociología* 37, no. 3 (1975): 767–88. On women organizations and consumer activism, see Rosemblatt, *Gendered Compromises*, 116–21. On labor and increase in the cost of living in Chile, see Thomas M. Klubock, *Contested Communities: Class, Gender, and Politics in Chile's El Teniente Copper Mine, 1904–1951* (Durham, NC: Duke University Press, 2000), 226–32; Jody Pavilack, *Mining for the Nation: The Politics of Chile's Coal Communities from the Popular Front to the Cold War* (University Park: Pennsylvania State University Press, 2011), 259–65.

90. "Salario mínimo," *Nuestra voz* (Santiago), March 18, 1932, 3; and "Igualdad de salarios para ambos sexos," *Nuestra voz* (Santiago), June 3, 1932, 3.

91. "Concentración de presidentes de la Confederación de Profesores," *Ariel* (Santiago), October 27, 1932, n.p.

92. Dirección del Trabajo, Decreto 276, September 12, 1932.

93. Inspección Provincia del Maule, Memoria Anual, 1932, ARNAD, DT, vol. 372.

94. Julio Inostroza Quiroz, Inspector Provincial del Trabajo, Linares, December 10, 1932, ARNAD, DT, vol. 374.

95. Since the late 1920s, the International Labor Organization had supported the establishment of an adequate living wage and encouraged national governments to develop effective mechanisms to fix wages, especially in the case of "classes of unfavourably situated workers." ILO, C026—Minimum Wage-Fixing Machinery Convention, 1928 (no 26). For a larger discussion on the convention see International Labour Organisation, *Report on Minimum Wage Fixing Machinery* (ILO: Geneva, 1928). It was in Mexico, however, that minimum wage legislation had made more progress in the Americas. The Mexican constitution of 1917 had established the principle of minimum wage. "Minimum Wage Cases in Some Mexican States," *International Labor Review*, vol. 22, no. 1 (1939): 70–77. For a discussion of the Mexican experience and other American countries see International Labour Organisation, Second Labour Conference of the American States which Are Members of the International Labour Organisation, "Minimum Wage Regulation in the Countries of America," Havana, Cuba, November 1939.

96. Inspección del Trabajo, Circular 25, May 29, 1933, cited in Inspección del Trabajo de Cautín, Temuco, October 8, 1934, ARNAD, DT, vol. 475.

97. While Latin American countries such as Chile, José Méndez wrote in 1950 in the ILO review, "treat the cost of living as the main factor to be taken into account in fixing wages, though they differ as to what should be included in the concept of a 'living wage.'" Méndez, "Minimum Wages in Latin America," *International Labour Review* (Geneva) 62, no. 2 (1950): 116–40.

98. Memoria Inspección del Trabajo de Valdivia, Valdivia, April 12, 1933, ARNAD, DT, vol. 453.

99. Dragoni and Burnet, "L'Alimentation populaire."

100. Juan Carlos Yáñez, "Por una legislación social en Chile: El movimiento de los panaderos (1888–1930)," *Historia* vol. 41, no. 2 (2008): 495–532; Henríquez, *En "estado sólido"*, 194–204.

101. It was also common that workers slept in the bakery, making it even harder to prove that they were actually working at night. In the legal case *Lorenzo Rosselot v. Inspección del Trabajo*, the labor inspector had found sixteen workers at 3:00 AM inside Rosselot's bakery. While Rosselot argued that they were not in the work area but sleeping in a different room, the Labor Department presented evidence that the workers were wearing their work clothes. The Supreme Court ruled that having people sleeping in the workplace violated the law prohibiting night work and fined the employer. *Gaceta de los Tribunales* 1926, Second Semester, 308–11.

102. Inspección General del Trabajo, Cautín, Temuco October 8, 1934, ARNAD, DT, vol. 475.

103. Labor union to minister of labor, Viña Casa Blanca, Lontué, January 11, 1933. ARNAD, DT, 373.

104. Loveman, *Struggle in the Countryside,* 73, 99–100, and 142–44.

105. The joint board system failed to fix the minimum wage in the countryside, and, in 1953, the Ministry of Labor established special regulations for a mandatory minimum salary for agricultural workers. Héctor Humeres, *Patrones y obreros* (Santiago: Editorial Jurídica de Chile, 1954), 76–79.

106. Ministerio de Fomento, Ley 5,350, article 48 and artículo transitorio, in Contraloria General de la Republica, *Recopilación de leyes*, vol. 20 (Santiago: Imprenta Nascimento, 1934), 223–38.

107. Inspección del Trabajo, Antofagasta, March 17, 1934, ARNAD, DT, vol. 457.

108. Rosemblatt, *Gendered Compromises*, 63–71.

109. "Acta reunión mensual de directorios de las organizaciones sindicales," Iquique, October 17, 1934.

110. Partido Radical Independiente, Iquique, May 31, 1934. ARNAD, DT, vol. 465.

111. "Salario familiar," Resolución XIII, in *Conferencia del trabajo de los estados de América miembros de la Organización Internacional del Trabajo. Santiago de Chile, 2 al 14 de enero de 1936. Actas de las sesiones* (Geneva: ILO, 1936), 388.

112. Ibáñez Aguila's intervention. International Labour Organisation, *Record of Proceedings: Second Labour Conference of the American States which Are Members of the International Labour Organisation, Havana (Cuba), 1939* (Montreal: ILO, 1941), 109–10.

CHAPTER 6. INCOMPLETE REFORMS

1. P. T. Ellsworth, *Chile: An Economy in Transition* (New York: Macmillan, 1945), chapter 2; Gabriel Palma, "From an Export-Led to an Import-Substituting Economy: Chile 1914–1939," in *An Economic History of Twentieth-Century Latin America*, vol. 2, ed. Rosemary Thorp (Oxford: Palgrave, 2000), 43–70.

2. Eduardo Saraos, "De como nació el Comité de Defensa de la Industria Metalúrgica," *Músculo* (Santiago), August 17, 1940, 1 and 10.

3. "Una escuela industrial nocturna para los obreros," *Músculo* (Santiago) May 21, 1941, 5; "Calificación industrial de la juventud laboriosa," *Músculo* (Santiago), May 21, 1942, 4.

4. Ricardo Ffrench-Davis, Oscar Muñoz, José Miguel Benavente, and Gustavo Crespi, "The Industrialization of Chile during Protectionism, 1940–82," in *An Economic History of Twentieth-Century Latin America*, vol. 3, ed. Rosemary Thorp (Oxford: Palgrave, 2000), 114–53.

5. Brian Loveman, *Chile: The Legacy of Hispanic Capitalism*, 3rd ed. (New York: Oxford University Press, 2001), chapter 8.

6. On the labor movement during the Popular Front, see Jody Pavilack, *Mining for the Nation: The Politics of Chile's Coal Communities from the Popular Front to the Cold War* (University Park: Pennsylvania State University Press, 2011); Sebastián Leiva Flores, "Vida y trabajo de la clase obrera chilena. Los trabajadores textiles y metalúrgicos entre las décadas de 1930 y 1960" (PhD diss., Universidad de Santiago, 2018). On rural workers, see Brian Loveman, *Struggle in the Countryside: Politics and Rural Labor in Chile, 1919–1973* (Bloomington: University of Indiana Press, 1976).

7. A. A. Dawson, "The United Nations and Full Employment," *International Labour Review* 67, no. 5 (May 1953): 401–33.

8. William H. Beveridge, *Full Employment in a Free Society (a summary)* (London: New Statesman and Nation and Reynolds News, 1944), 10 and 18. This is a summary of his longer report.

9. John M. Keynes, *The General Theory of Employment, Interest, and Money* (London: MacMillan, 1936).

10. International Labour Organisation, "Declaration Concerning the Aims and Purposes of the International Labour Organisation" (Declaration of Philadelphia), May 1944.

11. "National Action to Promote Full Employment," *International Labour Review* 59, no. 6 (June 1949): 684–98.

12. For an overview of Latin America during World War II, see David Rock, ed., *Latin America in the 1940s: War and Postwar Transitions* (Berkeley: University of California Press, 1994).

13. Marcelo Rougier and Juan Odisio, *Argentina será industrial o no cumplirá sus destinos. Las ideas sobre el desarrollo nacional (1914–1980)* (San Martín, Argentina: Imago Mundi, 2017), 91–93.

14. Ministerio del Trabajo, *La Conferencia Internacional del Trabajo de Nueva York* (Santiago: Imprenta Universitaria 1942), 52.

15. By the early 1940s, copper, controlled by US companies, was Chile's most important export commodity. Between 1942 and 1946, the US government fixed the price of copper (including copper produced in Chile) at 12 cents per pound. After the United States lifted price controls, the price for copper almost doubled. Clark W. Reynolds, "Development Problems of an Export Economy: The Case of Chile and Copper," in *Essays on the Chilean Economy*, ed. Markos Mamalakis and Clark Winton Reynolds (Homewood, IL: Richard D. Irwin, 1965), 242.

16. Decreto Supremo 56 (January 1942), cited by Clara Williams de Junge, "Organización del Departamento Nacional de Colocaciones," *Servicio Social* 17, no. 2 (1943): 14–18.

17. Ángela Vergara, "Cuando los obreros no trabajan: una aproximación a la historia del desempleo en América Latina," in *Trabajadores y sindicatos en Latinoamérica: conceptos, problemas y escalas de análisis*, eds. Silvia Simonassi y Daniel Dicósimo (San Martín, Argentina: Imago Mundi, 2018), 3–18.

18. Ministerio de Hacienda, "Ley 6528: Reorganiza los servicios del trabajo" (February 10, 1940).

19. Ministerio del Interior, "Decreto 6" (August 26, 1942).

20. Williams de Junge, "Organización del Departamento Nacional de Colocaciones."

21. Juan Antonio Ríos, *Mensaje de S.E. el Presidente de la República don Juan Antonio Ríos en la apertura de las sesiones ordinarias del Congreso Nacional: 21 de mayo de 1943* (Santiago: n.p., 1943), 256–57.

22. The Dirección General de Estadística included data from the Placement Offices in *Estadística Chilena* (1928–1960) and sometimes (e.g., 1948, 1949) estimated the number of people who did not register (*cesantía no-inscrita*).

23. Ministerio del Trabajo, "Decreto 1,184: Reglamento orgánico general de los servicios del trabajo" (December 10, 1942), *Boletín de leyes y decretos*, December 1942, 3182–490.

24. My description of placement services in the 1940s is based on Alberto Aranda Ocaranza, "La desocupación obrera" (thesis, Universidad de Chile, 1951); René Carvallo Montenegro, "El servicio de colocación pública en Chile y la colocación pública en los principales países" (thesis, Universidad de Chile, 1947); and

Herminia Navarro Lane, "Algunos aspectos de la desocupación en Chile" (thesis, Universidad de Chile, 1945).

25. Law 7747 approved emergency measures to confront the economic problems caused by World War II. Some of these measures included rent control, rationing of imports and raw materials, and expansion of price controls. The law also mentioned the design of a new plan for agricultural development and reformed the Comisariato de Precios y Subsistencias (renamed Consejo Superior de Subsistencias y Precios). Ministerio de Hacienda, "Ley 7,747 (Ley económica)" (December 24, 1943).

26. Ministerio del Trabajo, "Reglamento de artículo 27, letra (B) de la Ley No 7,747 que se refiere a reducción de faenas y paralizacion de empresas" (January 20, 1945).

27. Corte Suprema, "Ríos, Orlando y otros (recurso de queja)," August 8, 1949, *Revista de Derecho y Jurisprudencia* 47, nos. 1–2 (March/April 1950): 20–24, 20.

28. Decreto 50, "Exceptúa faenas que señala, de las obligaciones impuestas por los Nos. 1 y 2 del Decreto 98" (January 7, 1949); Decree 335, "Exceptúa a la Fundición Nacional de Paipote Ltda., de la obligación que le impone el art. 86 del Código del Trabajo para deshauciar obreros en las faenas de construcción e instalación de la fundición que se indica" (April 6, 1949); and "Exceptúa a la Empresa Nacional de Electricidad S.A." (July 5, 1949). These decrees are included in *Repertorio de legislación y jursiprudencia chilenas* (Santiago: Editorial Jurídica, 1958), 150–54.

29. Pedro R. Davis, *Jurisprudencia del trabajo* (Santiago: Carlos E. Gibbs A. Editor, 1963), 78.

30. The case went first to the Corte del Trabajo of Concepción (November 1945) and then to the Supreme Court (January 1946). The supreme court argued that women were working illegally at night and, therefore, had to be fired. The company, the court argued, had also made some efforts to protect workers including paying the dismissed women a compensation equivalent to fifteen day of work (half of what the law required in cases of collective dismissal) and firing women whose husbands worked at the company. Corte Suprema, "Henríquez y otras contra Fábrica de Loza Penco," January 9, 1946, *Revista de Derecho y Jurisprudencia* 43, nos. 1–2 (March/April 1946): 45–46.

31. Corte Suprema, "Ríos, Orlando, y otros" (recurso de queja)," August 8, 1949, *Revista de Derecho y Jurisprudencia* 47, nos. 1–2 (March/April 1950): 20–24.

32. Ángela Vergara, *Copper Workers, International Business, and Domestic Politics in Cold War Chile* (University Park: Pennsylvania State University Press, 2008), 74–76.

33. William H. Beveridge, *Social Insurance and Allied Services* (London: His Majesty's Stationary Office, 1942).

34. International Labour Organization, *Conference of the International Labour Organisation, New York and Washington DC 1941* (ILO: Montreal, 1941), 12.

35. Gøsta Espin-Anderson, *The Three Worlds of Welfare Capitalism* (Cambridge: Polity, 1990), see chapter 1.

36. Desmond King, *Actively Seeking Work? The Politics of Unemployment and Welfare Policy in the United States and Great Britain* (Chicago: University of Chicago Press, 1995).

37. *Final Act of the Inter-American Conference on Problem of War and Peace, Mexico City 1945* (Washington, DC: Pan American Union, 1945). See resolutions XLVIII, LXI, and LVIII.

38. Third Conference of American States Members of the International Labour Organization, Mexico City, April 1946, *Director Report* (Montreal: ILO, 1946).

39. Luis Orlandini, "Orientaciones sobre la seguridad social," *Mensaje* 12, no. 123 (1960): 545–53.

40. México, Secretaría del Trabajo y Previsión Social, "Ley de Seguro Social," *Diario Oficial* (Mexico), January 19, 1943.

41. N. Bonino and García Repetto, "Protección frente al desempleo estacional y bolsas de trabajo en Uruguay (1944–1979)," *Revista uruguaya de historia económica* 3, no. 4 (2013): 46–55.

42. According to Moisés Poblete Troncoso, the number of active insured people in the CSO in 1947 was between 971,697 and 1,145,736. Moisés Poblete Troncoso, *El derecho del trabajo y la seguridad social en Chile* (Santiago: Editorial Jurídica, 1949), 138–39.

43. For an overview of Chile's social security system see Rodrigo Henríquez, *En "estado sólido": políticas y politización en la construcción estatal, Chile 1920–1950* (Santiago: Pontificia Universidad Católica de Chile, 2014), see chapter IV; Francisca Rengifo, "Desigualdad e inclusión: la ruta del estado de seguridad social chileno, 1920–1970," *Hispanic American Historical Review* 97, no. 3 (2017): 485–521. For a detailed description of the different funds and legislation see: Alfredo Gaete Berríos, *La seguridad social* (Santiago: Prensas de la Universidad de Chile, 1946) and Poblete Troncoso, *El derecho del trabajo*, chapter VI.

44. Pedro Aguirre Cerda, *Mensaje de S.E. el Presidente de la República en la apertura de las sesiones ordinarias del Congreso Nacional, 21 de mayo de 1941*, 261–62.

45. Salvador Allende Gossens, *La realidad medico-social chilena* (Santiago: Ministerio de Salubridad, Previsión y Asistencia Social, 1939).

46. Consejo Nacional de Economía, *Informe de la comisión de trabajo, salarios y prevision social del Consejo Nacional de Economía: sobre el proyecto de reforma a las leyes 4054 y 4055*, (Santiago: n.p., 1947).

47. Bernardo Araya, *Una CTCH unida combatiendo en defensa de la clase obrera y del pueblo: II Conferencia Nacional de la Confederación de Trabajadores de Chile* (Santiago: CTCH, 1946).

48. After the economic crisis of the early 1930s, there was a rapid increase in unionization. The number of legal labor unions increased from 421 in 1932 to 1,888 in 1940. A legal labor union (*personalidad jurídica*) not only represented workers in labor negotiations and collective bargaining but also offered a wide

range of services to its members. Labor unions offered benefits to members such as medical and dental care and sponsored social and sport events. In addition, some unions provided cash subsidies in case of sickness, death, and other emergencies. James O. Morris and Roberto Oyaneder, *Afiliación y finanzas sindicales en Chile, 1932–1959* (Santiago: INSORA, 1962).

49. *La voz del sindicato Weiss* (Valdivia), no. 1, 2, November 4, 1939, 1.

50. Poblete Troncoso, *El derecho del trabajo,* 29–30.

51. Metal and copper workers successfully expanded severance pay through collective bargaining. See: Leiva Flores, "Vida y trabajo de la clase obrera chilena"; Vergara, *Copper Workers.*

52. The Department of Social Aid originated in the Unemployment Board. In April 1940, President Pedro Aguirre Cerda gave the Unemployment Board the status of a permanent department, the Unemployment Department (Dirección General de Cesantía), and placed it under the direct authority of the Ministry of Interior. Its focus on unemployment faded, and the department turned almost exclusively to serving the indigent. In 1942, the Ministry of Interior merged the department with the service of workers' restaurants and shelters (Servicio de Restaurantes Populares y Hospederías) and formed a Department of Social Aid (Dirección General de Auxilio Social). In 1947, the Dirección General de Auxilio Social passed to the presidency and in 1948 was renamed Servicio Social del Trabajo. In the mid-1950s, following the recommendations of the Klein-Saks mission, the office was relocated to the Ministry of Interior. In 1953, it became the Servicio Nacional de Bienestar y Auxilio Social and, in 1959, the Dirección de Auxilio Social. For a summary of these administrative changes, see Germán Urzúa Valenzuela, *Evolución de la administración pública chilena* (Santiago: Editorial Jurídica, 1970), 165 and 220–23.

53. The project is included in Navarro Lange, "Algunos aspectos de la desocupación en Chile," 33–35.

54. Navarro Lange, "Algunos aspectos de la desocupación en Chile," 35.

55. Navarro Lange, "Algunos aspectos de la desocupación en Chile," 54.

56. Hugo Martini M., *Estudio jurídico práctico del auxilio de cesantía* (Santiago: Editorial Universitaria, 1961).

57. Gaete Berríos, *La seguridad social,* 136.

58. Salvador Ocampo, *Diario de sesiones del Senado,* October 7, 1952, 1924.

59. Corte de Apelaciones de La Serena, "Contra José de la C. Miranda—vagancia," *Gaceta de los tribunales,* 1942 (first semester), 208–10.

60. "Social Services in Chile," *Studies and Reports, Series M (Social Insurance)* (Geneva), no. 11 (1933): 823–44.

61. Ministerio del Trabajo, Decreto 551, "Determina las funciones que corresponde a los Servicios de Cesantía," (June 27, 1934), *Boletín de leyes y decretos,* book 103 (June 1934): 1816–18.

62. Comisión de Cesantía, "Memoria anual y general de los Servicios de Cesantía durante el año de 1936," ILO Archives, Unemployment Files 10/01/12.

63. Juan Carlos Yáñez Andrade, "'Alimentación abundante, sana y barata': los restaurantes populares en Santiago (1936–1942)," *Cuadernos de Historia* (Santiago), no. 45 (2016): 117–42. Other Latin American countries established similar programs to feed workers and expand modern ideas of food consumption and nutrition. See for example: Paulo Drinot, "Food, Race, and Working-Class Identity: *Restaurantes Populares* and Populism in 1930s Peru," *Americas* 62, no. 2 (2005): 245–70.

64. Elena Yávar, "Dirección General de Auxilio Social del Estado. Servicio Social," *Servicio Social* 17, no. 2 (1943): 31–35.

65. These changes can be followed through the following laws and decrees: Ministerio Interior, Decreto 1779 (April 26, 1940), *Boletín de leyes y decretos* (April 1940): 893–96; Ministerio Interior, Decreto 6 / 4,817 (September 9, 1942); Ministerio Interior, Decreto 2,596 (April 27, 1948); Ministerio del Interior, DFL 186 (August 5, 1953); Ministerio del Interior, DFL 20 (November 20, 1959). For a summary of these administrative changes, see Urzúa Valenzuela, *Evolución de la administración pública chilena*, 165 and 220–23. For an overview of the service and its responsibility in 1960, see Ministerio de Hacienda, Chile, *Manual de organización del gobierno de Chile* (Santiago: Guttenberg, 1960), 79–81.

66. Ríos, *Mensaje de S.E.*, 18–20.

67. Karin Alejandra Rosemblatt, *Gendered Compromises: Political Cultures and the State in Chile, 1920–1950* (Chapel Hill: University of North Carolina Press, 2000), 124–25 and 135–40.

68. Navarro Lane, "Algunos aspectos de la desocupación en Chile," 31.

69. Elena Yávar, "Iniciación de desarrollo del Servicio en el actual servicio denominado Servicio Social del Trabajo," *Servicio Social* 45, no. 1 (1950): 41–44.

70. Rosemblatt, *Gendered Compromises*,135.

71. "Círculo de estudios sociales," *Servicio Social*, vol. 22, 1 (1948): 69–77.

72. "Informe sobre el Servicio Nacional de Salud (extractos)," December 6, 1957, in *The Chilean Stabilization Program and the Work of the Klein and Saks Economic and Financial Mission to Chile* (Santiago, 1958), chapter 45, 4.

73. Julia Vives Infantes, "La importancia del servicio social en las parroquias" (thesis, Escuela de Servicio Social Elvira Matte Cruchaga, 1938).

74. For a description of the work of Hogar de Cristo in 1950, see: letter from Alberto Hurtado to Alvaro Lavín, Santiago, May 25, 1950, in *Cartas de San Alberto Hurtado, S.J.*, ed. Jaime Castillo (Santiago: Ediciones Universidad Alberto Hurtado).

75. In 1961–1963, the University of Chile published a comprehensive list of institutions providing social assistance in Santiago. The research identified 374 institutions including 269 private, 70 semipublic, and 35 public. The big majority of these agencies provided medical care, education, and shelter for women and children. Seminario de Investigaciones Sociales del Instituto de Servicio Social, *Instituciones de asistencia social de Santiago* (Santiago: Universidad de Chile, 1966).

76. María Angélica Illanes, *Ausente señorita: el niño chileno, la escuela para pobres y el auxilio 1890/1990 (hacia una historIa social del siglo XX)* (Santiago: Junta Nacional de Auxilio Escolar y Becas, 1990).

77. In his study of Spain during the Franco regime, Antonio Cazorla argued that the family became the "the fundamental tool to survive" in a country with limited social security. The extended family, Cazorla continued, provided for the elderly, took care of small children, and redistributed meager resources among its members. In many of these cases, finding help within the family was preferable to experiencing the humiliation and mistreatment of welfare and charity institutions. To what extent the Chilean working family provided a safety net in case of unemployment, sickness, and other emergencies remains to be studied. Antonio Cazorla, *Miedo y progreso: los españoles de a pie bajo el franquismo, 1938–1975* (Madrid: Alianza Editorial, 2010), 128–29.

78. Joaquín Fernández, *El ibañismo (1937–1952): Un caso de populismo en la política Chilena* (Santiago: Universidad Católica, 2007); Tomás Moulián, *El gobierno de Ibáñez. 1952–1958* (Santiago: FLACSO, 1986).

79. "Chile Is Confronted by Financial Crisis," *New York Times,* January 7, 1953.

80. "Social Security in Chile: Reform of Social Insurance," *Industry and Labour* 9, no.2 (January 15, 1953): 52–59; Ministerio de Salubridad, Previsión y Asistencia Social, Ley 10383 (August 8, 1952). For an accessible description of benefits and payments see Servicio de Seguro Social, *Manual de consultas del SSS.*

81. Servicio de Seguro Social, *Estadísticas,* 1960, 4.

82. Alfredo Gaete Berríos, *Tratado de derecho del trabajo chileno* (Santiago: Editorial Jurídica, 1960), 116.

83. DFL 243, "Establece la indemnización por años de servicios para los obreros," in Héctor Humeres, ed., *Código del Trabajo, leyes complementarias* (Santiago: Editorial Jurídica, 1958).

84. Ministerio de Hacienda, Ley 13,305 (April 4, 1959).

85. República de Chile, Servicio de Seguro Social, *Estadísticas 1960*, 23 and 25. This volume also breaks down information per economic sector, and agricultural workers represented the largest group (28.7 percent in 1957; 28.4 percent in 1958; 28.3 percent in 1959; and 27.9 percent in 1960), followed by manufacturing (26.7 percent in 1957; 26.9 percent in 1958; 27.0 percent in 1959, and 27.5 percent in 1960).

86. Chile's economic and development problems and uncontrolled inflation attracted a myriad of international agencies and technical advisors. In 1955, President Carlos Ibáñez del Campo hired the Klein-Saks Economic and Financial Mission to study the problem of inflation—the cost of living had increased 56 percent in 1953 and 84 percent in 1955—and design a stabilization program. The mission recommended the reduction of public expenditure, the rationalization of the public administration, and the elimination of subsidies and economic protections. Klein-Saks emphasized a technical view of social, economic, and political issues, present-

ing itself as "an objective adviser on the over-all aspects of a balanced program, and as an originator of technically sound policies in various specific fields of action." *The Chilean Stabilization Program and the Work of the Klein and Saks Economic and Financial Mission to Chile* (Santiago: n.p., 1958), 6–7. Its recommendations, Brian Loveman argues, were highly unpopular, favoring "conventional, hard-line, anti-inflationary policies." Other technical missions followed, advising the government to introduce reforms in agriculture, forestry management, health care, social security, and education. Brian Loveman, *Chile: The Legacy of Hispanic Capitalism*, 3rd ed. (New York: Oxford University Press, 2001), 223.

87. República de Chile, Servicio de Seguro Social, *Estadísticas 1960*, 54.

88. República de Chile, Servicio de Seguro Social, *Estadísticas 1960*, 71.

89. International Labour Organisation, *Informe al Gobierno de Chile sobre la organización del Servicio Nacional del Empleo y el programa de informacion sobre el mercado de empleo* (Geneva: ILO, 1959).

90. Graciela Miranda Yáñez, "La colocación obrera y el contrato de enganche" (thesis, Universidad de Chile, 1962), 84–86.

91. República de Chile, *XII Censo de población y vivienda*, vol. 1 (Santiago: Servicio de Estadística y Censo, 1952).

92. Ingrid Liebeskind Sauthier, "Histoire de la défenition du chômage," *Courrier des statistiques* no. 127 (2009): 5–12.

93. International Labour Office, Eighth International Conference of Labour Statisticians, "Employment and Unemployment Statistics," report IV, Geneva 1954.

94. International Labour Office, "Meeting of Experts on Measurement of Unemployment," working paper no. 2, August 1963.

CHAPTER 7. FULL EMPLOYMENT AND LABOR RIGHTS DURING THE LONG 1960S

1. Between 1957 and 1969, Jorge Montes represented the congressional district of Concepción, Talcahuano, Yumbel, and Coronel. In 1969, he was elected senator for the region of Ñuble, Concepción, and Arauco. Originally from Chillán, Montes was a teacher and union organizer.

2. Chile, Cámara de Diputados, *Diario de sesiones* October 25, 1966, 935.

3. Chile, Cámara de Diputados, *Diario de sesiones*, October 11, 1966, 460.

4. United Nations, General Assembly, Resolutions adopted, "1710 (XVI), United Nations Development Decade: A programme for international economic co-operation."

5. Gerry Rodgers et al., *The International Labour Organization and the Quest for Social Justice, 1919–2009* (Geneva: International Labour Office, 2009).

6. ILO, "Convention Concerning Employment Policy" (C122), 1964.

7. Conventions are the ILO's most important legal instrument and represent international labor standards. Approved by the General Assembly, conventions re-

quired the ratification of member countries and, once ratified, have the same status as an international treaty. After ratification, countries should make efforts to incorporate the new standards in their labor laws and practice. If a country does not enforce an approved convention, workers and employers as well as other countries may file a complaint to the ILO Governing Body.

8. The ILO includes three bodies: General Conference, the Governing Body (executive council), and the ILO office. In addition to its headquarters in Geneva, Switzerland, the ILO maintains regional offices around the world.

9. The first Latin American countries to ratify C 122 were: Costa Rica (1966), Peru (1967), Chile (1968), Brazil (1969), and Paraguay (1969).

10. ILO, Fifty-Fourth Session, "Summary of Reports on Ratified Conventions" (Geneva: ILO, 1970), 157.

11. ILO, Fifty-Fifth Session, "Summary of Reports on Ratified Conventions" (Geneva: ILO, 1971).

12. ILO Century Project, transcription of the interview of Victor Tokman by Gerry Rodgers and Eddy Lee, June 10, 2008, ILO Geneva.

13. Eric Zolov, *The Last Good Neighbor: Mexico in the Global Sixties* (Durham, NC: Duke University Press, 2020), 1.

14. Octava Conferencia de los Estados de América Miembros de la Organización Internacional del Trabajo, Ottawa, Septiembre 1966, *Actas*, 125.

15. ILO, "Ottawa Plan: A Regional Programme for Employment Creation and Skill Formation," D. 28 (1), 1968.

16. International Labour Conference, *The World Employment Programme. Report of the Director-General* (Geneva: ILO, 1969).

17. Paul E. Bangasser, *The ILO and the Informal Sector: An Institutional History* (Geneva: ILO, 2000), 5.

18. Manuel Délano and Gérard Thirion, *PREALC 25 años* (Geneva: ILO, 1993).

19. ILO Century Project, transcription of the interview of Victor Tokman by Gerry Rodgers and Eddy Lee, June 10, 2008, ILO Geneva.

20. International Labour Office, *Towards Full Employment in Colombia. Summary of an Employment Programme for Colombia, prepared by an inter-agency team organised by the International Labour Office* (Geneva: International Labour Office, 1970).

21. Eduardo Frei Montalva, *Primer mensaje del Presidente de la República de Chile don Eduardo Frei Montalva al inaugurar el período de Sesiones Ordinarias del Congreso Nacional* (Santiago: Departamento de Publicaciones de la Presidencia de la República, 1965), 8.

22. For an overview of the Eduardo Frei administration and the Revolution in Liberty, see Biblioteca del Congreso Nacional, ed., *Eduardo Frei Montalva: fe, política y cambio Social* (Santiago: Ediciones Biblioteca de Congreso Nacio-

nal, 2013); Carlos Huneeus and Javier Couso, eds., *Eduardo Frei Montalva: un gobierno reformista. A 50 años de la Revolución en Libertad* (Santiago: Editorial Universitaria, 2016); and Michael Fleet, *The Rise and Fall of Chilean Christian Democracy* (Princeton, NJ: Princeton University Press, 2014). On the role of the United States, see Sebastián Hurtado-Torres, *The Gathering Storm: Eduardo Frei's Revolution in Liberty and Chile's Cold War* (Ithaca, NY: Cornell University Press, 2020). On the relationship between President Frei and the labor movement see Luis Thielemann, "La perspectiva parcial: el movimiento obrero frente a la política salarial del gobierno de Frei Montalva, 1964–1967," *Economía y política* 1, no. 6 (2019): 85–116.

23. Although outside the scope of this chapter, the process of agrarian reform and the unionization of rural workers, the most emblematic reforms of the Frei administration, also influenced employment policies. Both national and international experts agreed that the urban economy was not growing fast enough to provide jobs to rural migrants. The redistribution of land, the modernization of production, and the improvement of rural employment conditions could contribute to creating new and better jobs in the countryside, as well as increase rural families' purchasing power. The Agrarian Reform Law and the Law of Rural Unionization, both enacted in 1967, were the symbols of the Christian Democrats' agrarian policy. In tandem with these laws, the government expanded technical training and assistance, facilitated credit, and supported the organization of social and political institutions in the countryside.

24. Eduardo Frei Montalva, "Mensaje presidencial," in República de Chile, *Sesiones del Congreso Nacional,* Congreso Pleno, May 21, 1966, 44.

25. Jorge Ahumada, *En vez de la miseria* (Santiago: Editorial del Pacífico, 1958) and *La crisis integral de Chile* (Santiago: Editorial Universitaria, 1966).

26. Sergio Molina, *El proceso de cambio en Chile: la experiencia 1965–1970* (Santiago: Editorial Universitaria, 1972), Patricio Silva, *In the Name of Reason: Technocrats and Politics in Chile.* (University Park: Penn State Univ Press, 2012).

27. For an overview of the concept of marginality see: Cristóbal Kay, *Latin American Theories of Development and Underdevelopment* (London: Routledge, 2010), chapter 4, and Janice E. Perlman, *The Myth of Marginality: Urban Poverty and Politics in Rio de Janeiro* (Berkeley: University of California Press, 1976), part II.

28. Roger Vekemans, and Ramón Venegas, "Marginalidad y Promoción Popular," *Mensaje* 15, no. 149 (June 1966): 218–22.

29. Alberto Quijano, "Notas sobre el concepto de marginalidad social" (Santiago: CEPAL, División de Asuntos Sociales, 1966); José Nun, *Marginalidad y exclusión social* (Mexico: Fondo de Cultura Económica, 2001).

30. Pía Montalva Díaz and Yalile Uarac Graf, "Promoción Popular, 'el pueblo organizado,'" in Biblioteca del Congreso Nacional, ed., *Eduardo Frei Montalva,* 241–64.

31. Molina, *El proceso de cambio en Chile*, 94.

32. For a firsthand account of employment policies under Frei, see Pablo Huneeus, *El problema de empleo y recursos humanos: ideas para una política* (Santiago: Andres Bello, 1970).

33. William Thayer, *Trabajo, Empresa y Revolución* (Santiago: Zig-Zag, 1968), 98.

34. Mario Cerda, *El Instituto de Capacitación Profesional de Chile (INACAP)* (Paris: UNESCO, 1975). For a longer discussion about training and the labor market, see Kirsten Sehnbruch, *The Chilean Labor Market: A Key to Understanding Latin American Labor Markets* (New York: Springer, 2006).

35. Ministerio del Trabajo y Previsión Social, DFL 5, May 30, 1967.

36. Regional Employment Program for Latin America and the Caribbean, *Empleo y el proceso de desarrollo en Chile, 1960–1970*. (Santiago: PREALC, 1973), vol. 4, chapter XII.

37. Regional Employment Program for Latin America and the Caribbean, *La búsqueda de trabajo y los mecanismos de sobrevivencia en el Gran Santiago, 1976* (Santiago: PREALC, 1977).

38. "Informe de la Comisión de Relaciones Exteriores," Chile, Cámara de Diputados, *Diario de sesiones* August 23, 1966, 4400–41.

39. Regional Employment Program for Latin America and the Caribbean, *Empleo y El Proceso de Desarrollo en Chile, 1960–1970* (Santiago: PREALC, 1973), vol. 1, chapter 1.

40. Eduardo Frei Montalva, *Quinto mensaje del Presidente de la República de Chile don Eduardo Frei Montalva al inaugurar el período de sesiones ordinarias del Congreso Nacional, 21 de Mayo de 1966* (Santiago: Departmento de Publicaciones de la Presidencia de la República, 1969).

41. James Petras, "Chile," *New Left Review*, 1, no. 54 (Mar/April 1969): 54–59.

42. FOSL, Conferencia Nacional Textil, "Acuerdos y resoluciones de una jornada gremial sindical, con los trabajadores textiles del país," June 1965.

43. Ángela Vergara, "Conflicto y modernización en la Gran Minería del Cobre (1950–1970)," *Historia (Chile)*, no. 37 (2004): 419–36.

44. Chile, Cámara de Diputados, *Diario de sesiones*, June 9, 1965, 752–54.

45. "Laura," in Teresa Marshall et al., *Mujeres de la ciudad: Historia de vida en doce episodios*, Documento de Trabajo (Santiago: Ediciones Sur, 1984), 295–317.

46. Chile, Cámara de Diputados, *Diario de sesiones*, June 9, 1965, 752–54.

47. "Report on the Committee on the Termination of Employment," ILO 47th Conference (1963) *Proceedings*, 578–79.

48. "Report on the Committee on the Termination of Employment," ILO 46th Conference (1962) *Proceedings*, 438–44.

49. "Text of the Proposed Recommendation concerning Termination of Employment," ILO 47th Conference (1963), *Proceedings*, 589–91.

50. Chile, Cámara de Diputados, *Diario de sesiones*, May 25, 1965, 61.

51. Ministerio de Hacienda, Ley 16.250, Article 92, April 20, 1965.

52. Chile, Cámara de Diputados, *Diario de sesiones* December 1, 1965, 2580.

53. Protections were renewed twice in June and in December 1965. Ministerio del Trabajo y Previsión Social, Ley 16.270, June 18, 1965, and Ministerio del Trabajo y Previsión Social, Ley 16.404.

54. "Mensaje de S.E. el Presidente de la República" in Chile, Cámara de Diputados, *Diario de sesiones*, December 14, 1965, 2906.

55. Francisco Tapia, "Presentación," *Chile 1970: el país en que triunfa Salvador Allende*, ed. Pedro Milos (Santiago: Editorial Universidad Alberto Hurtado, 2013).

56. *Fallos del Mes*, July 1967, 167.

57. Ministerio del Trabajo y Previsión Social, Ley 16, 455 (Normas para la terminación del contrato de trabajo), April 5, 1966, and Decreto 464, "Aprueba reglamento para la aplicación de la ley número 16,455" (June 3, 1966). See also Alfredo Gaete Berríos, *La ley 16,455 sobre contrato de trabajo frente a la jursiprudencia judicial y administrativa* (Santiago: Editorial Jurídica, 1971).

58. *Presencia*, no. 14 (1970), 4.

59. *Fallos del mes* 9, no. 100 (March 1967): 24–25.

60. *Fallos del mes* 10, no. 120 (November 1968): 259–60.

61. *Fallos del mes* 10, no. 115 (November 1968): 112–13.

62. OIT and PREALC, "La situación del empleo y el proceso de desarrollo en Chile," Documento de trabajo, September 1971.

63. Salvador Allende, Victory Speech, September 5, 1970.

64. Márcia Carolina de Oliveira Cury, *El protagonismo popular chileno: Experiencias de clase y movimientos sociales en la construcción del socialismo (1964–1973)* (Santiago: LOM Ediciones, 2018); Franck Gaudichaud, *Poder popular y cordones industriales: testimonios sobre el movimiento popular urbano, 1970–1973* (Santiago: LOM Ediciones, 2004); Peter Winn, *Weavers of Revolution: The Yarur Workers and Chile's Road to Socialism* (New York: Oxford University Press, 1986). For a general overview of Allende's government see: Claudio Llanos, *Cuando el pueblo unido fue vencido: estudios sobre la vía chilena al socialismo* (Valparaíso: Ediciones Universitarias de Valparaíso, 2014); Peter Winn, *La revolución chilena* (Santiago: LOM Ediciones, 2013).

65. *Presencia*, no. 30, March 3, 1973, 1.

66. *Presencia*, no. 5, 1968, 5.

67. Central Única de Trabajadores de Chile y Gobierno, *Normas básicas de participación de los trabajadores en la dirección de las empresas de las áreas social y mixta* (Santiago: Odeplan, 1971).

68. Manuel Barrera, *Worker Participation in Company Management in Chile: A Historical Experience* (Geneva: United Nations Research Institute for Social Development, 1981).

EPILOGUE. UNEMPLOYMENT, DICTATORSHIP, AND NEOLIBERALISM (1973–1989)

1. Augusto Pinochet Ugarte, *Mensaje Presidencial: 11 septiembre 1974.*
2. Jaime Ruiz-Tagle, "Cesantía y alza de precios," *Mensaje* 23, no. 232 (September 1974): 394–97.
3. José Aldunate, "Remuneraciones y costo de vida. Situación real de los trabajadores de ingresos mas bajos," *Mensaje* 23, no 235 (December 1974): 634–36.
4. Pierre Dubois, *Un prêtre français au Chili. 50 ans au service du monde ouvrier* (Paris: Éditions Karthala, 2012), 3–4.
5. Jaime Ruiz-Tagle, "El sindicalismo chileno entre 1973 y 1990," in *Libertad sindical y derechos humanos. Análisis de los informes del Comité de Libertad Sindical de la OIT (1973–1990)*, ed. Elizabeth Lira and Hugo Rojas (Santiago: LOM Ediciones, DIBAM, Universidad Academia de Humanismo Cristiano, 2009), 19.
6. Ministerio del Interior, Decreto Ley 6, September 6, 1973, "Declara en calidad de interino las personas que se indican."
7. Ángela Vergara and Peter Winn, "'Los empresarios hacen lo que quieren': sindicatos y trabajadores bajo la dictadura de Pinochet," in *Un país desigual a la fuerza: complicidad económica con la dictadura chilena*, eds. Juan Pablo Bohoslavsky, Karinna Fernández, and Sebastián Smart (Santiago: LOM Ediciones, 2019).
8. "Análisis y aspiraciones de los trabajadores chilenos a 44 meses de gobierno militar," *Solidaridad*, separata, no. 9, 1977.
9. Junta de Gobierno, Acta 123, May 14, 1974.
10. Economists have debated the persistency of unemployment in the 1970s. While some argued that wage controls inhibited job creation and rapid demographic growth put new pressures on the labor market, others pointed out the combination of external shocks and the government economic policies. See: Alejandra Cox de Edwards, "Mercado laboral chileno durante la década de 1974–1983: Problemas de ajuste," *Cuadernos de Economía* 24, no. 72 (1987): 165–95; R. Lagos & ILO Multidisciplinary Technical Advisory Team, "Effects of extreme de-regulation of the labour market: Chile 1974–1990," *Documentos de trabajo*, no. 17 (1995).
11. Alejandro Foxley, "Políticas de estabilización," *Estudios CIEPLAN* 2 (1979): 37–74.
12. Manuel Gárate Chateau, *La revolución capitalista en Chile (1973–1990)* (Santiago: Universidad Albterto Hurtado, 2012); Juan Gabriel Valdés, *Pinochet's Economists: The Chicago School of Economics in Chile* (Cambridge: Cambridge University Press, 1995).
13. Dominique Hachette, Rolf Lüders and Guillermo Tagle, "Five Cases of Privatization in Chile," in *Privatization in Latin America*, ed. Manuel Sánchez and Rossana Corona (Washington, DC: Inter American Development Bank, 1993), 41–100, 41–42.
14. The influence of neoliberalism on the Chilean military was not automatic nor homogenous, but it grew between 1973 and 1975 and, eventually, displaced

those traditional military groups that favored a stronger role of the state in the economy. For a discussion of this transition, see Verónica Valdivia Ortiz de Zárate, "Estatismo y neoliberalismo: un contrapunto militar. Chile 1973–1979," *Historia* (Santiago) 34 (2001): 167–226.

15. Rolf Lüders and Nora Cabrera, "Employment and Technology: The Chilean Case," Meeting of Experts on Fiscal Policies for Employment Promotion, 4–8 January 1971, ILO, Geneva, 1970.

16. According to Patricio Meller, on the eve of the military coup the state owned more than four hundred companies and banks. By 1980, it owned only forty-five. Patricio Meller, *Un siglo de política económica chilena (1890–1990)* (Santiago: Ugbar, 2016).

17. Meller, *Un siglo de política económica chilena.*

18. Azun Candina Polomer, *Clase media, Estado y sacrificio: la Agrupación Nacional de Empleados Fiscales en Chile contemporáneo (1943–1983)* (Santiago: LOM Ediciones, 2013), 157–75.

19. Claudio Llanos, "La dictadura militar en Chile frente al desempleo: algunos aspectos de la mirada política 1973–1978," *Estudios Ibero-Americanos*, 44, no 2 (2018): 311–25.

20. Regional Employment Program for Latin America the Caribbean, *Pobreza y mercado de trabajo en el Gran Santiago, 1969–1985* (Santiago: PREALC, 1987), 8.

21. Desmond King, *Actively Seeking Work? The Politics of Unemployment and Welfare Policy in the United States and Great Britain* (Chicago: University of Chicago Press, 1995), see chapter 5.

22. Matías Sepúlveda Momberg, "Del trabajo protegido al trabajo subsidiado. Intervención, libre mercado y la situación de los trabajadores del PEM y POHJ, 1974–1984," in *Instituto de Historia*, Seminario Simon Collier 2014 (Santiago: Instituto de Historia, 2015), 213–44.

23. Verónica Valvidia, Rolando Álvarez Vallejos, and Karen Donoso Fritz, *La alcaldización de la política: los municipios en la dictadura pinochetista*, (Santiago: LOM Ediciones, 2012).

24. Ministerio del Trabajo, Decreto Ley 603, August 10, 1974, "Crea Sistema de subsidio de cesantía."

25. Decreto Ley 1,446.

26. Banco Central de Chile, *Indicadores económicos y sociales 1960–1985* (Santiago: Dirección de Estudios, Banco Central de Chile, 1986), 281–82.

27. Jaime Ruiz-Tagle, "Cesantía y solidaridad nacional: El Programa de Empleo Mínimo," *Mensaje* 24, no. 242 (September 1975): 341–44. See also Rolando Álvarez Vallejos and Verónica Valdivia, "Platita poca, pero segura: los refugios laborales de la dictadura," in *La alcaldización de la política*; PREALC, *El Plan de Empleo Mínimo en Chile*, ILO 1979.

28. The survey included eighty-five unemployed people living in peripheral neighborhoods in Santiago.

29. Regional Employment Program for Latin America and the Caribbean, *La búsqueda de trabajo y los mecanismos de sobrevivencia en el Gran Santiago, 1976* (Santiago: PREALC, 1977), "La búsqueda de trabajo y los mecanismos de sobrevivencia de los desocupados en el Gran Santiago, 1976."

30. Ascanio Cavallo, Manuel Salazar, and Oscar Sepúlveda, *La historia oculta del régimen militar. Memoria de una época* (Santiago: Mondadori, 1997), 300–302.

31. Cox de Edwards, "Mercado laboral chileno."

32. The Plan Kelly is cited in *Chile informativo*, no. 142, May 1978.

33. Junta de Gobierno, Acta N 343-A, Santiago, April 24, 1978.

34. *Chile Informativo*, no. 144, June 1978, 44.

35. Jaime Ruiz-Tagle, "El caso CRAV: lecciones y consecuencias," *Mensaje* no. 300, July 1981, 305.

36. María Ester Aliaga, "CRAV: trago amargo para un dulce monopolio," *APSI* no. 100 (1981), 11–12; María Ester Aliaga, "Después de CRAV: Diabetes del modelo," APSI no. 102 (1981), 11–12.

37. Peter Winn, "No Miracle for Us: The Textile Industry in the Pinochet Era, 1973–1998," in *Victims of the Chilean Miracle: Workers and Neoliberalism in the Pinochet Era, 1973–2002*, ed. Peter Winn (Durham, NC: Duke University Press, 2004), 125–63.

38. Patricio Frías Fernández, Magdalena Echeverría, Gonzalo Herrera, and Christian Larraín, *Industria textil y del vestuario en Chile* (Santiago: PET, 1987).

39. Augusto Pinochet, *Mensaje Presidencial*, September 11, 1982.

40. Augusto Pinochet, *Mensaje Presidencial*, September 11, 1983.

41. Alison Bruey, *Bread, Justice, and Liberty" Grassroot Activism and Human Rights in Pinochet's Chile* (Madison: University of Wisconsin Press, 2018). Mariana Skolnik and Berta Teitelboim, *Pobreza y desempleo en poblaciones: la otra cara del modelo neoliberal* (Santiago: PET, 1988).

42. Viviana Bravo Vargas, *Piedras, barricadas y cacerolas: las jornadas nacionales de protesta. Chile 1983–1986* (Santiago: Ediciones Universidad Alberto Hurtado, 2017).

43. Clarisa Hardy, *Hambre + dignidad = ollas comunes* (Santiago: PET, 1986).

BIBLIOGRAPHY

ARCHIVES

Archivo Histórico Nacional
    Intendencias: Antofagasta, Cautín, Chiloé, Concepción, and Santiago.
Archivo Nacional de la Administración del Estado
    Dirección del Trabajo
    Ministerio de Fomento
    Ministerio del Trabajo
ILO-BIT archives
    Diplomatic series

DIGITAL ARCHIVES AND COLLECTIONS

Biblioteca del Congreso Nacional
    Diario de sesiones de la Cámara de Diputados
    Diario de sesiones del Senado
    Junta de Gobierno, Actas
    Ley Chile
    Mensajes presidenciales
The ILO Century Project
    ILO Conventions
    International Labour Conference: Resolutions
    International Labour Conference: Record of Proceedings
    American Regional Meetings: Reports and other official documents

PERIODICALS

APSI (Santiago, Chile)
Anuario Estadístico (Santiago, Chile)
Barómetro Económico (Santiago, Chile)
Boletín del Departamento Nacional del Trabajo (Buenos Aires, Argentina)
Boletín de la Oficina del Trabajo (Santiago, Chile)
Boletín Oficial de la Unión Industrial de Obreros de Gath y Chaves (Santiago, Chile)
Boletín de leyes y decretos (Santiago, Chile)

Boletín Médico de la Caja de Seguro Obligatorio (Santiago, Chile)
Boletín Minero (Santiago, Chile)
Chile Informativo
El comercio (Viña del Mar, Chile)
El empleado (Valparaíso, Chile)
El laborista (Temuco, Chile)
Estadística chilena (Santiago, Chile)
Fallos del Mes (Santiago, Chile)
International Labour Review (Geneva, Switzerland)
La Gaceta de los Tribunales (Santiago, Chile)
Mensaje (Santiago, Chile)
Músculo (Santiago, Chile)
Oro (Santiago, Chile)
Presencia (Santiago, Chile)
Revista del Trabajo (Santiago, Chile)
Revista de Derecho y Jurisprudencia (Santiago, Chile)
Servicio Social (Santiago, Chile)
Sucesos (Santiago, Chile)

PUBLISHED PRIMARY SOURCES

"The Hospital and the Hospital System of Chile." *Modern Hospital* 11, no. 6 (December 1918): 440–44.

"Price Control and Rationing in Foreign Countries during the War." *Monthly Labor Review* 61 (November 1945): 882–89.

Alessandri, Arturo. *Mensaje leído por S.E. el Presidente de la República en la apertura de sesiones ordinarias del Congreso Nacional*. Santiago: Imprenta fiscal de la penitenciaría de Santiago, 1922.

Allende Gossens, Salvador. *La realidad medico-social chilena*. Santiago: Ministerio de Salubridad, Previsión y Asistencia Social, 1939.

Aranda Ocaranza, Alberto. "La desocupación obrera." Thesis, Universidad de Chile, 1951.

Araya, Bernardo. *Una CTCH unida combatiendo en defensa de la clase obrera y del pueblo: II Conferencia Nacional de la Confederación de Trabajadores de Chile*. Santiago: CTCH, 1946.

Banco Central de Chile. *Indicadores económicos y sociales 1960–1985*. Santiago: Dirección de Estudios, Banco Central de Chile, 1986.

Banco Central de Chile. *Séptima memoria anual presentada a la Superintendencia de Bancos, año 1932*. Santiago: Dirección General de Prisiones, 1933.

Baraona Puelma, Jorge. *El paro forzoso*. Santiago: Imprenta Cervantes, 1923.

Barros Jarpa, Ernesto. "How Chile Has Met the Depression." *Foreign Affairs* 13, no. 4 (1935): 638–46.

Behm Rosas, Héctor. *El problema de la habitación mínima*. Santiago: Leblanc, Stanley y Urzúa, 1939.

Benavente, David. *A medio morir cantantando: rastrojos de la memoria chilena 1978–1998*. Santiago: Catalonia, 2007.

Beveridge, William H. *Full Employment in a Free Society (a summary)*. London: New Statesman and Nation and Reynolds News, 1944.

Beveridge, William H. *Social Insurance and Allied Services*. London: His Majesty's Stationery Office, 1942.

Beveridge, William H. *Unemployment: A Problem of Industry*. 3rd ed. London: Longmans, Green, 1912.

Bureau International du Travail. *Une politique des travaux publics*. Études et Documents, série C (chômage), no. 19 (1935).

Cámara de Diputados. *Compañía de Salitre de Chile (COSACH)*. Santiago: El Imparcial, 1933.

Cañas O'Ryan, Carlos. *Seguros sociales*. Santiago: Imprenta y Litografía La Ilustración, 1922.

Carvallo Montenegro, René. "El servicio de colocación pública en Chile y la colocación pública en los principales países." Thesis, Universidad de Chile, 1947.

Castillo, Jaime, ed. *Cartas de San Alberto Hurtado, S.J.* Santiago: Ediciones Universidad Alberto Hurtado.

Central Única de Trabajadores de Chile y Gobierno. *Normas básicas de participación de los trabajadores en la dirección de las empresas de las áreas social y mixta*. Santiago: Odeplan, 1971.

Cerda, Mario. *El Instituto de Capacitación Profesional de Chile (INACAP)*. Paris: UNESCO, 1975.

Conference International du Chômage. *Compte rendue de la conference international du chômage*, 3 vols. Paris: Secrétariat général de la conference du chômage and Librairies de science politiques et sociales, 1911.

Consejo Nacional de Economía (Chile). *Informe de la comisión de trabajo, salarios y prevision social del Consejo Nacional de Economía: sobre el proyecto de reforma a las leyes 4054 y 4055*. Santiago: n.p., 1947.

Contraloría General de la República. *Recopilación de leyes*. Vol. 20. Santiago: Imprenta Nascimento, 1934.

Contreras Labarca, Carlos. *La defensa del proletariado contra el riesgo profesional de la desocupación*. Santiago: Imprenta del Instituto Sordo-Mudos y Ciegos, 1923.

Cruz Roja. *Memoria de la Presidenta de la Cruz Roja de las Mujeres de Chile Sra Carmela Prieto de Ramírez, 1931*. Santiago: Imprenta Lagunas y Quevedo, 1932.

Cruzat, Ximena, and Eduardo Devés, eds. *Recabarren: Escritos de prensa*, vol. 4, *1919–1924*. Santiago: Nuestra América y Terranova Editores, 1987.

D'Ambrossio, Manlio Andrea. *La passivité économique*. Paris: M. Giard & E. Brière, 1912.

Dávila, Carlos. *El Presidente Dávila y la revolución de junio*. Santiago: Imprenta Socialista, n.d.

Davis, Pedro R. *Jurisprudencia del trabajo*. Santiago: Carlos E. Gibbs A. Editor, 1963.

de Bray, Leo. *Asistencia social y cesantía*. Santiago: Imprenta Universitaria, 1934.

de la Fuente Lillo, Benito. *Tema: Ley No 6020 que mejora la situacion económica de los empleados particulares*. Santiago: Dirección General de Prisiones, 1939.

Dragoni, Carlo, and Etienne Burnet. "L'Alimentation populaire au Chili: première enquête générale de 1935." *Apartado de la Revista Chilena de higiene y medicina preventiva* 1, nos. 10–12 (1938): 407–611.

Dubois, Pierre. *Un prêtre français au Chili. 50 ans au service du monde ouvrier*. Paris: Éditions Karthala, 2012.

Ellsworth, P. T. *Chile: An Economy in Transition*. New York: Macmillan, 1945.

Frei Montalva, Eduardo. *Primer mensaje del Presidente de la República de Chile don Eduardo Frei Montalva al inaugurar el período de Sesiones Ordinarias del Congreso Nacional*. Santiago: Departamento de Publicaciones de la Presidencia de la República, 1965.

Frei Montalva, Eduardo. *Quinto mensaje del Presidente de la República de Chile don Eduardo Frei Montalva al inaugurar el período de sesiones ordinarias del Congreso Nacional, 21 de Mayo de 1966*. Santiago: Departmento de Publicaciones de la Presidencia de la República, 1969.

Fuenzalida, César. *¿Hemos vencido la crisis?* Santiago: Editorial Nascimento, 1934.

Gaete Berríos, Alfredo. *La ley 16,455 sobre contrato de trabajo frente a la jursiprudencia judicial y administrativa*. Santiago: Editorial Jurídica, 1971.

Gaete Berríos, Alfredo. *Tratado de derecho del trabajo chileno*. Santiago: Editorial Jurídica, 1960.

Gaete Berríos, Alfredo. *La seguridad social*. Santiago: Prensas de la Universidad de Chile, 1946.

González Videla, Gabriel. *Discurso pronunciado por el presidente de la república Excmo. Sr. Gabriel González Videla, en la ceremonia de inauguración de la planta de Huachipato, 25 de noviembre de 1950*. Santiago: Artes y Letras, 1950.

Grez Toso, Sergio. *La "cuestión social" en Chile: ideas y debates precursores, 1804–1902*. Santiago: Dirección de Bibliotecas, Archivo y Museos, Centro de Investigaciones Diego Barros Arana, 1995.

Guerra, Gregorio. *Desocupación y miseria*. Santiago: Editorial Problemas, 1937.

Guzmán, Nicomedes. *La sangre y la esperanza*. Santiago: Orbe, 1943.

Humeres, Héctor. *Código del Trabajo, leyes complementarias*. Santiago: Editorial Jurídica, 1958.

Humeres, Héctor. *Patrones y obreros*. Santiago: Editorial Jurídica de Chile, 1954.

Huneeus, Pablo. *El problema de empleo y recursos humanos: ideas para una política*. Santiago: Andres Bello, 1970.

International Labour Organisation. *Creación de empleos y absorción del desempleo en Chile. La experiencia de 1971.* Geneva: International Labour Office, 1972.

International Labour Organisation. *Informe al gobierno de Chile sobre la organización del Servicio Nacional del Empleo y el programa de información sobre el mercado de empleo.* Geneva: ILO, 1959.

International Labour Organisation. *The International Labour Organization and Unemployment.* Geneva: ILO, 1926.

International Labour Organisation. *Methods of Compiling Statistics of Unemployment. Replies of the Governments.* Geneva: ILO, 1922.

International Labour Organisation. *Remedies for Unemployment.* Geneva: ILO, 1923.

International Labour Organisation. *Report on Minimum Wage Fixing Machinery.* ILO: Geneva, 1928.

International Labour Organisation. *Towards Full Employment in Colombia. Summary of an Employment Programme for Colombia, prepared by an inter-agency team organised by the International Labour Office.* Geneva: International Labour Office, 1970.

Ivovich, Esteban, and Isauro Torres. *Orígenes y desarrollo de la beneficencia pública en Chile.* Santiago: Imprenta Universitaria, 1933.

Izquierdo, Adriana. "Como se organizó la ayuda a los cesantes y la participación que a ella le corresponde a la escuela de servicio social Elvira Matte de Cruchaga." Thesis, Escuela de Servicio Social Elvira Matte de Cruchaga, July 1932.

Klein-Saks. *The Chilean Stabilization Program and the Work of the Klein and Saks Economic and Financial Mission to Chile.* Santiago: n.p., 1958.

Klein-Saks. *El Sistema de prevision chileno: Informe de la Misión Klein and Saks.* Santiago: n.p., 1958.

League of Nations. *Report on Unemployment: Prepared by the Organising Committee for the International Labour Conference, Washington, 1919.* London: Harrison & Sons, n.d.

Lira Vergara, J. Toribio. *El seguro contra el paro forzoso.* Santiago: Talleres Gráficos La Aurora, 1938.

Macchiavello Varas, Constantino. "Contribución al estudio de nuestro problema de la carestía de la vida frente al problema de las subsistencias." Thesis, Universidad de Chile, 1933.

Macchiavello Varas, Santiago. *Política económica nacional: antecedentes y directivas.* Santiago, Chile: Establecimientos Gráficos Balcells, 1931.

Marshall, Teresa, et al. *Mujeres de la ciudad: Historia de vida en doce episodios.* Documento de Trabajo. Santiago: Ediciones Sur, 1984.

Martini M., Hugo. *Estudio jurídico práctico del auxilio de cesantía.* Santiago: Editorial Universitaria, 1961.

Méndez, Jorge. "Minimum Wages in Latin America." *International Labour Review* (Geneva), 62, no. 2 (1950): 116–40.

Ministerio de Bienestar Social, Chile. *Memoria del Ministerio de Bienestar Social correspondiente al año 1929.* Santiago: La Ilustración, 1930.

Ministerio de Hacienda, Chile. *Manual de organización del gobierno de Chile*, Santiago: Gutenberg, 1960.

Ministerio de Relaciones Exteriores, Perú. *Memoria del Ministro de Relaciones Exteriores.* Lima, Peru: Imprenta Americana, 1914.

Ministerio del Trabajo, Chile. *La Conferencia Internacional del Trabajo de Nueva York.* Santiago: Imprenta Universitaria 1942.

Ministro del Interior, Chile. *Memoria del Ministro del Interior.* Santiago: Imprenta Nacional, 1921.

Miranda Yáñez, Graciela. "La colocación obrera y el contrato de enganche." Thesis, Universidad de Chile, 1962.

Navarro Lane, Herminia. "Algunos aspectos de la desocupación en Chile." Thesis, Universidad de Chile, 1945.

Olavarría Bravo, Arturo. *Durante la tiranía.* Santiago: La Alianza, 1931.

Pérez Canto, Julio. "La industria salitrera y la intervención del Estado." *Revista universitaria* 5–6 (September 1933): 571–76.

Poblete Troncoso, Moisés. *El derecho del trabajo y la seguridad social en Chile.* Santiago: Editorial Jurídica, 1949.

Poblete Troncoso, Moisés. *El subconsumo en América del Sur, alimentos, vestuario y vivienda.* Santiago: Nascimento, 1946.

Poblete Troncoso, Moisés. *La organización sindical en Chile y otros estudios sociales.* Santiago: Imprenta R. Brias, 1926.

Poblete Troncoso, Moisés. *The Rise of the Latin American Labor Movement.* New York: Bookman Associates, 1960.

Poblete Troncoso, Moisés, and Oscar Álvarez Andrews. *Legislación social obrera chilena. (recopilación de leyes y disposiciones vigentes sobre el trabajo y la previsión social).* Santiago: Imprenta Santiago, 1924.

Regional Employment Program for Latin America and the Caribbean. *Empleo y el proceso de desarrollo en Chile, 1960–1970.* Santiago: PREALC, 1973.

Regional Employment Program for Latin America and the Caribbean. *La búsqueda de trabajo y los mecanismos de sobrevivencia en el Gran Santiago, 1976.* Santiago: PREALC, 1977.

Regional Employment Program for Latin America and the Caribbean. *Pobreza y mercado de trabajo en el Gran Santiago, 1969–1985.* Santiago: PREALC, 1987.

República de Chile. *Código del Trabajo.* Santiago de Chile: Editorial Nascimento, 1932.

República de Chile, Dirección General de Estadística. *Resultados del X censo de la población efectuado el 27 de noviembre de 1930*, 2 vols. Santiago: Imprenta Universo, 1931.

República de Chile. *XII Censo de población y Vivienda.* Santiago: Servicio de Estadística y Censo, 1952.

Rodríguez, Simón. *La estadística del trabajo*. Santiago: Imprenta Cervantes, 1908.

Rowe, L. S. *Early Effects of the European War upon the Finance, Commerce and Industry of Chile*. New York: Oxford University Press, 1918.

Rowe, L. S. *Early Effects of the War upon the Finance, Commerce and Industry of Peru*. New York: Oxford University Press, 1920.

Schmidt, Teodoro. *Los trabajos públicos y la cesantía 1931–1934*. Santiago: Imprenta Nascimento, 1934.

Seminario de Investigaciones Sociales del Instituto de Servicio Social. *Instituciones de asistencia social de Santiago*. Santiago: Editorial Jurídica de Chile, 1966.

Sociedad San Vicente de Paul. *Memoria de la Sociedad San Vicente de Paul*. Santiago: Dirección General de Prisiones, 1932.

Soria, Carmen, ed. *Letras anarquistas: José Santos González Vera, Manuel Rojas*. Santiago: Planeta, 2005.

Thayer, William. *Trabajo, Empresa y Revolución*. Santiago: Zig-Zag, 1968.

Thomas, Émile. *Histoire des ateliers nationaux*. Paris: M. Lévy frères, 1848.

Ulianova, Olga, and Alfredo Riquelme. *Chile en los Archivos Soviéticos 1922–1991*. Vol. 2, *Komintern y Chile entre julio de 1931 y febrero de 1935 crisis e ilusión revolucionaria*. Santiago, Chile: Centro de Investigaciones Barros Arana, LOM Ediciones, 2005.

Vives Infantes, Julia. "La importancia del servicio social en las parroquias." Thesis, Escuela de Servicio Social Elvira Matte Cruchaga, 1938.

Walker Linares, Francisco. *Esquema del derecho del trabajo y de la seguridad social en Chile*. Santiago: Editorial Jurídica, 1965.

Walker Linares, Francisco. *Panorama del derecho social chileno*. Santiago: Editorial Jurídica de Chile, 1947.

Wilson Hernández, Santiago. "Nuestra crisis económica y la desocupación obrera." Thesis, Universidad de Chile, Santiago, 1933.

Zañartu Prieto, Enrique. *Hambre, miseria e ignorancia*. Santiago: Editorial Ercilla, 1933.

SECONDARY SOURCES

Ahumada, Jorge. *En vez de la miseria*. Santiago: Editorial del Pacífico, 1958.

Ahumada, Jorge. *La crisis integral de Chile*. Santiago: Editorial Universitaria, 1966.

Álvarez Vallejos, Rolando. "'¡Viva la revolución y la patria!': Partido Comunista de Chile y nacionalismo, 1921–1926." *Revista de historia social y de las mentalidades*, no. 7 (2003): 25–44.

Alberti, Manfredi. *La 'scoperta' dei disoccupati: Alle origini dell'indagine statistica sulla disoccupazione nell' Italia liberale (1893–1915)*. Florence: Firenze University Press, 2013.

Amenta, Edwin. *Bold Relief: Institutional Politics and the Origins of Modern American Social Policy*. Princeton, NJ: Princeton University Press, 1998.

Araya Espinoza, Alejandra. "Guerra, intolerancia a la ociosidad y resistencia: los discursos ocultos tras la vagancia, Ciudad de México, 1821–1860." *Boletín Americanista.*, no. 52 (2002): 23–55.

Balderrama, Francisco E., and Raymond Rodriguez. *Decade of Betrayal: Mexican Repatriation in the 1930s.* Rev ed. Albuquerque: University of New Mexico Press, 2006.

Bangasser, Paul E. *The ILO and the Informal Sector: An Institutional History.* Geneva: ILO, 2000.

Barrera, Manuel. *Worker Participation in Company Management in Chile: A Historical Experience.* Geneva: United Nations Research Institute for Social Development, 1981.

Barría Serón, Jorge I. *El movimiento obrero en Chile: síntesis histórico-social.* Santiago: Ediciones de la Universidad Técnica del Estado, 1971.

Barría Serón, Jorge I. *Los movimientos sociales de Chile desde 1910 dasta 1926: Aspecto político y social.* Santiago: Editorial Universitaria, 1960.

Barr-Melej, Patrick. *Reforming Chile: Cultural Politics, Nationalism, and the Rise of the Middle Class.* Chapel Hill: University of North Carolina Press, 2001.

Bauer, Arnold J. *Chilean Rural Society from the Spanish Conquest to 1930.* Cambridge: Cambridge University Press, 1975.

Bertolo, Maricel. "Estado y trabajadores en Argentina. El Departamento Nacional del Trabajo ante el fenómeno de la desocupación, 1907–1934." PhD diss., Universidad de Buenos Aires, Argentina, 2008.

Biblioteca del Congreso Nacional, ed. *Eduardo Frei Montalva: fe, política y cambio social.* Santiago: Ediciones Biblioteca de Congreso Nacional, 2013.

Blakemore, Harold. *British Nitrates and Chilean Politics, 1886–1896: Balmaceda and North.* London: Athlone Press for the Institute of Latin American Studies, 1974.

Blum, Ann S. *Domestic Economies: Family, Work, and Welfare in Mexico City, 1884–1943.* Lincoln: University of Nebraska Press, 2009.

Blum, Ann S. "Speaking of Work and Family: Reciprocity, Child Labor, and Social Reproduction, Mexico City, 1920–1940." *Hispanic American Historical Review* 91, no. 1 (2011): 63–95.

Bohoslavsky, Ernesto. "Casa tomada. Pobreza, desempleo y asaltos populares en el sur de Chile en los '30." *Entrepasados. Revista de Historia*, no. 23 (2002): 101–22.

Bonino, N., and García Repetto. "Protección frente al desempleo estacional y bolsas de trabajo en Uruguay (1944–1979)." *Revista uruguaya de historia económica* 3, no. 4 (2013): 46–55.

Brahm García, Enrique. "La visión de la diplomacia alemana sobre un momento de crisis del régimen de gobierno chileno: la caída del presidente Carlos Ibáñez del Campo en julio de 1931." *Revista de estudios histórico-jurídicos* no. 33 (2011): 487–510.

Bravo Acevedo, Guillermo. "La crisis de 1929 y los problemas de la sociedad urbana de Valparaíso." In *Valparaíso 1536–1985*, edited by Instituto de Historia, 171–83. Valparaíso: Universidad Católica de Valparaíso, 1987.

Bravo Vargas, Viviana. *Piedras, barricadas y cacerolas: las jornadas nacionales de protesta. Chile 1983–1986.* Santiago: Ediciones Universidad Alberto Hurtado, 2017.

Brown, Juan, et al. "Economía chilena 1810–1995: estadísticas históricas." *Documento de Trabajo* (Facultad de Economía, Universidad Católica) no. 187 (2000).

Bruey, Alison. *Bread, Justice, and Liberty: Grassroot Activism and Human Rights in Pinochet's Chile.* Madison: University of Wisconsin Press, 2018.

Burnett, John. *Idle Hands: The Experience of Unemployment, 1790–1990.* London: Routledge, 1994.

Candina Polomer, Azun. *Clase media, Estado y sacrificio: la Agrupación Nacional de Empleados Fiscales en Chile contemporáneo (1943–1983).* Santiago: LOM Ediciones, 2013.

Cariola Sutter, Carmen, and Osvaldo Sunkel. *Un siglo de historia económica de Chile, 1830–1930.* Santiago: Editorial Universitaria, 1990.

Cavallo, Ascanio, Manuel Salazar, and Oscar Sepúlveda. *La historia oculta del régimen militar. Memoria de una época.* Santiago: Mondadori, 1997.

Cazorla, Antonio. *Miedo y progreso: los españoles de a pie bajo el franquismo, 1938–1975.* Madrid: Alianza Editorial, 2010.

Cerón Blau, Nicky Antonio. "Por una vivienda digna de ser ocupada por seres humanos: Movimiento Social Arrendatario: dinámicas asociativas y de politización popular (1914–1925)." Thesis, Universidad de Chile, 2017.

Cohen, Lizabeth. *A Consumers' Republic: The Politics of Mass Consumption in Postwar America.* New York: Vintage Books, 2003.

Cohen, Lizabeth. *Making a New Deal: Industrial Workers in Chicago, 1919–1939*, 2nd ed. Cambridge: Cambridge University Press, 2008.

Cohen, Miriam, and Michael Hanagan. "Politics, Industrialization and Citizenship: Unemployment Policy in England, France and the United States, 1890–1950." *International Review of Social History* 9 :(1995) ,401–129.

Couyoumdjian, Juan Enrique. *Chile y Gran Bretaña: durante la Primera Guerra Mundial y la postguerra, 1914–1921.* Santiago: Editorial Andrés Bello.

Cox de Edwards, Alejandra. "Mercado laboral chileno durante la década de 1974–1983: Problemas de ajuste." *Cuadernos de Economía* 24, no. 72 (1987): 165–95.

Crew, David F. *Germans on Welfare: From Weimar to Hitler.* New York: Oxford University Press, 1998.

Cury, Márcia Carolina de Oliveira, *El protagonismo popular chileno: Experiencias de clase y movimientos sociales en la construcción del socialismo (1964–1973).* Santiago: LOM Ediciones, 2018.

Daniel, Claudia. "De crisis a crisis: la invención de la desocupación en La Argentina." *Revista de Indias* 73, no. 257 (2013): 193–218.

Délano, Manuel, and Gérard Thirion. *PREALC 25 años.* Geneva: ILO, 1993.

DeShazo, Peter. *Urban Workers and Labor Unions in Chile, 1902–1927.* Madison: University of Wisconsin Press, 1983.

De Ramón, Armando. *Santiago de Chile. Historia de una sociedad urbana*. Santiago: Catalonia, 2015.

Dinamarca, Manuel. *La República Socialista: orígenes legítimos del Partido Socialista*. Santiago: Documentas/Estudio, 1987.

Dirección General del Trabajo. *La Inspección General del Trabajo. El surgimiento de la fiscalización laboral, 1924–1934*. Santiago: Dirección del Trabajo, 2010.

Donoso, Ricardo. *Alessandri, agitador y demoledor. Cincuenta años de historia política de Chile*. Vol. 2. Santiago: Editorial Tierra Firme, 1954.

Drake, Paul W. *The Money Doctor in the Andes: The Kemmerer Missions, 1923–1933*. Durham, NC: Duke University Press, 1989.

Drake, Paul W. *Socialism and Populism in Chile, 1932–52*. Urbana: University of Illinois Press, 1978.

Drinot, Paulo. *The Allure of Labor: Workers, Race, and the Making of the Peruvian State*. Durham, NC: Duke University Press, 2011.

Drinot, Paulo. "Food, Race, and Working-Class Identity: Restaurantes Populares and Populism in 1930s Peru." *Americas* 62, no. 2 (2005): 245–70.

Drinot, Paulo, and Alan Knight, eds. *The Great Depression in Latin America*. Durham, NC: Duke University Press, 2014.

Elena, Eduardo. *Dignifying Argentina: Peronism, Citizenship, and Mass Consumption*. Pittsburgh: University of Pittsburgh Press, 2011.

Espin-Anderson, Gøsta. *The Three Worlds of Welfare Capitalism*. Cambridge: Polity, 1990.

Evans, Richard J., and Dick Geary. *The German Unemployed: Experiences and Consequences of Mass Unemployment from the Weimar Republic to the Third Reich*. New York: St. Martin's, 1987.

Feiertag, Olivier. "Réguler la mondialisation: Albert Thomas, les débuts du BIT et la crise économique mondiale de 1920–1923." *Les cahiers irice* 2, no. 2 (2008): 127–55.

Fernández, Joaquín. *El ibañismo (1937–1952): Un caso de populismo en la política Chilena*. Santiago: Universidad Católica, 2007.

Ffrench-Davis, Ricardo, and Ernesto Tironi, eds. *El cobre en el desarrollo nacional*. Santiago: Ediciones Nueva Universidad, 1974.

Fink, Leon. *Sweatshops at Sea: Merchant Seamen in the World's First Globalized Industry, from 1812 to the Present*. Chapel Hill: University of North Carolina Press, 2011.

Fink, Leon, ed. *Workers across the Americas: The Transnational Turn in Labor History*. New York: Oxford University Press, 2011.

Fink, Leon, and Juan Manuel Palacio, eds. *Labor Justice across the Americas*. Urbana: University of Illinois Press, 2018.

Fleet, Michael. *The Rise and Fall of Chilean Christian Democracy*. Princeton, NJ: Princeton University Press, 2014.

Flores, Jaime. "Un episodio de historia social de Chile 1934, Ranquil. Una revuelta campesina." MA thesis, Universidad de Santiago de Chile, 1993.

Fontes, Paulo. *Migration and the Making of Industrial São Paulo*. Durham, NC: Duke University Press, 2016.

Foxley, Alejandro. "Políticas de estabilización." *Estudios CIEPLAN* 2 (1979): 37–74.

Frías Fernández, Patricio, Magdalena Echeverría, Gonzalo Herrera, and Christian Larraín, *Industria textil y del vestuario en Chile*. Santiago: PET, 1987.

Gárate Chateau, Manuel. *La revolución capitalista en Chile (1973–1990)*. Santiago: Universidad Alberto Hurtado, 2012.

Garside, W. R. *British Unemployment, 1919–1939: A Study in Public Policy*. Cambridge: Cambridge University Press, 1990.

Garside, W. R. *The Measurement of Unemployment: Methods and Sources in Great Britain, 1850–1970*. Oxford: Basil Blackwell, 1980.

Gaudichaud, Franck. *Poder popular y cordones industriales: testimonios sobre el movimiento popular urbano, 1970–1973*. Santiago: LOM Ediciones, 2004.

Goicovic, Igor. "La crisis económica de 1929 y el retorno de los salitreros: efectos politicos y sociales en El Valle del Choapa (1929—1938)." *Espacio Regional* 1, no. 8 (2001): 51–68.

Goicovic, Igor. "Crisis económica y respuesta social. Choapa 1929–1935." *Notas Históricas y Geográficas* no. 4 (1993): 119–53.

Gómez Leyton, Juan Carlos. "Crisis, hambre y socialismo: Chile 1931–1932," *Andes*, no. 5 (1987): 101–59.

González Miranda, Sergio. *Hombres y mujeres de la pampa. Tarapacá en el ciclo del salitre*. Santiago: LOM Ediciones, 2002.

Grez Toso, Sergio. *El Partido Democrático de Chile: Auge y ocaso de una organización política popular (1887–1927)*. Santiago: LOM Ediciones, 2016.

Grez Toso, Sergio. *Historia del comunismo en Chile. La era de Recabarren (1912–1924)*. Santiago: LOM Ediciones, 2011.

Grez Toso, Sergio. "Una mirada al movimiento popular desde dos asonadas callejeras (Santiago, 1888–1905)." *Revista de Estudios Históricos* 3, no. 1 (2006): 158–93.

Greenberg, Cheryl Lynn. *To Ask for an Equal Chance: African Americans in the Great Depression*. New York: Rowman and Littlefield, 2009.

Guajardo, Guillermo. "La capacitación técnico manual de los trabajadores ferroviarios chilenos (1852–1914)." *Proposiciones* no. 19 (1990).

Guisti, Jorge. "Participación popular en Chile: antecedentes para su estudio, las JAP." *Revista Mexicana de Sociología* 37, no. 3 (1975): 767–88.

Guy, Donna J. *Women Build the Welfare State: Performing Charity and Creating Rights in Argentina, 1880–1955*. Durham, NC: Duke University Press, 2009.

Hachette, Dominique, Rolf Lüders, and Guillermo Tagle. "Five Cases of Privatization in Chile." In *Privatization in Latin America*, edited by Manuel Sánchez and Rossana Corona. Washington, DC: Inter American Development Bank, 1993.

Haney, Lynne A. *Inventing the Needy: Gender and the Politics of Welfare in Hungary*. Berkeley: University of California Press, 2002.

Hardy, Clarisa. *Hambre + dignidad = ollas communes*. Santiago: PET, 1986.

Henríquez, Rodrigo. *En "estado sólido": políticas y politización en la construcción estatal. Chile, 1920–1950*. Santiago: Pontificia Universidad Católica de Chile, 2014.

Herrera León, Fabián, Patricio Herrera González, and Juan Carlos Yáñez Andrade, eds. *América Latina y la Organización Internacional del Trabajo: redes, cooperación técnica e institucionalidad social (1919–1950)*. Morelia, Michoacán, México: Instituto de Investigaciones Históricas, Universidad Michoacana de San Nicolás de Hidalgo, 2013.

Hidalgo, Rodrigo. *La vivienda social en Chile y la construcción del espacio urbano en el Santiago del siglo XX*. Santiago: DIBAM, 2005.

Hirschman, Albert O. *Journeys toward Progress: Studies of Economic Policy-Making in Latin America*. Garden City, NY: Doubleday, 1965.

Hobsbawm, Eric J. *The Age of Extremes: A History of the World, 1914–1991*. New York: Vintage, 1996.

Hong, Young-Sun. *Welfare, Modernity, and the Weimar State, 1919–1933*. Princeton, NJ: Princeton University Press, 1998.

Huneeus, Carlos, and Javier Couso, eds. *Eduardo Frei Montalva: un gobierno reformista. A 50 años de la Revolución en Libertad*. Santiago: Editorial Universitaria, 2016.

Hurtado Ruiz-Tagle, Carlos. *Concentración de población y desarrollo económico. El caso chileno*. Santiago: Universidad de Chile, Instituto de Economía, 1966.

Hurtado-Torres, Sebastián. *The Gathering Storm: Eduardo Frei's Revolution in Liberty and Chile's Cold War*. Ithaca, NY: Cornell University Press, 2020.

Hutchison, Elizabeth Q. "La historia detrás de las cifras: la evolución del censo chileno y la representación del trabajo femenino, 1895–1930." *Historia* (Santiago), 33 (2000): 417–34.

Hutchison, Elizabeth Q. *Labors Appropriate to their Sex: Gender, Labor, and Politics in Urban Chile, 1900–1930*. Durham, NC: Duke University Press, 2001.

Illanes, María Angélica. *Ausente señorita: el niño chileno, la escuela para pobres y el auxilio 1890/1990 (hacia una historia social del siglo XX)*. Santiago: Junta Nacional de Auxilio Escolar y Becas, 1990.

Illanes, María Angélica. *Cuerpo y sangre de la política: la construcción histórica de las visitadoras sociales, Chile, 1887–1940*. Santiago: LOM Ediciones, 2007.

Illanes, María Angélica. "Ella en Lota-Coronel: poder y domesticación. El primer servicio social industrial de América Latina." *Mapocho*, no. 49 (2001): 141–48.

Illanes, María Angélica. *"En el nombre del pueblo, del estado y de la ciencia": historia social de la salud pública Chile 1880–1973*. Santiago: Colectivo de Atención Primaria, 1993.

Ioris, Rafael. "'Fifty Years in Five' and What's in it for Us?' Development Promotion, Populism, Industrial Workers and Carestia in 1950s Brazil." *Journal of Latin American Studies* 44, no. 2 (2012): 261–84.

Jacobs, Meg. *Pocketbook Politics: Economic Citizenship in Twentieth-Century America*. Princeton, NJ: Princeton University Press, 2007.

Jobet, Julio César. *Historia del Partido Socialista*. Santiago: Documentas/Estudio, 1987.

Kay, Cristóbal. *Latin American Theories of Development and Underdevelopment*. London: Routledge, 2010.

Keynes, John M. *The General Theory of Employment, Interest, and Money*. London: MacMillan, 1936.

Keyssar, Alexander. *Out of Work: The First Century of Unemployment in Massachusetts*. Cambridge: Cambridge University Press, 1986.

King, Desmond. *Actively Seeking Work? The Politics of Unemployment and Welfare Policy in the United States and Great Britain*. Chicago: University of Chicago Press, 1995.

Klubock, Thomas Miller. *Contested Communities: Class, Gender, and Politics in Chile's El Teniente Copper Mine, 1904–1951*. Durham, NC: Duke University Press, 1998.

Klubock, Thomas Miller. *La Frontera: Forests and Ecological Conflict in Chile's Frontier Territory*. Durham, NC: Duke University Press, 2014.

Kott, Sandrine, and Joëlle Droux, eds. *Globalizing Social Rights: The International Labour Organization and Beyond*. New York: Palgrave Macmillan, 2013.

LaBarbera-Twarog, Emily. *Politics of the Pantry: Housewives, Food, and Consumer Protest in Twentieth-Century America*. New York: Oxford University Press, 2017.

Lecerf, Éric. "Les conférences internationales pour la lutte contre le chômage au début du siècle." *Mil neuf cent*, no. 7 (1989): 99–126.

Leiva Flores, Sebastián. "Vida y trabajo de la clase obrera chilena. Los trabajadores textiles y metalúrgicos entre las décadas de 1930 y 1960." PhD diss., Universidad de Santiago, 2018.

Lira, Elizabeth, and Brian Loveman. *Los actos de la dictadura. Comisión investigadora 1931*. Santiago: DIBAM, 2006.

Lira, Elizabeth, and Hugo Rojas, eds. *Libertad sindical y derechos humanos. Análisis de los informes del Comité de Libertad Sindical de la OIT (1973–1990)*. Santiago: LOM Ediciones, DIBAM, Universidad Academia de Humanismo Cristiano, 2009.

Llanos, Claudio. *Cuando el pueblo unido fue vencido: estudios sobre la vía chilena al socialismo*. Valparaíso: Ediciones Universitarias de Valparaíso, 2014.

Llanos, Claudio. "La dictadura militar en Chile frente al desempleo: algunos aspectos de la mirada política 1973–1978." *Estudios Ibero-Americanos* 44, no. 2 (2018): 311–25.

López, A. Ricardo, and Barbara Weinstein, eds. *The Making of the Middle Class: Toward a Transnational History of the Middle Class.* Durham, NC: Duke University Press, 2012.

Loveman, Brian. *Chile: The Legacy of Hispanic Capitalism.* 3rd ed. New York: Oxford University Press, 2001.

Loveman, Brian. "The Political Architecture of Dictatorship: Chile before 1973," *Radical History Review* 125 (January 2016): 11–42.

Loveman, Brian. *Struggle in the Countryside: Politics and Rural Labor in Chile, 1919–1973.* Bloomington: Indiana University Press, 1976.

Loveman, Brian, and Elizabeth Lira. *Arquitectura política y seguridad interior del estado: Chile, 1811–1990.* Santiago: DIBAM, Universidad Alberto Hurtado, 2002.

Loveman, Brian, and Elizabeth Lira. *Las suaves cenizas del olvido: vía chilena de reconciliación política, 1814–1932.* Santiago: LOM Ediciones, 1999.

Loveman, Brian, and Elizabeth Lira. *Poder Judicial y conflictos políticos. Chile 1925–1958.* Santiago: LOM Ediciones, Universidad Alberto Hurtado, 2014.

Loveman, Mara. *National Colors: Racial Classification and the State in Latin America.* Oxford: Oxford University Press, 2014.

Lüders, Rolf, and Nora Cabrera. "Employment and Technology: The Chilean Case." Meeting of Experts on Fiscal Policies for Employment Promotion, ILO, Geneva, January 4–8, 1971.

Maldonado, Carlos. *La Milicia Republicana: historia de un ejército civil en Chile, 1932–1936.* Santiago: WUS, 1988.

Mamalakis, Markos, and Clark Winton Reynolds. *Essays on the Chilean Economy.* Homewood, IL: Richard D. Irwin, 1965.

Mansfield, M., Robert Salais, and Noel Whiteside. *Aux sources du chômage, 1880–1914: Une comparaison interdisciplinaire entre la France et La Grande-Bretagne.* Paris: Belin, 1994.

Marfán, Manuel. "Políticas reactivadoras y recesión externa, 1929–1938." *Estudios CIEPLAN* no. 12 (1984): 89–119.

Marx, Karl. *Capital*, vol. 1. New York: Vintage, 1977.

Matus, Mario. *Crecimiento sin desarrollo. Precios y salarios reales durante el ciclo salitrero en Chile (1880–1930).* Santiago: Editorial Universitaria, 2012.

Matus, Mario, and Isabel Jara Hinojosa, eds. *Hombres del metal: trabajadores ferroviarios y metalúrgicos chilenos en el ciclo salitrero, 1880–1930.* Santiago: Universidad de Chile, 2009.

McKillen, Elizabeth. *Making the World Safe for Workers: Labor, the Left, and Wilsonian Internationalism.* Urbana: University of Illinois Press, 2013.

Meller, Patricio. *Un siglo de política económica chilena (1890–1990).* Santiago: Ugbar, 2016.

Milanesio, Natalia. *Workers Go Shopping in Argentina: The Rise of Popular Consumer Culture.* Albuquerque: University of New Mexico Press, 2015.

Milos, Pedro, ed. *Chile 1970: el país en que triunfa Salvador Allende*. Santiago: Editorial Universidad Alberto Hurtado, 2013.

Molina, Sergio. *El proceso de cambio en Chile: la experiencia 1965–1970*. Santiago: Editorial Universitaria, 1972.

Monsalvo Mendoza, Edwin, and Roberto González Arana. "Contra la moral i las buenas costumbres: el control de la vagancia y la prostitución en la frontera sur de Antioquia, Manizales, Colombia, 1850–1870." *Caravelle* no. 104 (2015): 153–75.

Monteón, Michael. *Chile and the Great Depression: The Politics of Underdevelopment, 1927–1948*. Tempe: Center for Latin American Studies Press, Arizona State University, 1998.

Monteón, Michael. *Chile in the Nitrate Era: The Evolution of Economic Dependence, 1880–1930*. Madison: University of Wisconsin Press, 1982.

Monteón, Michael. "The *Enganche* in the Chilean Nitrate Sector, 1880–1930." *Latin American Perspectives* 6, no. 3 (1979): 66–79.

Montgomery, David. *Workers' Control in America: Studies in the History of Work, Technology, and Labor Struggles*. Cambridge: Cambridge University Press, 1979.

Mooney, Jadwiga E. Pieper. *The Politics of Motherhood: Maternity and Women's Rights in Twentieth-Century Chile*. Pittsburgh: University of Pittsburgh Press, 2009.

Morris, James O. *Élites, Intellectuals, and Consensus: A Study of the Social Question and the Industrial Relations System in Chile*. Ithaca, NY: School of Industrial and Labor Relations, Cornell University, 1966.

Morris, James O,, and Roberto Oyaneder. *Estudio de afiliación y finanzas sindicales en Chile, 1932–1959*. Santiago: INSORA, Universidad de Chile, 1962.

Moulián, Tomás. *El gobierno de Ibáñez. 1952–1958*. Santiago: FLACSO, 1986.

Nelson, Daniel. *Unemployment Insurance: The American Experience, 1915–1935*. Madison: University of Wisconsin Press, 1969.

Nun, José. *Marginalidad y exclusión social*. Mexico: Fondo de Cultura Económica, 2001.

O'Brassill-Kulfan, Kristin. *Vagrants and Vagabonds: Poverty and Mobility in the Early-American Republic*. New York: New York University Press, 2019.

O'Brien, Thomas F. *The Nitrate Industry and Chile's Crucial Transition, 1870–1891*. New York: New York University Press, 1982.

Ochoa, Enrique. *Feeding Mexico: The Political Uses of Food since 1910*. Wilmington, DE: Scholarly Resources, 2000.

O'Connor, Alice. *Poverty Knowledge: Social Science, Social Policy, and the Poor in Twentieth-Century U.S. History*. Princeton, NJ: Princeton University Press, 2001.

Ortíz, Eduardo. *La gran depresión, 1929. Impacto en Chile*. Santiago: Liberalia, 2014.

Palacio, Juan Manuel. *La justicia peronista: la construcción de un nuevo orden legal en la Argentina*. Buenos Aires: Siglo XXI, 2018.

Palma, Gabriel. "Chile 1914–1935: de economía exportadora a substitutiva de exportaciones." *Estudios CIEPLAN* no. 12 (1984): 61–88.

Panettieri, José. *Ayer y hoy: desocupación y subocupación en La Argentina.* Buenos Aires: Grupo Editor Universitario, 1997.

Parker, David S. *The Idea of the Middle Class: White-Collar Workers and Peruvian Society, 1900–1950.* University Park: Pennsylvania State University Press, 1998.

Parker, David S., and Louise E. Walker, eds. *Latin America's Middle Class: Unsettled Debates and New Histories.* Lanham, MD: Lexington Books, 2013.

Patriarca, Silvana. *Numbers and Nationhood: Writing Statistics in Nineteenth-Century Italy.* New York: Cambridge University Press, 1996.

Pavilack, Jody. *Mining for the Nation: The Politics of Chile's Coal Communities from the Popular Front to the Cold War.* University Park: Pennsylvania State University Press, 2011.

Pénin, Marc. *Charles Gide, 1847–1932: l'esprit critique.* Paris: L'Harmattan, 1997.

Pérez Sáinz, Juan Pablo. *Mercados y bárbaros: la persistencia de las desigualdades de excedente en América Latina.* San José: FLACSO, Sede Costa Rica, 2014.

Perlman, Janice E. *The Myth of Marginality: Urban Poverty and Politics in Rio de Janeiro.* Berkeley: University of California Press, 1976.

Pernet, Corinne A. "L'OIT et la question de l'alimentation en Amérique latine (1930–1950). Les problémes poses par la definition internationale des norms de niveau de vie." In *L'Organisation Internationale du Travail: origines, développment, avenir,* edited by Isabelle Lespinet-Moret and Vincent Viet. Rennes: Presses Universitaires, 2011.

Pinto Vallejos, Julio. *Desgarros y utopías en la pampa salitrera: La consolidación de la identidad obrera en tiempos de la cuestion social, 1890–1923.* Santiago: LOM Ediciones, 2007.

Pinto Vallejos, Julio. *Episodios de historia minera: estudios de historia social y económica de la minería chilena, siglos XVIII–XIX.* Santiago: Editorial Universidad de Santiago, 1997.

Pinto Vallejos, Julio. *Trabajos y rebeldías en la pampa salitrera: El ciclo del salitre y la reconfiguración de las identidades populares (1850–1900).* Santiago: Editorial Universidad de Santiago, 1998.

Pinto Vallejos, Julio, and Valdivia Ortiz de Zárate, Verónica. *¿Revolución proletaria o querida chusma?: socialismo y alessandrismo en la pugna por la politización paml pina (1911–1932).* 1st ed. Santiago: LOM Ediciones, 2001.

Ponce de León Atria, Macarena. *Gobernar la pobreza: prácticas de caridad y beneficencia en la ciudad de Santiago, 1830–1890.* Santiago: Editorial Universitaria, Centro de Investigaciones Diego Barros Arana, 2011.

Quadagno, Jill. *The Color of Welfare: How Racism Undermined the War on Poverty.* New York: Oxford University Press, 1995.

Quijano, Alberto. "Notas sobre el concepto de marginalidad social." Santiago: CEPAL, División de Asuntos Sociales, 1966.

Recabarren, Floreal. *La matanza de San Gregorio 1921: crisis y tragedia*. Santiago: LOM Ediciones, 2003.

Rengifo, Francisca, "Desigualdad e inclusión: la ruta del estado de seguridad social chileno, 1920–1970." *Hispanic American Historical Review* 97, no. 3 (2017).

Rock, David ed. *Latin America in the 1940s: War and Postwar Transitions*. Berkeley: University of California Press, 1994.

Rodgers, Daniel T. *Atlantic Crossings: Social Politics in a Progressive Age*. Cambridge, MA: Belknap Press of Harvard University Press, 1998.

Rodgers, Gerry, et al. *The International Labour Organization and the Quest for Social Justice, 1919–2009*. Geneva: International Labour Office, 2009.

Rodogno, Davide, Bernhard Struck, and Jakob Vogel, eds. *Shaping the Transnational Sphere: Experts, Networks, and Issues from the 1840s to the 1930s*. New York: Berghahn Books, 2015.

Rodríguez, Julia. *Civilizing Argentina: Science, Medicine, and the Modern State*. Chapel Hill: University of North Carolina Press, 2006.

Rojas Flores, Jorge. *Historia de la infancia en el Chile republicano: 1810–2010*. Santiago: Junta Nacional de Jardines Infantiles, 2010.

Rojas Flores, Jorge. *La dictadura de Ibáñez y los sindicatos (1927–1931)*. Santiago, Chile: Centro Barros Arana, DIBAM, 1993.

Rojas Flores, Jorge, Alfonso Murúa Olguín, and Gonzalo Rojas Flores. *La historia de los obreros de la construcción*. Santiago: Programa de Economía de Trabajo, 1993.

Rosemblatt, Karin Alejandra. *Gendered Compromises: Political Cultures and the State in Chile, 1920–1950*. Chapel Hill: University of North Carolina Press, 2000.

Rosenblitt, Jaime. "El ministerio de Gustavo Ross y la configuración del estado nacional desarrollista." *Historia* 25 (1995–1996): 405–42.

Rougier, Marcelo, and Juan Odisio. *Argentina será industrial o no cumplirá sus destinos. Las ideas sobre el desarrollo nacional (1914–1980)*. San Martín, Argentina: Imago Mundi, 2017.

Ruggiero, Kristin. *Modernity in the Flesh: Medicine, Law, and Society in Turn-of-the-Century Argentina*. Stanford, CA: Stanford University Press, 2004.

Sábato, Hilda, and Luis Alberto Romero. *Los trabajadores de Buenos Aires: la experiencia del mercado, 1850–1880*. Buenos Aires: Editorial Sudamericana, 1992.

Salais, Robert, Nicolas Baverez, and Bénédicte Reynaud. *L'invention du chômage: Histoire et transformations d'une catégorie en France des années 1890 aux années 1980*. 1st ed. Paris: Presses universitaires de France, 1986.

Salais, Robert, and Roger Lionnet. *Enquêtes sur l'emploi 1968 et 1969; Principaux résultats*. Paris: I.N.S.E.E., 1971.

Salazar, Gabriel. *Ferias libres: espacio residual de soberanía ciudadana*. Santiago: Ediciones Sur, 2003.

Salazar, Gabriel. *Labradores, peones y proletarios: formación y crisis de la sociedad popular chilena del siglo XIX*. Santiago: Ediciones Sur, 1985.

Sánchez Lovell, Adriana. "El problema de la vagancia: una propuesta de enfoque teórico desde la historia del trabajo, a partir del caso de Costa Rica en el siglo XIX." *Diálogos* 17, no. 2 (2016): 161–90.

Santibáñez Rebolledo, Camilo. "Los trabajadores portuarios chilenos y la experiencia de la eventualidad: Los conflictos por la redondilla en los muelles salitreros (1916–1923)." *Historia* 50, no. 2 (2017): 699–728.

Santibáñez Rebolledo, Camilo. "Huelgas y lockouts portuarios por la redondilla: Los conflictos por el control de la contratación en los muelles chilenos (1916–1923)." MA thesis, Universidad de Santiago de Chile, 2016.

Salvatore, Ricardo. *Disciplinary Conquest: U.S. Scholars in South America, 1900–1945*. Durham, NC: Duke University Press, 2016.

Salvatore, Ricardo. *Wandering Paysanos: State Order and Subaltern Experience in Buenos Aires during the Rosas Era*. Durham, NC: Duke University Press, 2003.

Sanders, Nichole. *Gender and Welfare in Mexico: The Consolidation of a Postrevolutionary State*. University Park: Pennsylvania State University Press, 2011.

Sater, William. "Chile and the World Depression of the 1870s." *Journal of Latin American Studies* 11, no. 1 (1979): 67–99.

Saunier, Pierre-Yves. "Circulations, connexions et espaces transnationaux." *Genèses* 4, no. 57 (2004): 110–26.

Sauthier, Ingrid. "Histoire de la définition du chômage." *Courrier des statistiques* 127 (2009): 5–12.

Schatz, Ronald W. *The Electrical Workers: A History of Labor at General Electric and Westinghouse, 1923–60*. Urbana: University of Illinois Press, 1983.

Schkolnik, Mariana, and Berta Teitelboim. *Pobreza y desempleo en poblaciones: la otra cara del modelo neoliberal*. Santiago: PET, 1988.

Scott, James. *Seeing Like a State: How Certain Schemes to Improve the Human Condition Have Failed*. New Haven, CT: Yale University Press, 1998.

Sehnbruch, Kirsten. *The Chilean Labor Market: A Key to Understanding Latin American Labor Markets*. New York: Springer, 2006.

Sepúlveda Momberg, Matías. "Del trabajo protegido al trabajo subsidiado. Intervención, libre mercado y la situación de los trabajadores del PEM y POHJ, 1974–1984." In *Instituto de Historia*, Seminario Simon Collier 2014. Santiago: Instituto de Historia, 2015.

Shukla, Sandhya Rajendra, and Heidi Tinsman, eds. *Imagining Our Americas: Toward a Transnational Frame*. Durham, NC: Duke University Press, 2007.

Silva, J. Pablo. "The Origins of White-Collar Privilege in Chile: Arturo Alessandri, Law 6020, and the Pursuit of a Corporatist Consensus, 1933–1938." *Labor* 3, no. 1 (2006): 87–112.

Silva, Patricio. *In the Name of Reason: Technocrats and Politics in Chile*. University Park: Pennsylvania State University Press, 2008.

Skocpol, Theda. *Protecting Soldiers and Mothers: The Political Origins of Social Policy in the United States*. Cambridge, MA: Belknap Press of Harvard University Press, 1992.

Stallings, Barbara. *Class Conflict and Economic Development in Chile, 1958–1973*. Stanford, CA: Stanford University Press, 1978.

Stapleford, Thomas A. *The Cost of Living in America: A Political History of Economic Statistics, 1880–2000*. New York: Cambridge University Press, 2009.

Stickell, Arthur. "Migration and Mining: Labor in Northern Chile in the Nitrate Era, 1880–1930." PhD diss., Indiana University, 1979.

Strikwerda, Eric. *The Wages of Relief: Cities and the Unemployed in Prairie Canada, 1929–39*. Edmonton, Canada: Athabasca University Press, 2013.

Suárez-Potts, William J. *The Making of Law: The Supreme Court and Labor Legislation in Mexico, 1875–1931*. Stanford, CA: Stanford University Press, 2012.

Tenorio, Mauricio. *Mexico at the World's Fairs: Crafting a Modern Nation*. Berkeley: University of California Press, 1996.

Thielemann, Luis. "La perspectiva parcial: el movimiento obrero frente a la política salarial del gobierno de Frei Montalva, 1964-1967". *Economía y política* no. 1, 6 (2019): 85–116.

Thompson, E. P. *The Making of the English Working Class*. New York: Vintage, 1963.

Thompson, E. P. "The Moral Economy of the English Crowd in the Eighteenth Century," *Past and Present* 50 (1971): 76–136.

Thorp, Rosemary, ed. *An Economic History of Twentieth-Century Latin America*. Oxford: Palgrave, 2000.

Thorp, Rosemary. *Progress, Poverty, and Exclusion: An Economic History of Latin America in the 20th Century*. Washington, DC: Inter American Development Bank, 1998.

Topalov, Christian. *Histoires d'enquêtes: Londres, Paris, Chicago (1880–1930)*. Paris: Classiques Garnier, 2015.

Topalov, Christian. *Naissance du chômeur, 1880–1910*. Paris: A. Michel, 1994.

Urzúa Valenzuela, Germán. *Evolución de la administración pública chilena*. Santiago: Editorial Jurídica, 1970.

Valdés, Juan Gabriel. *Pinochet's Economists: The Chicago School of Economics in Chile*. Cambridge: Cambridge University Press, 1995.

Valdivia Ortiz de Zárate, Verónica. "Estatismo y neoliberalismo: un contrapunto militar. Chile 1973–1979." *Historia* (Santiago) 34 (2001): 167–226.

Valdivia Ortiz de Zárate, Verónica. *Las Milicias Republicanas. Los civiles en armas, 1932–1936*. Santiago: Centro de Investigaciones Diego Barros Arana, 1992.

Valdivia, Verónica, Rolando Álvarez, and Karen Donoso Fritz. *La alcaldización de la política: los municipios en la dictadura pinochetista*. Santiago: LOM Ediciones, 2012.

Valdivieso, Patricio. *Dignidad humana y justicia: la historia de Chile, la política social y el cristianismo, 1880–1920*. Santiago: Ediciones Universidad Católica, 2006.

Van Daele, Jasmien, ed. *ILO Histories: Essays on the International Labour Organization and its Impact on the World during the Twentieth Century*. New York: Peter Lang, 2010.

Viales Hurtado, Ronny, and Emmanuel Barrantes Zamora. "Mercado laboral y mecanismos de control de mano de obra en la cafilcultura centroamerica: Guatemala y Costa Rica en el período 1850–1930." *Revista de Historia*, no. 55–56 (2007): 15–36.

Vergara, Ángela. "Identifying the Unemployed: Social Categories and Relief in Depression-Era Chile (1930–1934)." *Labor* 15, no. 3 (2018): 9–30.

Vergara, Ángela. "Cuando los obreros no trabajan: una aproximación a la historia del desempleo en América Latina." In *Trabajadores y sindicatos en Latinoamérica: conceptos, problemas y escalas de análisis*, edited by Silvia Simonassi and Daniel Dicósimo, 3–18. San Martín, Argentina: Imago Mundi, 2017.

Vergara, Ángela. "Busquemos oro. Trabajo, lavaderos de oro y ayuda fiscal durante tiempos de crisis, Chile 1930–1936." *Tiempo Histórico*, no. 11 (2015): 75–92.

Vergara, Ángela. "Precios y raciones: La Anaconda Copper Company en Chile entre 1932 y 1958." *Investigaciones de historia económica* 3 (2012): 135–43.

Vergara, Ángela. *Copper Workers, International Business, and Domestic Politics in Cold War Chile*. University Park: Pennsylvania State University Press, 2008.

Vergara, Ángela. "Conflicto y modernización en la Gran Minería del Cobre (1950–1970)." *Historia (Chile)*, no. 37 (2004): 419–36.

Vergara, Ángela, and Peter Winn, "'Los empresarios hacen lo que quieren': sindicatos y trabajadores bajo la dictadura de Pinochet." In *Un país desigual a la fuerza: complicidad económica con la dictadura chilena*, edited by Juan Pablo Bohoslavsky, Karinna Fernández, and Sebastián Smart. Santiago: LOM Ediciones, 2019.

Videla Bravo, Enzo, Hernán Venegas Valdevenito, and Milton Godoy Orellana, eds. *El orden fabril: paternalismo industrial en la minería chilena, 1900–1950*. Valparaíso: América en Movimiento, 2016.

Wadauer, Sigrid, ed. *The History of Labour Intermediation: Institutions and Finding Employment in the Nineteenth and Early Twentieth Centuries*. New York: Berghahn Books, 2015.

Walkowitz, Daniel J. *Working with Class: Social Workers and the Politics of Middle-Class Identity*. Chapel Hill: University of North Carolina Press, 1999.

Walter, Richard. *Politics and Urban Growth in Santiago, Chile, 1891–1941*. Stanford, CA: Stanford University Press, 2005.

Williams, Raymond. *Keywords: A Vocabulary of Culture and Society*. New York: Oxford University Press, 1985.

Winn, Peter. *La revolución chilena*. Santiago: LOM Ediciones, 2013.

Winn, Peter, ed. *Victims of the Chilean Miracle: Workers and Neoliberalism in the Pinochet Era, 1973–2002*. Durham, NC: Duke University Press, 2004.

Winn, Peter. *Weavers of Revolution: The Yarur Workers and Chile's Road to Socialism*. New York: Oxford University Press, 1986.

Wright, Thomas C. *Landowners and Reform in Chile: The Sociedad Nacional de Agricultura, 1919–1940*. Urbana: University of Illinois Press, 1982.

Wright, Thomas C. "The Politics of Urban Provisioning in Latin American History." In *Food Politics and Society in Latin America*, edited by John C. Super and Thomas C. Wright. Lincoln: Nebraska University Press, 1985.

Yáñez Andrade, Juan Carlos. "'Alimentación abundante, sana y barata': los restaurantes populares en Santiago (1936–1942)." *Cuadernos de Historia (Santiago)* no. 2016) 45): 117–42.

Yáñez Andrade, Juan Carlos. *La intervención social en Chile y el nacimiento de la sociedad salarial, 1907–1932*. Santiago: RIL Editores, 2008.

Yáñez Andrade, Juan Carlos. *La OIT en América del sur: el comunismo y los trabajadores chilenos (1922–1932)*. Santiago: Ediciones Universidad Alberto Hurtado, 2016.

Yáñez Andrade, Juan Carlos. "Las bolsas de trabajo: modernización y control del mercado laboral en Chile (1914–1921)." *Cuadernos de Historia* no. 2007) 26): 107–34.

Yáñez Andrade, Juan Carlos. "Por una legislación social en Chile. El movimiento de los panaderos (1888–1930)." *Historia* 41 (2008): 495–532.

Yáñez Andrade, Juan Carlos. "Trabajo y políticas culturales sobre el tiempo libre: Santiago de Chile, década de 1930." *Historia (Santiago)* 49, no. :(2016) 2 595–629.

Zárate, María Soledad. "Al cuidado femenino. Mujeres y profesiones sanitarias, Chile, 1889–1950." In *Historia de las mujeres en Chile*, vol. 2, edited by Ana María Stuven and Joaquín Fermandois. Santiago: Taurus, 2014.

Zárate, María Soledad. *Dar a luz en Chile, s. XIX: de la ciencia de hembra a la ciencia obstétrica*. Santiago: DIBAM, Universidad Alberto Hurtado, 2007.

Zimmermann, Bénédicte. *La constitution du chômage en Allemagne*. Paris: Éditions de la Maison des sciences de l'homme, 2001.

Zimmermann, Eduardo A. *Los liberales reformistas: la cuestión social en la Argentina, 1890–1916*. Buenos Aires: Editorial Sudamericana, 1995.

Zoberman, Yves. *Une histoire du chômage: de l' antiquité à nos jours*. Paris: Perrin, 2011.

Zolov, Eric. *The Last Good Neighbor: Mexico in the Global Sixties*. Durham, NC: Duke University Press, 2020.

INDEX

Agricultural Export Board, 107
agricultural workers, 29–30, 46, 48, 107, 111, 208n23
Aguirre Cerda, Pedro, 18, 118, 131
Ahumada, Jorge, 142–43
aid to families. *See* family aid
albergues (public shelters), 41, 85–90, 95
Aldunate, José, 153
Alessandri, Arturo, 17, 41, 45, 64, 72–73, 93
Allende, Salvador, 127, 138, 150, 151
Álvarez, Rolando, 44
anarchism, 12, 90
Araya, Bernardo, 127
Arbeitslosigkeit, 8
Argentina: placement offices, 35; unemployment policies, 33–36; unemployment statistics, 34–35
Article 92 of wage increase law, 147
Austria, 10

bakery workers, 110, 111, 198n101, 201n30
bankruptcies, 160–61
Baraona, Jorge, 37, 48
Beltrán, Juan G., 27, 33
Benavente, David, 19
Bernier, Jennie, 82
Beveridge, William, 9, 23, 26, 119, 125, 126

blue collar/white collar distinction, 91–92, 122, 189n82
Blum, Ann, 87
Bolshevik revolution, 28
Bourgeois, Léon, 11, 23
Brazil, 126
Britain, 10
British National Insurance Act (1911), 26
Bunge, Alejandro, 34–35, 171n56
Bustos, Manuel, 160
Butler, Harold B., 29

Caja de Seguro Obrero (CSO), 127, 128, 134
Caja Nacional de Empleados Particulares, 129
Campillo, Horacio, 79, 80
Canada, 10
Cañas O'Ryan, Carlos, 48
Cantero, Manuel, 137, 147
Capital (Marx), 8
capitalism, 8, 12–13
Carvajal, Arturo, 146
Casa del Pueblo, 90
casework approach, 82–83
Catholic Church, 45, 80, 104, 132–33, 158, 186n20
census information and unemployment statistics, 10, 16, 75, 100, 135–36
charitable relief, 76–77, 80, 94, 132–33

237

Chicago Boys, 155–56, 159
child welfare. *See* family aid
chômage (massive unemployment), 8, 14, 38–42. *See also* mass layoffs
coal industry, 59
Cohen, Lizabeth, 76
collective bargaining. *See* labor unions
collective immobility, 123–24
Colombia, 142
Comintern, 12–13
Comisariato General de Subsistencias y Precios, 108–9
Comisión Nacional de Precios, 107–8
Comité Central de Ayuda a los Cesantes, 79
communism, 12–13
Communist Party, 44, 67, 90, 105
company script, 39, 58
company stores, 39, 61, 98–100
Concha Stuardo, Luis Malaquías, 23, 167n3
construction industry, 60–61
contract law, 46, 47–48, 55, 98
contract termination, 46–47
Contreras Labarca, Carlos, 11–12, 13, 37
Convention 122, ILO, 139
copper industry, 59–60, 146
COSACH (Compañía de Salitres de Chile), 68, 112, 182n88
Costa Rica, 139
cost of living, 101–4
crash, economic (1981–1983), 160–62
CRAV (sugar refinery), 161
Crew, David, 63
CSO (Caja de Seguro Obrero), 127, 128, 134
CTCH (National Confederation of Chilean Workers), 127
CUT (Central Única de Trabajadores), 154

D'Ambrosio, Manlio Andrea, 8–9
data. *See* statistics
Dávila, Carlos, 69, 72, 96, 108
de Bray, Leo, 62, 81, 82
de Castro, Sergio, 154, 159
Declaration of Philadelphia (1944), 139
Decree Law 939, 154
Decree Law 2,200, 160
Decree Law 2,258, 160
Decree Law 2,756, 160
Decree Law 3,648, 160
Decree Law 18,620, 160
de las Cases, Philippe, 11
del Fierro, Guillermo, 53, 80
del Río Gundián, Sótero, 79
Departamento de Beneficencia y Asistencia Social, 132
Department of Labor. *See* Labor Department (Oficina del Trabajo)
Department of Public Works, 64
Department of Social Aid, 131–32
deserving contrasted with undeserving poor, 71, 75, 93–94, 130–31, 133
DeShazo, Peter, 40
direct relief: and local governments, 76–78; and national government, 79–81
Dirección General de Cesantía, 70
dismissal. *See* firing
displaced workers, 14, 39–41, 55–56, 58, 76–77, 85
domestic workers, 9, 46, 48
Drake, Paul, 69
Drinot, Paulo, 13, 31
Dubois, Pierre, 154
Dussaillant, Alejandro, 111

Economic Commission for Latin America and the Caribbean (ECLAC), 138
economic crash (1981-1983), 160–62

economic development and jobs, 142–45
economic planning, 142–43
Elgueta, Carlos, 62
Ellsworth, P. T., 109
emergency shelters, 41, 85–90, 95
El empleado, 103, 104
empleados (white collar workers), 90–93, 129
Employment and Social Security Act (1941, Canada), 10
employment contract law. *See* contract law
Employment Policy Convention (1964), 139
employment services, 133–36
employment stability law (1966), 148
ENDESA (National Electrical Company) layoffs, 129
Errázuriz Larraín, Elías, 67
Escribar Mandiola, Héctor, 113
Estadística chilena, 16
evictions. *See* housing

Falkenberg, Ph., 27
family aid: during 1930s, 93–95; lack of framework for, 75, 76; and minimum wage, 110–11, 130–32; for mining families, 59; and PREALC report, 158–59; public shelters, 41; public work, 63. *See also* food, access to; public shelters
family wage, 110, 112, 113
Fernández, Joaquín, 133
firing, 46–47; arbitrary, 15, 146–48
First International Conference of the American States (1936), 112–13
First International Conference on Unemployment (1910), 12, 23, 24, 25–27, 29, 33, 120
FOCH (Federación Obrera de Chile), 43, 44, 67, 71, 90, 174n32
Foiguet, Rene, 106

Fontaine, Arthur L., 29
food, access to, 96, 97–101, 110, 162
Foxley, Alejandro, 155
Frei Montalva, Eduardo, 137, 138, 142–43, 145, 148, 157
Frías Collao, Eugenio, 28
Friedman, Milton, 154
Fuentealba, Clemente, 137
full employment, 119, 151
frictional unemployment, 14

Gaete Berríos, Alfredo, 129, 134
Gálvez, Manuel, 13, 33–34
gender roles: in Germany and US, 63; and minimum wage, 110; and public assistance, 132–33; and soup kitchens, 162; and stereotypes, 31, 87; women in the workforce, 9, 27
General Commissariat of Subsistence and Prices, 108–9
General Strike (1890), 42
Germany, 10, 28
Ghent system, 26
Gibbs House, 42–43, 43–44
Gide, Charles, 11, 23, 106, 167n1
The Gold Campaign, 70–71
gold panning and mining, 70–71
Gómez Leyton, Juan Carlos, 80
González Vera, José Santo, 43, 44
González Videla, Gabriel, 15–16, 124
Goodman, Roe, 136
Great Britain, 9, 10, 26
Great Depression, 6, 14, 41, 91, 96
Grove, Marmaduke, 69
Guy, Donna, 80

Hachette, Dominique, 155
Harberger, Arnold C., 154
Hirschman, Albert O., 72
Holzapfel, Clemente, 80
home life, intrusion on workers', 47, 48
Hott, Elena, 81

housing: evictions, 105–6; rent control, 97; rent subsidies, 105–6; tenant activism, 104–5; tenant leagues, 105
Hurtado, Alberto, 133

Ibáñez Águila, Bernardo, 113
Ibáñez del Campo, Carlos: and declining state revenue, 60; final days of first term and resignation, 62, 79; quoted, 53; second term, 133–34; support for labor laws, 17, 46; work relief programs, 64
idleness, contrasted with unemployment, 7–8, 10, 71–74, 85, 89
Illanes, María Angélica, 82
ILO (International Labor Organization): American states Mexico City meeting (1946), 126; conference (1941), 119; Conference of American states (1936), 112–13; history and purpose of, 12–13, 24; increasing diversity in, 140; influence in Latin America, 8, 30–31; and job creation, 138; Manpower Program, 139; Ottawa meeting (1966), 140–41; Philadelphia meeting (1944), 119; recommendations and guidance, 6, 45; on reforms to placement services, 135; and unemployment during the 1960s, 138–42; unemployment insurance, 28–30; vocational training, 144
INACAP (Instituto Nacional de Capacitación), 144, 157–58
industrialization, 15–16, 44, 117–18
inflation, 79, 154–55
Inter-American Conference on Social Security (1942), 126
International Association Against Unemployment, 24–28
Izquierdo, Adriana, 79, 84, 85

Jay, Raoul, 26–27
job creation, 69–71, 142–43, 145
Jörissen, Luisa, 81
Juan Verdejo, and satirical verse, 103–4
junta and military coup, 153–60
Junta de Beneficencia, 80–81, 82
Junta de Exportación Agrícola, 107
Juntas de Habitación Popular, 97

Kast, Miguel, 159
Kelly, Roberto, 159
Keynes, John, 119
Keyssar, Alexander, 8
Klein-Saks Mission, 6, 131, 132, 135
Klubock, Thomas, 67

Labarca, Amanda, 73
Labor Code (1931), 46, 110, 146; Article 48, 125; Article 86, 123, 124–25; reform (1978), 159–60
labor contract law reform (1966), 144
labor contracts, 47–48
Labor Department (Oficina del Trabajo): access to food and housing, 97–101; collection of statistics, 9–10, 100; and cost of living, 101; establishment (1907), 16, 44–45, 53–54, 177n3; and Gold Campaign, 70–71; and housing crisis, 104; and mass layoffs, 55, 61–62, 123; and placement services, 120–23; restructuring, 1960s, 144; work relief programs, 64
labor exchanges, 26, 40–41, 56–57
labor inspectors, 16, 53, 60, 67, 98–100, 101–2, 110
El laborista, 102
labor legislation (1924), 46
Labor Plan (1978), 160
labor rights, 145–52
labor shortages, 31
labor statistics. *See* statistics

labor unions: and benefits, 128; and job security, 42–44, 145–46; and labor conflicts, 45; and mass layoffs, 125; opposition to decree law reforms, 160; persecution after military coup, 154; and reform of labor code, 146; and regulation of layoffs, 125; teachers' union, 109–10
landlords. *See* housing
Law 4053, 6, 46, 98
Law 5105, 68
Law 6020, 6, 93
Law 7747, 123
Law 16,455, 148, 149
Lawrence, Thomas, 101
layoffs, mass, 42–43, 55, 123–25, 154
Lazard, Max, 30
Leyton, Leonidas, 65
Lira, Elizabeth, 7
Llanos, Claudio, 156
Los Prisioneros, 162
Loveman, Brian, 7
Lüders, Rolf, 155

Macchiavello Varas, Constantino, 106
marginality, theory of, 143
Marguerie, A. J. de, 27–28
Martner, Daniel, 106
Marx, Karl, 8
mass layoffs, 42–43, 55, 123–25, 154
Matte, Eugenio, 69
Matte, Ricardo, 105
Matte Cruchaga, Elvira, 82
Matus, Mario, 41
medical assistance, 134
Meller, Patricio, 162
Merino, Arturo, 159
metal workers, 117–18
Metal Workers Industrial Federation (FIOM), 117
Mexico: Federal Labor Law, 35; Social Security Act (1943), 126, 127

military coup and junta, 153–60
Minimum Employment Plan, 158, 161
minimum wage, 65–67, 101, 109–13, 197n95
minimum work, 158
Ministry of Development (Ministerio de Fomento), 16
Ministry of Labor (Ministerio del Trabajo), 144
Ministry of Social Welfare (Ministerio de Bienestar Social), 81, 100
Miranda, Luis E., 91–92
Montero, Belisario, 27
Montero, Juan Esteban, 17, 62, 64, 69, 79, 102–3
Montes, Jorge, 137
Montt, Balmaceda, 147
Morris, James, 45
Morse, David, 141
Mujica, Federico, 160
municipal regulations, 101–4

National Confederation of Chilean Workers (CTCH), 127
National Convention of Teachers, 109–10
National Employment Service (SENDE), 139–40, 144–45, 157–58
National Placement Service, 120–23
National Planning Agency (ODEPLAN), 143, 159
National Security Act (1911, United Kingdom), 9
National Statistic and Census Service, 100
Navarrete Concha, Víctor, 70, 80
Navarro, Herminia, 128–29
neoliberalism, 153–60
New Economy under Allende, 150–52
night work, 111, 198n101, 201n30
"nitrate pool" for stocks, 44

nitrate workers, 14, 38–42, 54–58, 112
nitrate workers, displaced, 55–56, 76–77, 85
nutrition. *See* food, access to

Ocampo, Salvador, 129–30
Occupational Disease and Accidents law (1968), 144
O'Connors, Alice, 82
ODEPLAN, 143, 159
Office of Social Security, 76
Oficina del Trabajo. *See* Labor Department (Oficina del Trabajo)
Oficina de Planificación Nacional (ODEPLAN), 143, 159
Oficina de Seguro Obrero, 76
Oficina de Socorro, 81
Oliveira, Inés, 84
organized labor. *See* labor unions
Ortiz Wormald, Ernesto, 54
Ottawa Plan, 140–41

Palma, Gabriel, 79
papal encyclical *Rerum Novarum,* 45
paro forzoso, 8
Passivita économica (D'Amrosio), 8–9
PEM (Plan de Empleo Mínimo), 158, 161
Perkins, Francis, 125–26
Peru, 13, 32–33
Pfau, Luisa, 88
Phelan, Edward J., 126
philanthropy. *See* charitable relief
Pinochet, Augusto, 153, 159, 161
Pinto, Aníbal, 140
Pissarjevsky, Lydia, 27
placement offices, 26, 40–41, 56–57
placement services, 118–23, 144
Plan Kelly, 159
planning, economic, 142–43
Plaza Yungay, Santiago, 1922 demonstration, 41–42

poblaciones, 161–62
Poblete Troncoso, Moisés, 5, 31, 45, 100
Palacio, Juan Manuel, 12
poor laws (Britain), 9
Popular Front, 113, 118, 131, 133
Popular Unity coalition, 150, 151
poverty: deserving contrasted with undeserving poor, 71, 75, 93–94, 130–31, 133; stigmatization of, 8–9, 31, 93–94, 129, 130–31, 133; urban, 143
Pradenas, Juan, 65, 66, 69
Prats, Gabriela, 86
PREALC (Employment Programme for Latin America and the Caribbean), 141–42, 145, 158–59
Prebisch, Raúl, 140
Presencia, 148, 151
price ceilings, 101–2, 103, 108
price controls, 97, 98, 106–9
price councils, provincial, 107–8
print workers, 109
privacy, and workers' home life, 47, 48
private donations. *See* charitable relief
private/public collaboration on aid projects, 80–81
privatization, 155
Progressive Era (US), 23–24
protests. *See* social unrest; strikes
public labor exchanges. *See* labor exchanges
public/private collaboration on aid projects, 80–81
public shelters, 41, 85–90, 95
public works. *See* work relief programs

Quevedo, Abraham, 61

railroad construction, 61
Ranquil peasant uprising, 67
Recabarren, Luis Emilio, 43

Red Cross, 88
redondilla rotation system, 43
relief offices, 81–82
rent control, 97. *See also* housing
rent subsidies, 105–6
Rerum Novarum, 45
Revista del Trabajo, 37
Richmond, Mary E., 82
"right to work," 139
Ríos, Juan Antonio, 120, 122, 131
Rodgers, Daniel, 24
Ross, Gustavo, 72–73
Rosseti, Juan Manuel, 133–134
Rowe, Leo, 32–33
Ruiz-Tagle, Jaime, 153
rural unionization law (1967), 144

Salvatore, Ricardo, 32
San Gregorio strike, 1921, 42–43
Santiago, 81–84
Saraos, Eduardo, 117
Schiavi, Alessandro, 26
Schmidt, Teodoro, 60, 63, 64, 71, 73, 79
seasonal unemployment, 14
seasonal workers. *See* agricultural workers
SENCE (Servicio Nacional de Capacitación y Empleo), 157
SENDE (National Employment Service), 139–40, 144–45, 157–58
Serani Burgos, Alejandro, 36
Servicio de Cesantía, 73–74, 93–95
Servicio de Seguro Social (SSS), 134–36
Servicio Nacional de Estadística y Censos, 100
Servicio Nacional de Salud (SNS), 134
severance pay, 42–43, 128
shantytowns, 161–62
shelters, public, 41, 85–90, 95
socialism, 69–71

Socialist Republic, Chile, 64, 69–70, 96–97, 107–9
social legislation, 44–49
social marginality, 143
social problem, unemployment as, 71–74
social security, 76, 95, 119
Social Security Act (1934, US), 10
Social Security Service, 134–36
social unrest, 30, 67–68, 69, 71, 102–3
social workers, 81–85, 92
social work schools, 81
Sociedad de Empleados Públicos Cesantes, 92
Società Umanitaria de Milan (1906 conference), 24
Society of Saint Vincent de Paul, 80, 87. *See also* charitable relief
Solís, Luis, 6
soup kitchens, 80, 84–85, 162
Soviet Union, 13
statistics: Argentina, 34–35; challenges in collection of, 16–17, 25–26, 145; cost of living, 100; global, 29; importance of, 9–10, 25, 135–36; National Statistic and Census Service, 100
strikes, 39, 42–43, 103
subsistence, workers'. *See* food, access to

Tagle, Guillermo, 155
Tapia, Francisco, 148
teachers' union, 109–10
technical education, 144, 157–58
tenants. *See* housing
termination. *See* firing
Termination of Employment Recommendation, 147
textile workers, 7, 145–46, 161
Thayer, William, 144, 148
Thomas, Albert, 12, 28, 30, 31
Thompson, E. P., 37

Tokman, Victor, 140, 141–42, 156
Topaze, and satirical verse, 103–4
Torres, Isauro, 119
trade unions. *See* labor unions
Treaty of Versailles, 28
Trucco, Manuel, 68

underemployment, 149
unemployment: contrasted with idleness, 7–8, 10, 71–74, 85, 89; definitions of, 7–8, 9, 29, 30, 72, 75, 136; functional unemployment, 14; history of, global overview, 7–13; history of, overview in Chile, 13–16, 150–52; measurement of, 9–10, 16–17; as national problem, 58–62; scholarship on, 30–33; as social problem, 71–74; stigmatization of unemployed workers, 8, 54, 71–72, 73, 74, 89–90, 93
Unemployment: A Problem of Industry (Beveridge), 26
Unemployment Board, 130–31
Unemployment Department, 131
unemployment insurance: establishment of in Chile, 134–35; global trends, early 20th century, 10, 26–27, 125–26; ILO recommendations, 29–30; lack of support for in Chile, 48–49, 95, 127–30; under military Junta (1974), 156–57; Poblete's proposal for, 45–46; social security movement in Latin America, 126–27; for white collar employees, 93
unions. *See* labor unions
United Kingdom (Britain), 9, 10, 26
United National Development Programme (UNDP), 144
United Nations: Economic and Social councils, 119; technical education, 144

United States: consumer economy, 97; perceptions of unemployment, 8; Progressive Era, 23–24; social security, 10, 125–26; WPA (Works Progress Administration), 63
Universal Declaration of Human Rights, 139
Uruguay, 127

vagrancy, 8, 10, 15, 31, 58, 94, 130
Valenzuela Valderrama, Héctor, 147
Varlez, Luis, 28
Vekemans, Roger, 143
Vilcuya, Los Andes, company store, 98–100
vocational training, 157–58

wage increase law, 147
wages. *See* minimum wage
Walker Linares, Francisco, 45, 106
Weimar Republic, 28
WEP (World Employment Programme), 141
Werkmeister, Enrique, 80
Westergaard, Harold, 25
whale processing plants, 146
white collar workers, 90–93, 129
Williams, Clara, 81
Williams, Raymond, 7
Wilson Hernández, Santiago, 48, 57, 65, 85, 90
Winn, Peter, 7
women's roles, 9, 162. *See also* gender roles
workers' restaurants, 131
workers' subsistence. *See* food, access to
work relief programs, 62–69
work security, 145–52
World War I, economic impact of, 28, 32, 39
World War II, economic impact of, 118–19

WPA (Works Progress Administration, US), 63
Wright, Thomas C., 100, 107

Yunge, Roberto, 68–69, 79, 81–82, 187n28

Zaberman, Yves, 15
Zañartu Prieto, Enrique, 106–7
Zolov, Eric, 140